D1163769

# The Backstory of

# WALLPAPER

## Paper-Hangings
## 1650-1750

## Robert M. Kelly

HUDSON AREA LIBRARY

Lee, Massachusetts, USA

Editorial services by Angela Kipp and Rebecca McNamara

Book design by Encircle Publications LLC, Farmington, Maine

Photography by Bill Hock Photography, LLC

Cover design by Robin Locke Monda

Published by WallpaperScholar.Com

Copyright © 2013 by Robert M. Kelly

Library of Congress Control Number: 2012940376

International Standard Book Number 978-0-9856561-0-2

The paper used in this publication is acid free.




Library of Congress Cataloging Information:

Kelly, Robert M.

    The backstory of wallpaper : paper-hangings 1650-1750 /

Robert M. Kelly.

        p. cm.

    Includes bibliographical references and index.

    ISBN: 978-0-9856561-0-2

1. Wallpaper—History.  2. Interior walls—Decoration.  3.

Decoration and ornament, Early American.    I. Title.

NK3400 .K64 2013

747—dc23

                                        2012940376

# Acknowledgements

For inspiration, Isabel O'Neil; for more inspiration, Catherine Lynn, Richard Nylander and Guy Cooper; also, Anthony Wells-Cole, Christine Woods, Eric Entwisle, Geoffrey Beard, and Patrick Baty; Bernard Jacqué, Philippe de Fabry and Patrice Mauny; Joe Rock and Ian Gow; Eloy Koldeweij; Mrs Leask and David Skinner; also, Don Carpentier, Chris Ohrstrom, Joanne Warner, Greg Herringshaw, Robert Furhoff, Bill Seale, Alan Campbell, Karie Diethorn, Richard McKinstry, Matt Mosca, Martha Rowe, Margaret Pritchard, Max Ferro, Richard Byrne, Gail Cariou, Elizabeth McLane, Elizabeth Redmond, and Susan Nash.

I'm thankful to staff and collections departments at the Cooper-Hewitt National Design Museum, the Wintherthur Libary, the Museum of Early Southern Decorative Arts, the Boston Research Library, the American Antiquarian Society, the Essex Institute, Historic New England, the Victoria and Albert Museum, and the Library of Congress. I am also indebted to researchers who cared enough to leave notes about wallpaper discoveries: among them are Davida Deutsch, Robert Rales, and Nancy Gomes.

A special note of thanks to the members of the Wallpaper History Society based in Manchester, England, the keepers of the flame. And to Mary and Susan, for personal support.

# Table of Contents

# Table of Figures

# Illustration Credits

1, Trustees of the British Library (Harley 5942.40); 2, Joe Rock Photography; 3, 4, 5, 6, 7, 8, 9, 10, 11, 12, 13, 14, 15, 18, 28, 29, public domain; 16, Trustees of the British Museum (Reg. No. Heal, 91.50); 17, The Montreal Museum of Fine Arts, Gift of the Canada Steamship Lines, Ltd. Photo: Christine Guest; 19, Country Life Picture Library; 20, 21, Royal Commission Ancient and Historical Monuments, Scotland and Joe Rock Photography; 22, Trustees of the British Museum (Reg. No. Banks, 28.33); 23, Courtesy of the New York State Parks Department. Attributed to the Manuscripts and Archives Division, The New York Public Library; 24, American Antiquarian Society (Georgia Gazette, 1767-04-15, Iss: 186, p. 4); 25, 26, 27, author's copyright.

## At the Blew Paper Warehouse in Aldermanbury LONDON.

Are sold the true sorts of Figured Paper Hangings in pieces of twelve yards long and others after the mode of real Tapistry, and in imitation of Irish Stich, and flowered Damask and also of marble & other Coloured Wainscot, fitt for the hanging of rooms, and stair-Cases, with great variety of Skreens, Chimney pieces, sashes for windows and other things of Curious figures and Colours.

The Patentees for the Sole making thereof doe hereby Signify that their s. pieces are not only more substantial and ornamental as well as Cheaper than the Counterfeits sold in other places but are also distinguished by these words on the back of each piece as their true mark viz!

### (Blew Paper Society's Manufacture)

Where are also sold Blew sugar loafe and Purple paper in Reams (they being the only Patentees for the making thereof) and Linnen Cloth Tapistry Hangings very Cheap.

You may observe the following method in the putting up the said figured Paper Hangings. First Cutt your Breadths to your intended heights then tack them at the top and bottom with small Tacks, and between each Breadth leave a vacancy of about an inch for the borders to Cover, then cut out the borders into the same lengths and tack them strait down over the Edges of the Breadths and likewise at the top of the room in imitation of a Cornish and the same (if you please) at the bottom as you see described in the figure below without borders and with borders.

But if you will putt up the same without borders, then cutt one of the Edges of each piece or breadth smooth and even, then tack itt about an Inch over the next breadth and so from one to another.

But whether you putt them up with or without Borders gently wett them on the back side with a moist spunge or Cloth which will make them hang the smoother.

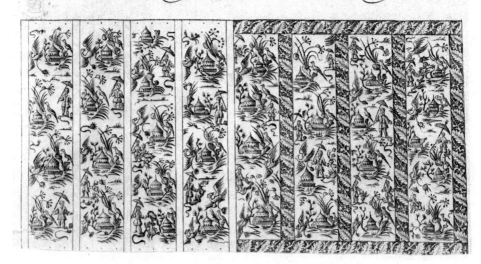

Figure 1: An advertisement for the Blew Paper Warehouse, c. 1700.

CHAPTER 1:

# Rediscovering Wallpaper

The year is 1741. Someone walks into the parlour of Hannah Shaw, near the south bank of the River Liffey in the Temple Bar section of Dublin, with a wrapped bundle of rolls. A glue-pot bubbles on the fire and spreads a musty odour throughout the room. Someone clicks a pair of shears. Wallpaper cascades onto a table, unfurling under the watchful eyes of a family, causing a commotion of 'oohs' and 'aahs'. A little girl wanders off to one side...

**A Little Girl's Reverie**

*...the red flowers were huge. That's all 10-year old Linna Shaw could think: the red flowers were huge. But, she loved them, and they made her smile. Now she knew why Father had said 'we'll see flowers all winter'. Yesterday, Mother let her watch as the man and woman slopped the paper with water for a long while (some spilled on the floor!) and finally peeled the paper from the canvas. Then they made a racket beating on sharp little nails with stubby hammers. As soon as the big people left, Shawn, her brat of a brother, chased her and cornered her and pulled a patch of canvas over her head. The canvas smelt vaguely like the barn they visited in the summer. It was damp and scratchy. She struggled and screeched till Shawn gave up and let go. Now she was still thinking of ways to get even when she was jolted by a woman's voice. 'Mrs Shaw? Mrs Shaw? Shall I come back tomorrow or start papering this room now?'...*

We don't really know if Hannah had children (or if one was a brat) but we do know that Hannah Shaw testified in a Dublin courtroom in 1742 that Catharine Mac Cormick came to her house a year earlier to paper a room.[1] This book is about Hannah's and Catharine's and Linna's and Shawn's world. This is a world of sinewy paper, powdery pigments, wide bristle brushes, and wet paste. Wallpaper was never again so unimpeachable. Wallpaper has travelled a long road, and this *backstory* explains the earliest part of the journey.

The topic is decoration, but the question of whether we should investigate or not is at the heart of all the humanities. Is it necessary to revisit the past in order to understand the present? Perhaps not, if we think the past is expendable. But if the past is not expendable

– if how our ancestors felt about decoration and how they feathered their nests matters to us – then a different picture is painted. Assuming that we *should* connect to our decorative past, how can we do that? Is it as simple as going online, past the computer wallpaper on our desktop, plunging through the years and surrounding ourselves with words and pictures? The sheer accumulation is impressive. Yet, we live in an age when sensory overload is not just a figure of speech, but a reality. We are the custodians of a wealth of texts and images which are as exhausting as they are exhilarating.

In particular the role of images must be addressed. Computer images can be very convincing. Our screens can even show real wallpaper to good effect, with its intricate ornament, rough and pleasing texture, and smooth and satiny lustre in millions of colours. Nevertheless, these beautiful images remain stuck in two dimensions, behind glass, beyond our reach. Pictures of wallpaper in art books suffer a similar deficiency. These are illuminated, yet limited, by a glossy veneer. We need more depth. The path toward understanding wallpaper, or any real thing, begins with the leap from visual to material. This book is an invitation to take that leap. The *backstory* of wallpaper is told here by paying strict attention to its materials during the first hundred years. This grounding is necessary for appreciating the main topic – the incredibly long-lived, rich, and still unfolding 365-year history of wallpaper.

Our touchstones are few – a handful of advertisements for the English trade and the drawings and memoirs of a troubled genius, the French wood engraver Jean-Michel Papillon. But, we travel with good fellows, sustained by the continuity of craft. Humans made wallpaper, humans installed wallpaper, and humans enjoyed wallpaper, and none of this has changed. Our mission is to establish, as best we can, how decorative paper made its first audacious leap to the perpendicular wall, how it was integrated into the home, and who was responsible for this integration.

This account is fragmentary because the subject is fragmentary. Nevertheless, a broad outline can be sketched. The major players in our hundred-year drama are the French, the Chinese, the English, and the Dutch. French Jesuit missionaries to China in the last half of the seventeenth century were amazed at the vast amount of paper used in Chinese interiors. Word got back to Europe. More important, an export wallpaper business sprang up, and soon 'India pictures' made especially for the West were getting back to Europe as well. The dominance of England and France in the early history 1650–1750 is well earned. They were prolific producers, and aggressive exporters. Dutch shippers played a vital role in facilitating trade worldwide. By the third quarter of the eighteenth century, the transatlantic wholesale wallpaper trade was booming. Even the American South was fertile ground; founding fathers like Jefferson and Washington took readily to wallpaper, though in a time beyond our reach.

This material history of wallpaper use is underpinned by a few convictions: that with a leap of imagination we *can* walk through Hannah's parlour door into the early modern era; that wallpaper is worthwhile for its own sake; and that this worth comes from the people who surrounded it when it was new. If decorating with wallpaper has remarkable continuity and value – as I assert – then it's best studied from the beginning.

Wallpaper can be defined simply as portable decoration, serial in nature. It wasn't meant to last. Styles changed with every generation – often sooner. After that, the questions get harder: decoration for whom? At what cost? To what purpose? Although style certainly mattered to wallpaper shoppers, few appear to have taken it as seriously as design historians. Bills, letters, and diaries tell us that cost, custom, and convenience mattered as much. But if wallpaper is not design, or, *not only* design, then what is it? How is it different from other decorative paper? That question will be considered in the next chapter, but, for the moment, at least four design-free traits of paper-hangings stand out: their uselessness, their portability, their cheapness, and their versatility.

Paper-hangings are supremely *useless*. Unlike foundations and studs, they don't support and hold up buildings; unlike tiles, thatch, or windows, they don't keep weather out; unlike plaster or panelling, they don't insulate; unlike paint, they don't protect. They are merely delightful.

The *portability* of paper-hangings developed from practices in fine art and murals in the late-seventeenth century. Portrait painters abandoned solid supports in favour of stretched canvas. Muralists took a slightly different path to achieve the same end. Painting on canvas in public spaces had long been difficult, especially in high places. Marouflage made the work a lot easier. With this technique, art could be created in a studio on fabric, rolled up, taken elsewhere, and then installed with adhesives. Portable decoration had been invented. Brushing ink on paper, rolling it up, and sending it elsewhere also caught on.

Throughout history the vast majority of wallpaper has been little more than cheap ink on cheap paper. This intrinsic *cheapness* works against wallpaper as a collectible. Silverware and sculpture, gilt frames and wood benefit from ageing. They develop a patina. Wallpaper shows its age and falls apart, much to the despair of paper conservators.

Yet, true to its *versatility*, wallpaper can confound these generalities. When produced with superior verve, workmanship and materials, it can compete head-to-head with luxury wall furnishings like silk and gilded leather. Significantly, overachieving paper-hangings are usually described not as 'expensive' but as 'less expensive' than competing materials.

It's not hard to find pasted sheets on a wall before 1650, but they become more numerous after 1650. Documentation shows that wallpaper was well established in France and England by around 1680. There must have been a ramping up to that point of steady use. It's hard to know what the earliest consumers thought about wallpaper. They must have liked it, and recommended it with enthusiasm to others. Nothing else could account for its rapid growth. By 1712 it was ripe for taxation by the English government. Despite the popularity of wallpaper there remain reasonable doubts about the extent of the market for paper-hangings in the early modern period. How many people could afford luxury paper-hangings, (indeed, *any* paper-hangings) in the mid-seventeenth to mid-eighteenth centuries? How expensive was it? What was the going rate? These questions are taken on here. Several sets of figures have been compiled, some based on bills for a single year – 1741. Some newly discovered statistics about the wholesale trade to the New World are tabulated and compared.

The terms 'wallpaper' and 'paper-hangings' have distinct roots. Around 1660, during the Restoration of the monarchy, fixed fabric hangings (tapestry, velvet, silk, linen, or cotton) came to England. The term for the paper version (paper-hangings) was dominant for more than two hundred years. At long last *wall-paper* began overlapping with *paper-hangings* around 1880. As the new century approached, a slight adjustment was made; *wallpaper* was favoured. Perhaps *paper-hangings* and *wall-paper* simply looked old-fashioned at the turn of the century. *Wallpaper* was soon standard, but for a surprisingly short time; by 1975, the introduction of vinyl and other substrates had forced another shift in terminology: to *wallcoverings*.

This book is organized by function. The text proceeds through definitions, artisanry, consumption, specialized types, and costs.

2. *Antecedents* looks at the roots of wallpaper. The differences between decorative papers, *dominos*, and lining papers are sorted out. Off-cuts of paper from the book trade were increasingly used for domestic decoration. Eastern designs both attracted and confounded the young wallpaper industry.

In 3. *'Printed, Painted, or Stained'*, paper, ink and methods of printing are surveyed. Materials, so taken for granted these days, were of great importance. Artisans worked around their limitations and played off of their strengths.

4. *Papillon And His Drawings* brings us face to face with techniques that must have been widespread on the continent; Jean-Michel's apprenticeship, artisanry, and legacy are explored. A unique type of French printing – the counter-proof – is explained.

Distribution takes up two chapters: 5. *The Paper-Hangings Trade* and 6. *Wallpaper Shopping*. Home furnishing companies and wallpaper tradesmen had not yet appeared, but somehow paper-hangings found a market. Advertising, guides to the trades, and selling customs are examined.

7. *'where there is wall'* tells how joiners, plasterers, and upholsterers prepared rooms for paper-hangings. Contemporary rules for panelling are given.

8. *Paperhanging* examines period instruction sheets and tools. Nails and tacks were driven into wood while wheat paste and glue size were ideal for plaster walls. Linings of paper and canvas were important for higher quality installations. Borders finished, decorated, and protected wallpaper installations.

9. *Installers* looks at individuals, from princes of the trade like Thomas Phill, member of the Worshipful Company of Upholders, who actually worked for

princes, to Catharine Mac Cormick, who hung wallpaper when she was not printing it.

In 10. *Leather Hangings* a venerable trade shows surprising relevance. An unbroken line connects Henry Asgill, first prominent English leather gilder, and Thomas Bromwich, tradesman extraordinaire.

11. *Chinese Wallpaper And Flock Damasks* considers the colour and design influence of 'Japan' inks, shimmering grounds, and the absence of perspective in the Eastern product; flock damasks opened the door for many more types of roll paper.

12. *Papier-mâché, Early Print Rooms, Screens* explores variants. After walls and ceilings, screens were the most popular destination for wallpaper in the early period. Print rooms became somewhat typecast in the late-eighteenth century, but the earliest forms were free-wheeling. The low cost, versatility, and tasteful application of papier-mâché ornaments are worth knowing about.

In 13. *Pounds, Shillings And Pence* the question of affordability is addressed: what was the going rate? Bills are examined, and per-sheet and per-roll costs are collated for both sides of the Atlantic. Documented costs of a competing material, gilt leather hangings, serve as a cross-check.

14. *The American Colonies* traces the reception of wallpaper and decorating professionals in the New World. It considers how much wallpaper was being hung and who was hanging it, and tells how the colonies differed from Europe.

15. *Canada And The North American Wholesale Trade* is about wholesale costs and numbers of rolls from the records of Thomas Hancock in Boston, Robert and John Stenhouse in Montreal, and John Baird in Quebec. Canadian shipping records show substantial growth in wallpaper use.

In Chapter 16. *Bringing The Backstory Forward*, some conclusions are drawn from the first hundred years.

Also included are a *Glossary*; a selection of *Texts*; a *Bibliography*; Appendix A: *Table 1* and *Table 2*, and Appendix B: *Notes on Costs*. The tables and notes are specific to the cost comparisons in Chapter 13.

Some notes on the text: The reader may be perplexed at times about the atrocious spelling and grammar of our ancestors. Nevertheless, these mistakes are historic and retaining them is better than the alternatives. Unless qualified, all money is given in pounds sterling (£ s. d.). The bibliography includes works referenced in the text whether they were quoted from or merely consulted. 'See Texts:' always refers to the small group of historic texts from R. Campbell, John Rowland, and others which is in the back of this volume.

Despite the fact that 'wallpaper' was never used before 1750, it's a convenient singular for 'paper-hangings'. I use these terms freely and interchangeably. I have also appropriated the late-nineteenth century term 'sidewall'. In late-Victorian times, 'sidewall' differentiated the main wallpaper from other paper components: ceiling, frieze and dado. *Sidewall* in this text simply means 'main body' of wallpaper as opposed to borders, festoons, panels, fillets, stiles or rails. The ancient artisan called the 'upholder' was increasingly called the 'upholsterer' in the early-eighteenth century. However, this changeover was not complete in 1750. I have retained the old spelling for upholders in England, and used the new spelling for upholsterers in other parts of the world.

The next chapter is about antecedents; decorative paper was made for hundreds of years before wallpaper arrived. It's important to know this development, but lest we seem to be straying from our topic, fear not: in the following two chapters, devoted to paperstaining and Papillon, we plunge directly into the chaos of the paperstainer's and paperhanger's workshops which bristled with leaning ladders, work tables, steaming water, chalk lines, pasting brushes, and shears. So, onward – out of the parlour and into the backstory!

CHAPTER 2:

# Antecedents

In 1568, the Roman Catholic Church found Herman Schinkel, an influential member of the Reformed Religion in Delft (the Netherlands) guilty of printing heretical ballads. On 13 July he was led to the marketplace and beheaded. In Herman's last letter to his wife, he wrote that one of his workers had printed the offensive texts in his absence; when Herman returned to his shop, he refused to deliver them. He told her that he tossed the sheets into a corner, 'intending to print roses and stripes for the papering of attics'.[2]

This incident captures one of decorative paper's baby steps as it toddled away from books, drawers, and trunks to a new location – walls and ceilings. This chapter defines how paper-hangings differed from what had gone before. It's a difficult task because of the number of types.[3] For example, a Dutch study asserts that the inspiration for block printed paper can be traced to the *cartiers*, who produced durable and colourful playing cards from about 1600. Over time, the range broadened:

> Decorated paper was for young and old, high and low, church and world, the scholar and the illiterate, the archives and the sitting room. It could be bought at the stationers's or in the local marketplace [...] The variety of pattern was enormous: flowers and plants, birds and fruits, all sorts of overall motifs, imitations of lace designs, etc. The motifs were fanciful or drawn from nature, scattered or distributed evenly over the surface, arranged in broad or narrow rows, or set against a background of dots or lines.[4]

This description of 'cotton paper' (a byproduct of Dutch cotton mills) tells what was available around 1650 or so – and this was only one type! Some of these block printed papers wound up on walls, but most did not. In this book, *wallpaper* and *paper-hangings* have a particular meaning. Both are created specifically for display on walls in homes. This meaning can be extended to 'paper tapestry', a less familiar term. 'Paper tapestry' was used in France (*papiers de tapisseries*) and Germany (*papiertapete*) and again, this always means wallpaper. The words clearly point in a new direction – toward a design extending well beyond the single sheet.

*Papiers de tapisseries* evolved from the *dominos* of French shops. In eighteenth-century

French dictionaries, *domino* describes all sorts of decorative paper, including paper-hangings. Those intended for walls were sold in bundles: 'The sheets are printed and dried, then painted with various colours in distemper, then the pieces are assembled; which is usually done by those who buy them; being sold more commonly in a bundle [lit. *à la main*] than assembled'.[5] These bundles are known in Great Britain as quires; the origin of quires is specific to twenty-four, but twenty-five is seen just as often. Could the twenty-fifth sheet have been a wrapper or waste paper? Notwithstanding the fact that *domino* was the general term in France, *papiers de tapisseries* were a special type of *domino*, and the proof is found in Jean-Michel Papillon's drawings about printing and hanging wallpapers; his first plate is titled 'Planche I. des papiers de tapisseries'.

Since display is one of our touchstones, screens have a place in this book. Screens used textile supports to achieve a stable (though not solid) surface. As already stated, the development of paper-hangings is fragmentary; it's also circuitous. And, it's still unfolding as more is learned. In many books about wallpaper, the transfer of textile patterns to paper has been emphasized, almost as if this brought wallpaper into being. Yet, when the aptly named surface design is stripped away, the well-springs of wallpaper turn out to be two areas quite distinct from posh textiles – stationery and book-printing.

The intended paper-hangings from Herman Schinkel's shop were merely offcuts intended to use up the controversial ballads. As for the connection to book-printing, the Irish historian Ada K. Longfield supplies many of the details [emphasis in original]:

> The technique of wood blocks for illustrating books offered an initial means of decorating paper whether the black outline of the pattern thus supplied was left plain, filled in by hand-painting in tempera colours, or combined with the later technique for the separate block-printing of each colour [...] This initial alliance with the printing industry explains the *small size* of early pieces of wallpaper, for they were only specially ornamented versions of the ordinary sheets of paper, that could be mounted on wood or canvas and moved about like pictures. Thus the grotesques and religious scenes produced by the 'Dominotiers' in Normandy in the sixteenth century were frequently bought by peasants to put over their fireplaces.[6]

This use of small decorative sheets is close to our definition (paper hung for the purpose of display), although these sheets were probably pasted on wood or canvas rather than on walls. The new location over fireplaces and other central locations gave them a daily prominence which likely led to improvements in colour and design.

This process of domesticating the illustrated page led to the joining of sheets on flat wall surfaces. One instance took place in England around 1600, when an unknown artisan hammered flat-headed nails through paper into the wattle and daub walls of Bordon Hall.[7] This paper had a proper design: 'a simple scrolling design on a red ground; the leaves, stem, tendrils, and stars are printed in black, while the flowers are filled in with bright blue. A second paper [...] has a scrolling design with a strong black outline having formal leaves and flowers rudely painted in vermilion. The ground is hatched with horizontal lines'.[8]

These are some of the earliest wallpapers known, even if the installation was crude. There were good reasons for tacks and nails in the early years; these worked well with wooden walls. By 1650, paper was well-known in the West, but it was far from a household commodity. Instead, it was largely restricted to books. England in particular struggled to create a domestic industry, and imported paper long into the eighteenth century. It needs to be repeated that wallpaper can be easily misunderstood as simply any paper hung on walls. On the contrary, wallpaper has distinct qualities; to use something *as* wallpaper does not mean that it *becomes* wallpaper. *Decorative papers* (paste papers and marbled papers, for example) are a huge sub-category and were used hundreds of years before paper was tacked up at Bordon Hall.[9]

The Remondini company was founded in Italy in 1649 and sent block printed papers all over Europe for the next two hundred years. Yet, the question is always the same: were these used on walls? The answer for the Remondini papers appears to be no. Their smooth, glossy surfaces and elevated cost set them apart from our topic. Some authors press this point with passion and one claims that 'there were plenty of wallpaper makers all over Italy'.[10] But, the examples shown undermine the hypothesis. These small, beautifully decorated papers were used on small objects. Scant information is provided about their placement on walls.

Other red herrings are bronze varnished papers and gilded and stamped papers. Many of these were produced in Augsburg, Germany by specialists such as Simon Haichele. A related type is brocade, or embossed paper. These covered 'dissertations, festive songs, musical scores and calligraphic notebooks; the motifs were almost exclusively floral'.[11] Although many of these types were popular, they were not necessarily affordable.

What follows is a look at five types that have been called wallpaper to gauge how closely they come to the stated requirements of intention and display.

1. decorative paper
2. lining paper
3. *domino papers*
4. *papiers de tapisseries*
5. *papier peint*

*Decorative papers* is the broadest category. The more costly they were, the less likely it is that they were used on walls. Many spattered or other small-patterned stationer's wares – finely wrought papers, often with a glossy finish – have been mistaken as wallpapers by collectors and archivists. It doesn't help that authentic wallpapers were often repurposed as substitute book covers for worn-out daybooks and journals.

The *lining papers* in deed boxes and other receptacles are proto-wallpapers and command our attention. These were repurposed from printing waste. *Lining papers* were common throughout northern Europe, where many countries fostered printing throughout the 1500s. Many, if not most, of the lining papers in deed boxes had some kind of pattern, however small. This type of lining paper is not to be confused with the plain *lining paper* used as a buffer between a finish paper and the wall.

The *domino papers* preserved in museums look like early wallpapers. They have thick black borders, earthy colours, and simple designs, just like English single sheets. Helpfully, many of them have company names on their edges; certainly, some were hung on walls. But, it's a mistake to call them the first wallpapers. 'Domino' seems taken from the notion of a master (a domino, patron or stencil) and indicates a template. But, repetition of a close-patterned design isn't enough to make a paper worthy of display.

*Papiers de tapisseries* echoes the German term *papiertapete*, which probably predates it. It may come as a shock to Francophiles that Germany, too, has a claim on the early development of wallpaper – but it's true. 'Paper tapestry' implies that a pattern similar in spirit to a fabric tapestry is created, sheet by sheet, on the wall. These sheets cost more than common decorative paper. Confusingly, both types of paper were sold in single sheets. The difference is that although a common decorative paper *could* have been used on a wall, *papiers de tapisseries* were *intended* to be used on a wall. By linking to each other, *papiers de tapisseries* broke the bounds of the single sheet. They did this in a way that utilitarian decorative papers never could – with a flourish. Counter-proof designs went even further in this direction – they are practically black magic on the wall.

The French-language *papier peint* translates literally as 'painted paper'. The first appearance of *'papier peint'* is sometimes ascribed to a 1760s governmental order levying protective duties on foreign goods which was cited in Henry Havard's late-nineteenth century dictionaries about ornament.[12] *Papier peint* was the Anglicized term for 'French wallpaper' by the early-nineteenth century and remains in use today.

## France And New France

In early-seventeenth century Rouen there was some production of flocks (chopped wool sprinkled on glue or varnish which imitated velvet textiles). Flocks were put on fabric supports and perhaps on paper as well. Jean-Michel Papillon's account of his upbringing mentions that by 1684 his father, Jean Papillon II, was operating one of the earliest paperstaining workshops in France. William Chatto, a historian of wood engraving, says that a competing shop was run by the Le Sueur family.[13] Considering that there must have been years of development before 1684, the date of 1650 for the hypothetical 'birth of wallpaper' seems valid for France.

The Savary family provides some of the strongest evidence for early wallpaper use. The French commerce expert Jacques Savary wrote in *Le Parfait Negociant* that the goods shipped to New France from about 1650 to 1675 were a motley assortment.[14] Ports such as Quebec, Three Rivers and Louisbourg received the wares. The composition of these shipments varied according to their starting points. For Normandy, the list was long and included a large variety of textiles as well as writing paper, playing cards and 'all sorts of haberdashery and hardware'.[15] While this is not proof that paper-hangings were shipped, *dominotiers* were prominent craftsmen in Rouen, a major city in Normandy, and part of a group of artisans that included *cartiers* and writing paper makers. It is very possible and perhaps even probable that the shipments to New France from Normandy would have included decorative paper, including *papiers de tapisseries* for the finer homes. Without question, the Jesuit missionaries used sheets of paper in the seventeenth century in Canada to instruct the native population in the ways of Christianity. Two types were helpful – 'les petites images' and larger ones – 'tableaux' or 'peintures'. These were distributed in New France and Acadia.[16]

Savary's son, Jacques Savary des Brûlons, spent decades gathering information in the late-eighteenth century for the first commercial dictionary in France. His regular employment as a customs official helped him with this task. The dictionary was finally published in 1723. It is the tapestry aspect that stands out in Brûlons' dictionary definition for *dominotier*:

> A dominotier makes a sort of tapestry on paper, which for a long time was used by the peasants and the poorer classes in Paris to cover the walls of their huts or their rooms and shops [...] By the end of the seventeenth century, the technique had reached a high point of perfection and elegance. Quite apart from the larger quantities of paper that are sold for export abroad and in the principle cities of France, there is not a house in Paris, however grand, that does not contain some example of this charming decoration, even if only in a wardrobe or other private room.[17]

Like the Brûlons family, the House of Papillon is central to our story. Jean Papillon II (1661–1723) and his father, Jean Papillon I (1639–1710), were both renowned engravers, but it is the son who made his living printing paper-hangings beginning in the mid-1680s. Jean Papillon II's son, Jean-Michel Papillon (1698–1776) wrote *Traité historique et pratique de la gravure en bois* (hereafter the *Traité*) and illustrated the printing and hanging of wallpaper. Papillon's history of engraving clarifies that *domino* papers differed from the stock-in-trade of his father, Jean Papillon II. While *domino*s had many purposes, *papiers de tapisseries* had only one – to adorn the wall.

As noted, some of the quantities of paper sold aboard were used for missionary work with the native population in New France, though the lack of evidence for pasting on walls leaves them well shy of paperhanging. Instead, 'many were hung on blankets and other textiles draping altars of chapels, houses and cabins of Indians and missionaries'.[18] When Peter Kalm, the Swedish botanist, visited nuns' cells in his tour of New France in 1749, he saw 'paper pictures' of religious figures on the walls. Unfortunately, he did not note how these were adhered.[19]

Some early development of wallpaper can be traced in Sweden, where a paper thought to be from Germany and dated to 1564 survives on a ceiling in the convent of Wienhausen near Celle (Germany), and at Antwerp. The same pattern was found at the Rosenvinge house in Malmö and is dated to around 1570. In these examples block printed outlines were coloured in. A small tile-like paper in the German Renaissance style from Läckö Castle was rediscovered in a Swedish archive in the 1990s. This block printed

Figure 2: House of Dun wallpaper (off-cuts from a two-sheet design).

paper is thought to have been printed in Germany in the early-seventeenth century. The squares, triangles, octagons and circles give the paper a severe aspect, somewhat relieved by small landscape vignettes. This rediscovery and dating confirm that colour, design, paper, block printing and hand-colouring were all in place in Germany by the early-seventeenth century.[20]

Small-scale 'India papers' made especially for export markets may have started coming into Europe as early as 1675. Such early trading would explain a London advertisement of 1680: 'George Minnikin, Stationer at ye Kings head in St. Martins Legrand near Aldersgate makes & sells all sorts of Japan & other colour'd pap'rhangings both in sheets & Yards & sells all sorts of Stationary wares at reasonable rates'.[21]

A charming example of single-sheet production was hung at the House of Dun in Scotland within a cabinet in the master's suite. It seems to date from the 1730s, and might be older, based on the design. It's been described by Scottish scholar Ian Gow:

> The paper was printed from a woodblock in black on a white ground and then overstenciled in green and orange [...] The design is so elaborate, however, that it had to be built up in two separate sheets. The best preserved areas sadly comprise only the 'bottom' sheets of the full repeat. From fragments of the upper sheets it is clear that the lambrequin or pelmet was intended to support a vase of flowers, which included tulips, between a pair of exotic birds.

It looks like a simpler version of a Baroque high-style leather pattern. This domesticated armorial type still has a shield in the middle, except that the shield has become tasseled. Nearly all the pieces show the same trim line (the lower half of the shield), indicating that they were trimmings from a larger and more important installation, probably in the master's bedroom. The installers must have known they didn't have enough matching pieces to do a proper installation, so the half-pieces were all thrown together. The armorial style was used to embellish hallways in mansions. An earlier and more formal example is the black and white design at Besford Court in England, dated from 1550 to 1575.[22]

In summary, many of the elements needed for paper-hangings were present by 1600 in most European countries. Colour, design and technology then gathered in a cocoon of creativity. The butterfly soon to be known as wallpaper grew and was pulsing to burst forth. The ingredient that seems to have tipped the balance was a steady supply of strong and inexpensive paper. By 1650, wallpaper had emerged as a phenomenon in France and England, but the roots were widespread. As Geert Wisse wrote: 'clearly [...] wallpaper was a European phenomenon'.[23] Clouzot had observed much the same in 1935: 'Wallpaper is fundamentally European. Its decoration and manufacturing processes arise directly from the Middle Ages'.[24]

To conclude this survey of early terminology I'd like to introduce yet another term, hopefully one which will simplify the field. I offer the term *decorative lining paper* to replace what has been known as 'lining paper'. This middle ground may ease the confusion between *decorative paper* on one hand (meant for small objects), and *paper-hangings* on the other (meant for walls). *Decorative* signifies that it's more than plain paper, and *lining paper* recognizes that it has not yet been created for display on a wall. This in-between term will not satisfy everyone; yet, there's clearly a difference between decorative paper for handheld or household objects and decorative paper meant for walls. The parameters of cost, utility and visual effect of the two types are quite different. It seems likely that these differences would have been observed in the period.

Two flags have been suggested for *decorative lining papers*: 1.) the smallness of the pattern, and 2.) a self-contained design.[25] To these might be added: 3.) repurposed materials, and 4.) absence of display. Most of the early decorative lining papers had small designs for small spaces; in contrast, papers meant for the wall often had larger designs which came into their own as sheets were aligned and linked on the wall. Larger designs were better able to exploit positive and negative space. On the other hand, decorative lining papers had little need for elaboration. Though they sometimes wound up on walls, their sketchy geometric patterns register poorly at normal viewing distances of four to eight feet. Decorative lining papers often recycled leftover stock, like that from Herman Schinkel's shop. Decorative patterns were printed on either the printed or the back side. And since they were placed within closed objects, such as deed boxes, drawers and trunks, rather than on walls, the aspect of display was conspicuously absent.

The Cambridge fragments, which date from 1509 and are sometimes called one of the earliest wallpapers in England, were decorative lining papers. A 16" by 11" carved wood block imprinted a decorative pattern on waste paper from a press run. The discarded paper just happened to include a poem lamenting the death of Henry VII and a 'Proclamation of Pardon' dating from the first year of Henry VIII's reign – a happy accident for history. Another example of the genre is the discarded pages of Thomas Hobbes' politically controversial *Leviathan*. These books were ordered to be overprinted with decorative designs (damasked): '11 Decr. 1673. Order of Bishop of London to damask The Leviathan [by Thomas Hobbes]'.[26]

Even as paper-hangings rose in importance, decorative lining papers continued to be used. Deed boxes papered as late as 1750 have been found. Patterns of this era are often larger and more elaborate, though still overprinted onto scrap paper. And yet, none of these secondary uses are quite like the radical use of a smartly printed wallpaper thrust into prominence over a roaring fireplace.

# CHAPTER 3:

# 'Printed, Painted, or Stained'

In 1712, the English wallpaper tax was created for paper which was '*Printed, Painted or Stained*', thus conferring official recognition on the explosive growth of wallpaper in the period 1650–1712.[27] One contributing factor was what the Jesuits found in China.

French missionaries to China from about 1650 discovered that the Chinese had long cultivated the art of paper decoration (see Texts: *History of China*). The East had ample supplies of raw material (plant and bamboo fibres). More important, perhaps, was cheaper labour. Chinese decorative paper traditions will be discussed in Chapter 11, but it's worth wondering if the prodigious use of paper in China may have spurred the development of wallpaper in Europe.

Whether they were following this model or not, Europeans began single-sheet production and installation around 1650 to 1675. The practicality of joining sheets of paper end-to-end before printing was soon realized in England. By 1693, the Warehouse for New-Fashioned Hangings in London was making and selling 'strong Paper-Hangings with fine India-Figures in pieces about 12 yards long and half Ell Broad'.[28] The full ell in England was about 45 inches wide; the half-ell was therefore about 22 ½ inches wide. The 'piece' was so-called to distinguish it from the sheets of paper which made up the piece. The scarceness of good paper explains the emphasis on 'strong'.

The terminology of the nascent industry included 'cartridge paper', 'cartouche', and 'cartoon'. Cartridge papers wrapped gunpowder charges, but the term was soon applied to sized, tough papers used as lining papers under the finer wallpapers. The familiar Baroque cartouche was a design mainstay of the time, and cartoons were made of large, stiff papers, and used for sketching designs.

Chinese scenic wallpapers, which were large and had many panels, were constructed very differently than Western paper-hangings. These were not put on thick paper, but were 'invariably painted on sheets of hand-made *hsuan* paper, pasted together with a 5–10 mm overlap and lined with one layer of unbleached bamboo or other paper'.[29] These two layers were sometimes supplemented by a third, all of which were thin, though the paper itself was strong. They were sometimes hung with textile supports and additional lining papers because of their delicacy and high cost.

Many countries have evidence for early use, if not nearly so early as England. The 'components' story traced here repeated itself in other places. There are three components to wallpaper: paper support and ground, colours, and printing.

## Paper Support And Ground

England depended on German, Italian and French imports for both decorative and plain paper in early modern times. John Briscoe's 1685 patent proposed 'paper for Writing, printing, and other uses [...] as white, as any French or Dutch paper'. It sounds like progress. However, even a dingy grey would have sufficed for paper-hangings, which were increasingly being covered by a priming (grounding) coat of paint.

Charles Hildeyerd on 16 February 1665 took out a patent for 'the way and art of making blew paper used by sugar-bakers and others'. In 1691 Nathaniel Gifford patented 'A new, better and cheaper way of making all sorts of blew, purple and other coloured paper'.[30] These references to blew paper are intriguing but they require definition. Blue art papers, 'blued' paper, and blue paper for paper-hangings are three separate things. From as early as the 1490s, Venetian artists such as Carpaccio worked with blue paper. These trends continued: 'Dutch 17th- and 18th-century papermakers were known for their production of finely crafted papers, especially those of a purplish colour. French importers of Dutch paper coined the term *Bleue Hollande* or *Dutch blue*'.[31]

'Blued paper' came into use as papermakers learned ways of enhancing low-quality white rags. Blue dye neutralized yellowy paper and thus made it acceptable for upper-class uses. Blue paper made specifically for paper-hangings could have been made from beaten blue rags. On the other hand, the Blew Paper Warehouse claimed that its products were 'dy'd through'. These dyes may have included woad, logwood and litmus. Mordants such as verdigris and alum, and metallic compounds such as copper and zinc sulphate fixed dyes onto fibres.[32] Low-grade blue paper stock was used for wrapping sugar cones, needles and other household wares; ream wrappers (which protected the paper during storage and shipment) were made of blue paper as well. It seems likely that, at first, paper-hangings were just another use, albeit in a new and portentous direction: the decoration of homes.

In 1691 the Blew (later Blue) Paper Company was founded on patents developed by William Bayly.[33] The fourteen-year patent called for printing paper 'with all sorts of figures and colours by several engines made of brass, without paint or stain, which will be useful for hanging in rooms'. Despite the mysterious wording, the company prospered. They outgrew their facilities in Aldermanbury in 1694 and sold paper from the 'large Japan Warehouse' in Henrietta St (in Covent Garden) and other locations.

A 1705 London advertisement hints about manufacturing processes. It states that

> At the Bible in Newgate-Street, Where is a Ware-house, and is sold all Sorts of Paper-Hangings, by Wholesale or Retale, very delightful for Rooms or Closets, of the newest Invention of Figures, as Irish and Diamond-Stitch, Carpet or Turky, and Forest-work, & c. Also most Sorts of Plain Colours,

Printed with a hot Role like your Stuffs: Sold very Cheap. You may likewise be furnish'd with *screens* ready made, at low prices and &c.[34]

Could plain colours have been impressed with hot metal plates and embossed with rollers, thus producing the patterns and figures sold by the 'Bible'? Was this also done at the Blue Paper Warehouse? It's just possible that the paper product may have been modelled after 'scorched' or 'damask' leather, which also used hot metal plates to impress patterns.

One of the Blue Paper Warehouse ads gives more details:

The patentees for making the said figur'd hangings (observing the same to be counterfeited upon a thin and common brown paper, daub'd over with a slight and superficial paint) do hereby give notice, that the said true sorts may be distinguish'd from counterfeits by their weight, strength, thickness and colour, dy'd through; and are every way more lasting and serviceable. At the same places are to be sold blue sugar-loaf and royal purple paper by the ream.[35]

But, even if this wallpaper was 'dy'd through', it's hard to see how it could have succeeded without the application of a ground coat which would have covered traces of glue or paste on the joined paper. Unfortunately, no samples survive to settle this question. Nevertheless, contemporary samples collected by museums show that wallpaper was increasingly being joined and then stained (*grounded*) with thin water-based colours prior to printing, stencilling, or brushwork. These ground coatings consisted of pigments and whiting mixed with a little binder. Often, the binder was a hide glue obtained locally from the skins of barnyard animals. Grounding gave the paper a uniform colour, but ground coats were not invariably opaque. *Stained* is the right word. It seems that clay, which aids opacity, was not widely used at first.

The 1712 Excise Duty on Stained Paper was a temporary tax imposed largely because of the War of the Spanish Succession until a 'good and lasting peace' could be achieved.[36] This period was optimistically estimated at 34 years (or, until 1746). 1746 came and went; the tax was finally removed in 1836! Charles Oman, co-author of a catalog of the Victoria and Albert museum wallpaper collection, cited the wallpaper tax, along with advertising, as evidence for his assertion that 'it is clear that by the end of the seventeenth century wallpaper was passing out of its infancy and was becoming an article of common use, though probably chiefly among people of the middle and lower classes'.[37]

In England, the typical printed piece was 21 inches wide and 12 yards long. When the 21" width is multiplied by 12 yards, the result is 9072 square inches. When this is divided by a square yard (1296 square inches), the result is 7 square yards. The wallpaper tax specified that a 'piece' consisted of 7 sq yd. It was clever of the tax authorities to specify square rather than linear measure, because the constituent sheets of some paper-hangings were run the 'other way' (landscape orientation). Because it produced fewer seams, this method was ideal for free-hand artwork and, ironically, landscape papers. Landscape papers featured hill and dale, rivers, and ruins, like those promoted by John Baptist Jackson in his *Essay* of 1754. All of the documented landscape papers have vertical seams every 27" or so. No doubt these types were also taxed at 7 sq yd per piece.[38]

Early decorative paper sizes are usually small, not larger than around 12" by 18". The most common constituent sheet size for paper-hangings found in England for the early-eighteenth century seems to be about 19" high by 22" wide.[39] This so-called elephant size soon grew to about 25" high, and by the late-eighteenth and early-nineteenth century, elephant was measuring anywhere from 28" to 30" high, though still in a 22" width.

Figure 3: An elephant watermark: seventeenth-century continental.

Elephant was so named because of its distinctive watermark. The origin of the seventeenth century watermark pictured here is not known; it may be Italian.[40] Papermakers used a team approach: a vatman plunged his papermaking mould and deckle into the pulp vat thousands of times a day. He was assisted by the coucher and the layman, who helped stack up and interleave wet sheets of paper at a rapid pace. While elephant sheets are not extremely large, and certainly not of the 36" dimension that has been mistaken for a standard, they're the largest that can be made efficiently. It's possible that the confusion about the 36" dimension crept in due to the popularity of chinoiserie sheets (Western imitation of Chinese motifs). These often measured 36" in one direction. Thus, twelve of them yielded the equivalent of a twelve yard piece (seven sq yds). The larger size of the chinoiserie sheets can be attributed to emulation of the good-sized Chinese 'India pictures'; the desire to avoid seams over a major motif; and the need for space to create balanced compositions.

## Colours

There is no standard term for paper-hangings' colouring materials. *Ink, distemper, ground, paint* and *colour* have been used. The paint historian Ian Bristow found that low-cost water-based paints were the norm for most interior house-painting over centuries. His charts show that the costs for organic red and yellow pigments from the colourman were perennially sky-high. Yet whiting, Paris white, and Satin white were cheap.[41] These base colours were easily tinted with small quantities of expensive pigments and lakes. The situation was no different with paper-hangings. Throughout 1650–1750 the most important ingredients were simple earthy pigments mixed with chalk in a glue binder. Pigments hide the paper and give colour. Bristow has written that in order to be acceptable, a pigment should not

> react with its fellows, other constituents of the paint, the atmosphere, or commonly encountered compounds to which it may be exposed. Pigments should also be light-fast, not fading on exposure, especially to sunlight. Even today it is not possible to meet these apparently simple conditions completely: much less was it feasible during the seventeenth and eighteenth centuries.[42]

In 1687, John Smith, in *The Art of Painting in Oyl*, wrote that 'those that list not to be at the trouble of grinding colours themselves, may have of any sort [...] ready ground, at the colour-shops, at reasonable rates, either in smaller or larger quantities'.[43] This advice must have been welcomed by the early paperstainers. They required vast amounts of pigments, and their workers could not have been eager to spend hours grinding clumps of clay into dust. Thick black registration lines around the perimeter of a sheet are commonly found on early single-sheet paper-hangings. Stencils for the design were placed on the sheet, and colours brushed in. A thin black outline was sometimes applied as well around the design itself. The papers were trimmed on one or two sides to the pattern and installed side by side to create tapestry-like designs.

In 1737, when Thomas Hancock in Boston wrote to John Rowe, stationer in London, about chinoiserie paper-hangings, he asked for water-based colours: 'I think they are handsomer and better than painted hangings done in oyle'.[44] Perhaps Thomas believed that distemper on paper was more vivid than oil paints on fabric hangings. In France, *dominos* were printed in distemper, but Jean Papillon II's *papiers de tapisseries* seem to have been printed and painted exclusively in oil. According to Philippe de Fabry, 'Papillon uses inks derived from walnut oil or from turpentine, and applies them by pinceautage'. Pinceautage is defined in Fabry's text as 'application of colour within the lines with brushes'.[45]

By around 1730 or so, Papillon's competitors Defourcroy and Boulard were using distemper. Nevertheless, Jean-Michel opposed it: 'the colour is so soluble that one can scarcely glue them and put them in place without having it come off on the fingers'.[46] This complaint might stem from his conviction that *dominos* were not true paper-hangings (and therefore not to be compared to the more advanced *papiers de tapisseries* associated with his family business). In any case, similar complaints about distemper are lacking in England. Eventually, Papillon came round. He included instructions for hanging distemper papers in an appendix of the *Traité*. Resistant to the end, he predicted that they will only succeed if they are hung with tacks, like upholstery.[47]

'Japan colours' on paper-hangings refers to the reflective quality of lacquerwork, a traditional Japanese method for coating wood. From the beginnings of the East India Company trade in 1662 lacquerware was imported to England; this was soon imitated by English painters with paint and varnish. The shimmer of Chinese grounds has been referred to as 'cicada-wing' by Von Gulik. Thus 'Japan colours' in an advertisement could refer to the ground, the design colours, or both. A greater contrast to the flat colours and folk-art-like black and white patterns of the early English domestic market can hardly be imagined. The Chinese grounds were described by Johann Beckmann:

> I once saw at Petersburg a kind of Chinese paper, which appeared all over to have a silver-coloured lustre without being covered with any metallic substance, and which was exceedingly soft and pliable. It bore a great resemblance to paper which has been rubbed over with dry sedative salt or acid of borax. I conjecture that its surface was covered with a soft kind of talc, pounded extremely fine.[48]

It's hard to say how this was done. Paper conservators have suggested that water-based inks were sized with glue or alum, hardening them.[49] It's likely that many extant eighteenth century Chinese scenics originally had shimmering grounds. This quality is lost when the grounds are overpainted with flat colours. Despite the shimmering grounds of the Eastern products, polished or glazed grounds are seldom found in Western wallpaper before 1750, though mica was strewn to add sparkle. In the nineteenth century, the situation changed radically; 'satin grounds' became a major category.

## Printing

It seems likely that stencilled outlines were considered *printed* by excise officials, yet there is little documentation for the stencilling process. It can be difficult to tell the difference between a rough block print outline and a stencilled one. Since even Chinese artisans, renowned for their freehand brushwork, used stencils for simple architectural features, and since closer examination has shown more and more evidence of stencilling on Western wallpaper, it's tempting to conclude that stencilling was a common if well-hidden tool of the trade for both occidental and oriental workshops.

Stencil patterns judged to have selling potential were carved into hardwood templates.

Blocks cost more, but gave sharper detail and lasted longer. Ordinarily, the carved surface of the block provided the impression, but details also came from pieces of metal hammered into the block face. Mallets were used to strike the block, but these gave way to levers and letter-press, which were less messy and gave sharper impressions. Nevertheless, village artisans continued with the old ways for a local clientele. Hundreds of these shops were active as late as the 1780s, according to Sugden and Edmundson. Though the city trade was highly developed and profitable for a handful of paperstainers, the majority continued to work in villages and small towns where the proprietor 'designed and produced his own blocks, printed his papers, sold them direct to the public, and (usually) hung them in the houses of his clients'.[50]

*Painted* denotes brushwork, or what Robert Dossie referred to in *The Handmaid to the Arts* as 'pencil work'. Painting seems to have been rarely done. It was far slower than printing with templates, and therefore more costly. Nevertheless, it could add variety to outlined designs. For instance, a close look at large repeating flower and bird patterns of the eighteenth century shows that flowers in alternating repeats were sometimes coloured differently.

We have *stained* to thank for 'paperstainer'. Sometimes a nicely grounded paper was enough. Plain papers were especially popular in picture galleries and hallways. Plain paper painted twice or thrice over *in situ* became popular, too. This was sometimes done on 'stamped elephant' – individual plain sheets subjected to the taxman's stamp. As this method gained in popularity, excise officials insisted that sheets coloured on the wall should be taxed at the standard rate for printed paper. It's safe to assume that much of it escaped this fate. The regulations state that 'supervisors and Officers must use every likely and legal means to discover where rooms have been hung with plain Paper, and afterwards Stained or Painted'.[51]

England and France were soon exporting to many countries. By 1750, even Russia was an export market.[52] These exports stimulated local production. When domestic paperstaining started in Sweden, 'manufacture was concentrated to the cities, mainly Stockholm. On the whole, the workshops were small, employing one to three people'.[53] Early workshops in Sweden produced simple stained papers (plain grounds). The earliest evidence in Sweden for domestic production is a set of patents registered by paperstainers from around 1730. Toward the middle of the century the Swedish paperstainers advanced to print on roll paper. Many countries have tantalizingly brief references to early wallpaper production. In Ireland, there were at least a half-dozen paperstainers active prior to 1750, though they left few traces. Other countries who turned to local production after a period of trade with the main wallpaper exporters included Norway and the Netherlands. The list would only grow.

By 1670, England had achieved self-sufficiency in the production of brown paper, according to Richard Hills.[54] Coloured papers were apparently often used for early paper-hangings. The text of the patent granted to Patrick Gordon of the Kingdom of Ireland in 1692 for 'an extraordinary way of making blue, purple, and all sorts of paper and pasteboards, and of embellishing and beautifying the same' certainly sounds like he had paper-hangings in mind.[55]

It's intriguing that in 1693 James Hamilton's mill in Scotland began producing 'coarse grey and blue paper, the attempts made to manufacture writing paper having failed'.[56] Coloured paper stock like this was exactly the type used for paper-hangings because it was stout enough to withstand printing, pasting, trimming and hanging. A historian noted that in Edinburgh around 1738 'painted paper, or paper for hanging rooms, was begun to be made [...] At first, Mr Esplin confined himself to two colours, and sold his paper at a shilling per piece, consisting of twelve yards'.[57] The description of Charles Esplin's operation seems almost a template for how primitive paperstaining workshops grew in secondary markets, where the clientele had less exacting needs than the citizens of London or Paris.

# CHAPTER 4

# Papillon And His Drawings

Figure 4: 'Au Papillon', the trademark of the Papillon family;
Papillon means 'butterfly' in French.

The French nation probably produced as much wallpaper as England in the early modern period, yet their methods were very different. French craftsmen ignored roll paper completely until 1750. And, printing was reversed: the French lowered the paper onto the block, instead of the other way round. It may be significant that roll paper doesn't lend itself to this method. Nevertheless, as Brûlons' comments in his commercial dictionary indicate, wallpaper grew in popularity and worked its way up in France just as it did in England. It should not be forgotten that Brûlons practically equates the *dominotier*

Figure 5: Planche 3.3; Papillon's shop opposite the St. Séverin fountain. The inscription reads: 'View of the old shop, where Papillon first put up his sign, in the rue St. Jacques by the fountain'.

Figure 6: Planche 3.3. [detail]; sheets are displayed just below the Papillon shop sign. A man on horseback may be picking up quires of paper in a leather satchel.

with the paperstainer. French archives contain many court actions among *dominotiers*, engravers and printers over the rights to make and sell paper-hangings. These arguments probably had little effect on the availability of the product. But they demonstrate how the trades operated, and prove that paper-hangings were worth fighting over.

In 1753 English flocks were hung at Lord Ablemarle's rented house in Passy by 28-year-old Jean-Baptiste Réveillon, and for a discriminating client at that; Ablemarle was the Ambassador to France. Réveillon was a mercer, or dry-goods merchant, who had completed a three-year apprenticeship a decade earlier. He could not legally make flock wallpaper. However, mercers had the right to refine products made by others. Thus, he was able to exploit the newfound popularity of English flocks by selling and installing them. He introduced battening and canvassing methods (or so he claimed). Whatever the truth of his claims, damp walls and raised wainscotting certainly were impediments to wallpaper installation, and they were neatly circumvented by these methods.

French craftsmen were soon profiting from the experience of copying English flocks. When they began producing roll (joined) paper, it was known as *raboute* (lit. end-to-end). The French used a smaller sheet size (roughly 18" by 18") and a smaller roll size (about nine yards). Réveillon and others were destined to take *papier peint* – as it was now called – to unprecedented heights in the latter years of the eighteenth century.[58] The future glories of French wallpaper, which included a healthy export business to the United States, cannot detain us just now. We're about to cross the threshold of a small Parisian workshop in the year 1755.

The *Encyclopédie,* one of the great achievements of the French rationalists, had a long gestation. By 1755, Denis Diderot, one of the editors, was beginning to understand why. As John Pannabecker has related, 'Diderot [...] became more aware of difficulties in representing the arts, noting that "each one has his own way of feeling and seeing" [...] he recounted how he had explained the same guidelines to two artist-authors: one a wallpaper hanger whose trade Diderot considered simple compared to that of another unnamed artisan employed in one of the most complex industries. The wallpaper hanger submitted ten or twelve plates filled with an enormous number of figures plus three thick folio-size notebooks with minuscule writing'.[59]

Oui! The unnamed wallpaper artisan could be none other than Jean-Michel of the Papillon dynasty, whose family shop had long endured on the rue St. Jacques. A pause must be made to point out that although Pannabecker in the quotation above refers to Jean-Michel Papillon as a 'wallpaper hanger', Jean-Michel no doubt would have bridled at the description; he had long since forsaken the everyday work of the trade, though certainly he was an expert on all aspects of it. He had become an unwilling apprentice to his father at the tender age of seven.

Jean-Michel's drawings bring us almost face to face with the mid-eighteenth century printer and installer. The drawings are the continental side of paperhanging. It seems probable that workers in neighbouring countries followed these methods. Surely no other single source about paperhanging rivals these simple but detailed drawings. Some explanatory notes follow. Yet, the best way to appreciate his drawings may be to give ourselves up to them. They allow us a place at the bench. If we listen, we can hear the scraping of walls, the clicking of shears, and the soft snapping of chalk lines, and feel the steam rising from a bubbling pot.

Ironically, the drawings on which Jean-Michel lavished so much time did not appear in Diderot's great work. Jean-Michel wrote several articles for Diderot which did appear. He also left a history of wood engraving. Whatever its shortcomings (for it is widely criticized) the *Traité* preserves the Papillon family's legacy, gives first-hand testimony about contemporary artisanry, and records how Jean-Michel mastered the trade. But, best of all, Jean-Michel's drawings from 1755 were miraculously found after a century and a half of obscurity. The drawings which had so bewildered Diderot are now celebrated as foundational documents of the wallpaper trade.

> 1766, extracts from the *Traité*:
> *...one of the first obstacles was the contrary attitude of my own father, whose firm opinion was that I should not make my career that of a fine engraver, but as an engraver exclusively of wallpapers; which were of course his line of business...*
>
> *...I was made to work all day printing wallpapers, as likely colouring them in when I was not cutting out the blocks, as going to houses of quality to attend to the hanging of papers...*
>
> *...in 1719 or 1720 I went to the village of Bagneux, near Mont-Rouge, where a Swiss officer, Captain de Greder, had a very pretty house. After I had decorated a small room for him, he asked me to put mosaic paper on his library shelves...*[60]

Jean-Michel was around 21 years old when he worked in Bagneux. He turned his back on the trade shortly after the death of his father a few years later. With a palpable sigh of relief, he then pursued what he considered his proper career – that of a fine engraver. His opinion of his engraving skill was so high that it's difficult to imagine him being pleased with his legacy. As noted, few examples of mid-eighteenth century wallpaper survive. It's hard to visualize, and even harder to understand how it was hung. Jean-Michel fills in many of these blanks. His drawings suggest that he was also a fastidious foreman. It's not too surprising, then, that Jean-Michel pursued his career as a fine engraver with a single-minded zeal bordering on obsession. Indeed, he suffered several episodes of what can only be described as nervous breakdown

His drawings show all the trimming possibilities for top, bottom, and sides of sheets. The sheets were trimmed according to how they would fall on the wall. Jean-Michel even labels each type of cut. It becomes clear why these cuts are needed when a coved ceiling is hung in fig. 77 and 78 (figure 10). In addition to a full range of paperhanging, he shows many patterns, including border designs, and illustrates the fine points of printing and colouring them. He includes the counter-proofing method, which magically transcended the bounds of the single sheet while yet remaining a single sheet. Remarkably, he shows

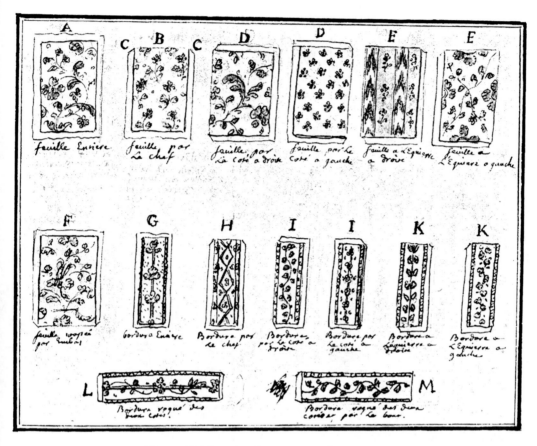

Figure 7: Planche 4.2.; types of trimming.

some landscape papers. These obvious forerunners to the French scenics have hardly been studied.[61]

There are seven plates with 27 strips containing 86 figures (scenes). Tools, workshops, rooms, and a variety of workers are all crowded together, an example of artistic license. We might pause here and wonder about his crew, who work with such purpose. Were they happy on the day Jean-Michel sketched them, as he leaned against a stray ladder? No doubt (like any crew) some were dour, others were wide-eyed newcomers, and some rollicked through their paces, humming tunes.

No rolled goods appear, nor are tacks shown adhering the papers, though many tacks are used for supports. The first planche (plate) is titled *des papiers de tapisseries* (paper tapestries). While few of the patterns are elaborate, all join into larger designs when hung. Clearly, these are what Europeans, and, by this time, colonists in New England and New France, knew as paper-hangings. They are not decorative paper repurposed for the walls.

The corners of picture frames are always set at ninety degrees. Alas, the corners and ceilings of rooms are usually not. Installers know how to hang paper so that the pattern is nicely fit to the space. Some of these techniques are displayed in Planche Five, fig. 61–63

Figure 8: Planche 2.3. and 2.4.; printing.

(Chapter 8), where a wayward ceiling line is brought under control with chalk lines.

As noted, Jean-Michel contributed a long article on engraving in wood and a shorter one on *dominos* to the *Encyclopédie*. He took the opportunity to disparage them. Nevertheless, he explains that the lower classes had a tradition of hanging *domino* papers above their fireplaces. Since they were used for display, they meet our definition as paper-hangings, even if some of them fell short of Jean-Michel's artistic standards.

Jean-Michel explains in the *Traité* that his father, at around 23 years old, began to engrave for the upholstery trade. He credits his father with the invention of *papiers de tapisseries*, commenting that they became popular 'around 1688'. It's not hard to believe that the continual development of paper-hangings resulted in a sort of breakthrough at about this time – it was certainly happening in England, as we've seen.

However, the newfound popularity on the walls for a product that had been popular elsewhere must have been the work of many hands. At the same time, Jean-Michel's father, Jean Papillon II, was certainly important. He's the first to be credited with installing paper in a tasteful and meticulous way.[62] These methods may well have included battening and canvassing. Fabric supports had long been used throughout Europe under leather and fabric, but perhaps the moment had arrived for their adaptation to a new material: paper-hangings. Almost certainly, his methods would have included borderwork.

Oddly, Papillon *pere* is not credited in the *Traité* with the counter-proofing method. It is perhaps the solitary opportunity missed by Jean-Michel to embellish his family history.

However, a counter-proof is shown and the printing process illustrated in fig. 31–35 of his drawings (figure 8). As already noted, this method exponentially extended the design. There are at least three surviving printed examples in collections. It must not be thought that these were common. On the contrary, they were the rarest of the rare.

## HOW IT WAS DONE: COUNTER-PROOF DESIGNS

First, a perfectly symmetrical pattern was worked out and a block carved. A proof was printed with walnut oil (for example, a 'd' sheet). Immediately, another sheet of paper was moistened and put on top of 'd'. Then, the pair went through a rolling press. The just-created counter-proof would supply a mirror image, a 'b' sheet. These could be coloured in, and then pasted, trimmed, and joined on the wall, always starting from the centre of the wall.

By reversing the next set, the installer complemented the first set (db, the top half of a design) with its own mirror image (qp, the bottom half of the design). This created a large design on the wall four times the size of the original sheet. The entire process was repeated toward the margins until the wall was filled with pattern. A completed counter-proof papiers de tapisseries is shown on the wall in figure 9.[63]

In the graphic image nearby and in the reconstruction of a counter-proof design on the back cover, the quadrants are separated to show the method of construction. In a wall installation, there would have been no gaps but rather a completed design. Other *papiers de tapisseries* are more complex, and some seem like proto-scenic papers. These small sets were joined side-to-side and top-to-bottom to create a landscape or scene, much like today's photo murals. Far too little is known about these advanced types.

A design attributed to the Papillon workshop in the short-lived Bizarre style has been published.[64] This may be a fabric design, but it works very well as a counter-proof wallpaper. Since larger patterns develop from it as the sheets are installed, the effect is just as symmetrical as the three known counter-proof types. The House of Dun pattern shown in Chapter 2 also makes larger units when installed, even if it is less ambitious; the pattern joins internally to make up one repeat, and it flows in a single direction.

Notes On The Drawings: These notes refer to Planche 2.3. and 2.4, Planche 3.4. (Chapter 7), Planche 4.1. (back cover), Planche 5 (Chapter 8), and to the four figures at the end of this chapter: Planches 6.1., 6.4, 7.1., and 7.2.[65]

Planche 2.3.:
fig. 30: Apprentices hang the printed sheets on waxed ropes to dry.
Planche 2.4. shows the counter-proofing method:
fig. 31: A stack of moist plain sheets (A); fig. 32 (B): A recently inked sheet is laid down; fig. 32 (C): A moist sheet is laid on the inked sheet; fig. 33: Both sheets are carried to the press; fig. 34: The counter-proof is made; fig. 35: Another view of the press.
Planche 3.4.:
Preparing plaster walls has not changed much; the men are raking out cracks, sponging down and scrubbing walls, sizing walls, filling cracks, and covering them with paper or fabric in preparation for installation.
Planche 4.1.:
Laying out the installation; fig. 49: Using the sheet as a measure, the walls are marked, beginning from the centre; the man on the right appears to be asking for a certain number of sheets; fig. 50: workers trim the sheets.
Planche 5:
fig. 54 and 55: The installers to the left are hanging to one side of a centre line, the installer on the far right has positioned his sheet straddling the centre line. The installers start from the middle and work toward the corners, which will be covered with borders. There is no glue pot – the basin probably contains wheat paste; fig. 57: A chalk line is snapped, probably for a vertical border; fig. 58: The workers are trimming and pasting borders, stringing plumb bobs, and chalking strings; fig. 59: A worker trims a border into place down one side of a corner; fig. 60: The worker is applying fabric or paper strips to cracks in the corner; fig. 61: To the left, *papiers de tapisseries* have been installed; to the right is a panelled

sidewall. Chalk lines are being snapped as guidelines for the borders.

Planche 6.1.:

The man in fig. 66 is snapping a vertical chalk line; the central panel in fig. 67 appears to be a *papiers de tapisseries*; the panelling and pillars in fig. 68 are nicely balanced.

Planche 6.4.:

fig. 76: The centre panel shows a virtuoso performance; fig. 77: The A (the sheet left untrimmed on all four sides) establishes horizontal continuity; the F sheet is trimmed only on the bottom; the B sheet is trimmed only on the top; fig. 78: Similarly, the G border is untrimmed and the H borders are trimmed on top. The H borders start at top left and top right with trimmed tops and proceed around the curve. Forty-five degree relief cuts (incisions) are indicated; these are made so that the sheets can follow the curve. The worker puts the last border in. The I borders start in the middle and move away from the centre with trimmed edges overlapping untrimmed ones.

Planche 7.1.:

Canvas is tacked directly to a wall and paper and border are pasted to it. When dry, these assemblies are remove, then tacked or pasted to wall spaces as needed. Papillon takes care to show that individual sheets of paper are being put into place. The apprentice holding the ladder cannot be very old.

Planche 7.2.:

fig. 81: This seems almost a diagram for print room practice, even if it's a rigid diagram. Differently-sized engravings, prints or pictures are arranged systematically on a wall divided by vertical borders. Although these arrangements were known as 'print rooms' all over the world, in France the style is known as 'English Decoration'. Though this term and 'print rooms' are interchangeable, neither of them are 'papiers en feuille', a single-sheet genre from the late-eighteenth century.[66]

Figure 9: Planche 6.1.; landscape, tapisseries, pillars.

Figure 10: Planche 6.4.; curved surfaces.

Figure 11: Planche 7.1.; canvas underlayments.

Figure 12: Planche 7.2.; English Decoration; creating and covering screens.

# CHAPTER 5:

# The Paper-Hangings Trade

## 1747

*My second room is not yet hung, not having been able to get any paper, to my mind, under an exorbitant price. At length, however, I have agreed for one and Bromwich comes to put it up tomorrow.*

Letter from Fanny Boscawen, while furnishing No. 14 Audley Street, London.[67]

Admiral Boscawen's wife probably meant that Thomas Bromwich himself was coming, whether to do part of the work, all of the work, or supervise. Fanny was one of the hostesses of the Blue Stockings Society – women who had the time and interest to indulge in literary conversation and lectures. But, who was Bromwich? She had called on Thomas K. Bromwich (1711?–87), son of John Bromwich, clerk of Bessesleigh in the county of Berkshire. There may have been paper in the blood – a William Bromwich is recorded as a bookseller at the 'Three Bibles' on Ludgate Street from 1677 to 1680.[68] Although no family connection has been found, it is an unusual surname. Thomas was indentured to the leather gilder Samuel Williams in 1727. When Thomas completed his apprenticeship in 1737, he graduated into the world of business. His trade card of around 1740 attests that he was soon making and selling leather hangings:

Thos. Bromwich at the Golden Lyon on Ludgate Hill, London. Makes and sells all manner of screens, window blinds, and covers for tables. Rooms, cabins, stair-cases, and c. hung with guilt leather, or India pictures. Chints's, callicoes, cottons, needlework, & damasks matched in paper to the utmost exactness, at reasonable rates.[69]

By 1744 his bill-head reads 'Leather Gilder & Paper Merchant'. Around 1748, he advertised as a linen draper and upholsterer, and began to supply and install Chinese scenics and papier-mâché. He was paid £3 13s. at Holkham Hall; £20 16s. 1d. at Uppark by Sir Matthew Fetherstonhaugh in 1748; and £50 for supplying Chinese wallpaper in 1750 for Longford Castle. In the years after 1750 he became well-known in London society for his stock of paper-hangings. Other shop-keepers had good selections of paper-hangings. Yet, only Thomas is repeatedly associated with large stock, bespoke work, and installation of the goods. It is unclear when he began running a shop and overseeing. By 1754 Horace Walpole referred to Bromwich's men installing paper during renovations at his Strawberry Hill residence, and complained about 'many jaunts to hurry Bromwich', presumably at his shop.[70] Despite all this activity, Thomas maintained his gilt leather business, and trained twelve men.[71]

Thomas exploited the wallpaper trade so much that when he ran for alderman in the 1760s he was routinely described as 'a paperhanger'. This is a misnomer – by then he was almost certainly selling paper-hangings and supervising their installation rather than installing them himself. He lost the election, but the results were reported on both sides of the Atlantic.[72] He was remembered at the time of his death as 'paper merchant' or 'papier-mâché maker'. He began as an apprentice and worked his way up through ten years of servitude; yet, his obituary records the acquisition of a 'genteel fortune'. He left his widow, Elizabeth, an income of £1,000 a year.[73] His career illustrates the fluidity of the eighteenth century trade environment and the importance of connections, both master/apprentice and client/supplier.

Remarkably, the word 'paperhanger' is missing throughout the entire 1650–1750 period; Thomas Bromwich was one of the first so-named. How, then, did the trade in paper-hangings develop? How did Thomas and others like him find wallpaper patterns and get them printed? First, it's important to understand what a tradesman was in the early-eighteenth century.

Daniel Defoe begins his book *The Complete English Tradesman* (1726) with a definition, logically enough, of the tradesman. He writes that a tradesman is not a merchant, nor 'a *mechanic*, such as a smith, a carpenter, a shoemaker, and the like, such as here we call a handicraftsman'. Also excluded are 'a tradesman such only as carry goods about from town to town [...] these in England we call petty chapmen, in the north pethers, and in our ordinary speech *pedlars*'.[74] Defoe's next category includes 'those who make the goods they sell'. Again, these are 'not called tradesmen, but *handicrafts* [...] who only make, or cause to be made, goods for other people to sell [...] manufacturers and artists, &c'. At length we come to those he calls *trading men*, or, simply, *tradesmen*. These are 'our grocers, mercers, linen and woollen drapers, Blackwell-Hall factors, tobacconists, haberdashers, whether of hats or small wares, glovers, hosiers, milliners, booksellers, stationers, and all other shopkeepers, who do not actually work upon, make, or manufacture, the goods they sell'.

The merchant is at the top of Defoe's hierarchy. For him, this title confers an 'honourable distinction'. *Merchants* are those who 'carry on foreign correspondences, importing the goods and growth of other countries, and exporting the growth and manufacture of England to other countries'. Despite their ambiguity, these descriptions help us understand the paper-hangings market and some of its leading figures. The *dominotiers*, who sometimes travelled around by horseback to village markets, were *pedlars*. Some of them had shops, some did not. But, either way, they fit his definition of *handicraft*: 'those who make the goods they sell'. The English paperstainers could have sold their own goods, and no doubt many did. Yet most of them must have fallen into the category of *handicraft* or *mechanic* because they made goods to be sold by others.

The *merchant* designation can be applied to businessmen who bought and sold paper-hangings on an international scale. Daniel Henchman and Thomas Hancock in Boston, John Rowe and Thomas Harris in London, and John Baird in Quebec all fit the description, and will be heard from later in this book. Thomas Hancock in particular was a paragon of trade. He was certainly one of the wealthiest men in America – yet not so successful that dabbling in paper-hangings was beneath him.[75]

Defoe's categories of *handicrafts* and *tradesman* apply to many in the wallpaper business. Among them are retailers such as George Minnikin, Edward Butling, and James Brooke, warehouse owners like Abraham Price and Robert Dunbar, and of course Thomas Bromwich. Thomas quickly transcended his *handicraft* speciality of gilded leather and, partly by trading on his installation know-how, became a quintessential *trading man* in the fields of dry goods, linen and wool, stationery, upholstery, papier-mâché, and wallpaper. It's not known if Thomas read Defoe. But surely he followed his advice: 'A *tradesman* ought to be able to turn his hand to any thing; that is to say, to lay down one trade and take up another, if occasion leads him to it, and if he sees an evident view of profit and advantage in it'.

Defoe (as usual), has more to say: 'mercers, linen-drapers, banking goldsmiths, and such considerable trades, are often, and indeed generally, carried on in partnership; but other meaner trades, and of less business, are carried on, generally speaking, single-handed'. There is no doubt where Thomas stood. Like many tradesmen of his time, he gained as much as £20 from agreeing to take on each of twelve apprentices. More important, apprentices provided unpaid help for at least three years. Thomas accepted the apprenticeships of J. Sherman in 1744, W. Cotton in 1747, and T. Willis in 1750. The three-year gap was a requirement of the Painter-Stainers' Company, the trade guild that Thomas belonged to. How he raised capital to acquire stock-in-trade is unknown, but a partnership seems likely. Certainly Bromwich & Leigh, his later business arrangement, was a formal partnership. Almost from the start, Thomas offered to match papers to fabrics 'to the utmost exactness', and often mentions paper-hangings in advertising – and yet these declarations are never placed first, and these paperstainers are never named. It seems highly likely that a partner or a subcontractor did the paperstaining work.

The Blue (formerly Blew) Paper Warehouse was fronted by Abraham Price beginning in 1724. In that year, his name appears in the Parish Poor Rate tax register, establishing that he was the property owner.[76] It could well be that day-to-day operations were supervised by foremen/paperstainers. Despite the charming depictions of wallpaper which grace eighteenth-century bill-heads, little is known about how the work was done. The images and descriptions of the goods in advertisements were aimed at contemporary consumers – not posterity. John Hall, a local paperstainer, succeeded Price in 1750. Robert Dunbar's Paper Warehouse left even fewer traces. Dunbar had a wife and four children and died in 1744. Robert Jr carried on the business until 1752, and died in 1766. These facts are nearly all that is left of a business spanning some thirty years.[77] See Texts: *A General Description* for more about early paperstaining shops.

## Calico-Printing: A Related Trade

We've learned about the 'paperstaining' tradesmen, but how did block printing develop? To find out, it's necessary to digress from the paperstaining trade to one that immediately preceded it – calico printing:

> The Indians paint all their calico with the pencil [brush]; which they do very expeditiously, at a prodigious low price [...] The honourable East India Company have been at a vast expense to find out the secret of their die, especially of red, but to no purpose [...] The European Method: We perform our printing in a different manner: it is properly printing. We took the hint from the Hamburghers, who first fell into that method. It is performed in this manner: the pattern is first drawn upon paper, the whole breadth of the cloth intended to be printed; the workman then divides the whole pattern into several parts according to its largeness, each part being about eight inches broad and twelve inches long; each distinct part of the pattern thus divided is cut out upon wooden types; the cloth to be printed is extended upon a table, and the types being covered with the proper colours, are laid on, and the impression is left upon the cloth.[78]

On the next page, Campbell states that 'Paper-Hangings are printed after the same manner, and may properly enough be called a Branch of this trade'. Secrecy was of the utmost importance in the trades, and calico printing was no exception. Campbell advises prospective apprentices that

> the chief care is to be taken in the choice of a master, who not only understands his trade, but is communicative of the secrets of his business: most of the calico-printers have some particular secret in the preparation of their colours, which they never reveal even to their apprentices, unless they are strongly obliged to it by the indentures: without the knowledge of these nostrums, the boy, though expert in cutting and printing, will never be esteemed a workman, nor can possibly set up for himself, with any prospect of success.[79]

One of the peculiarities of the seventeenth- and eighteenth-century paperstaining trade is that there are so very few who 'set up for himself' in the sense of having a retail presence. Instead, paperstainers are found selling to linen drapers, upholders, stationers, and warehouses. This reliance on a subcontracting system has had the odd effect of removing the paperstainer – the one who actually did the work – almost entirely from the historical record.

## Taxes And Tariffs

The wallpaper trade included far more than merely making and moving a product. Another side was the imposition of taxes and tariffs on the goods. Exports from French and English traders before 1700 must have been priced to account for the taxman's share. By 1700, paperstainers began targeting a new market, as potentially lucrative as it was close to hand – the finer goods for the finer people. The product was upgraded: design, fine materials and novelty came to the fore.

The 1712 wallpaper tax added to the existing tax on paper. This value-added tax proves that paper-hangings were making headway against silk, velvet and wool hangings. Paper-hangings were put into the same category as silks, which might suggest 'luxury' status. Yet this interpretation must be viewed with caution. It could be that they were put into this category not because of cost, but because they were printed on, like silk and other fabrics. It's possible, too, that the wallpaper tax inhibited the production of middling or lower-class wallpaper by elevating the cost of all wallpaper. If so, it would help to explain why these lower types survive so infrequently.

A few years after the wallpaper tax went into effect, the established paperstainers complained to the government that 'private and inferior workmen' were avoiding the tax and thereby underselling them. In 1716, the 'Printers, Painters, and Stainers, of Paper Hangings' petitioned Parliament: 'Since there is no provision made, as there is in the Case of the Callicoes, for the stamping the said Paper Hangings [it is] humbly propose[d] that every Sheet of the said Paper, so manufactured, either in Pieces, Reams or Quires, as well Stock in Hand [...] may [...] be stamped'.[80] Other writers have noted legislation predating 1716 which mandated the stamping of wallpaper, so this petition may have been simply urging stricter enforcement.[81] In any case, the tax burden fell on the manufacturer.

But perhaps the tax stamp has done more for historians than it did for eighteenth-century paperstainers. Wallpapers with tax stamps have been found all over the world. The stamp of a harp (denoting Ireland) was found on the rough linen support of a Réveillon arabesque hung around 1807 at the Lorenzo estate in Cazenovia, New York. A chinoiserie paper hung at Wotton-Under-Edge, England in around 1740 was thought to be a Chinese export paper until well into the twentieth century. Finally, during restoration in 1924 an English tax stamp was discovered on the reverse, shedding an entirely new light. It was perhaps the most spectacular misattribution in wallpaper literature.[82]

An obscure aspect of the tax is the *drawback,* described here by Dagnall:

> Wallpaper that was exported would already have received the various stamps and the duty would have been paid on it. However, since exported wallpaper was not liable to duty, the Statutes allowed a drawback (i.e. a refund) [...] the Charge Marks were cut off to indicate that the drawback had been allowed.[83]

The cutting off of the Charge Marks helps to explain why tax stamps are not always evident on paper-hangings sent overseas. Drawback amounts appear in a few eighteenth-century consumer bills in America. Other notations about paper-hangings subject to the drawback almost certainly lie in wait in ships' manifests and other wholesale archives. Since the tax statutes are known, documented drawback amounts may yet yield important information about costs and amounts of paper-hangings.[84]

## Copying And Creating

The paperstaining trade sprang up in places with two essential ingredients: consumers who could afford decoration, and artisans who could raise capital, grind and mix colours, get strong paper, and maintain a work force. Paper-hangings were printed and coloured in down-and-dirty workshops. Retail shops added a sheen of glamour as they were launched into the world. Trade cards show retail counters overflowing with attractive upholstery goods; no doubt these were managed and staffed by attractive people. But, in the absence of widespread newspaper advertising to publicize the product, how *were* paper-hangings sold?

Paper-hangings were first sold in local markets in villages and small cities, then graduated to stationer's shops.[85] The rural paperstainer, like other folk artists, probably heaved a sigh of relief the day his wares found a home within a stationery shop, where they settled next to account books, wrapping paper, and playing cards. After gaining a foothold among town retail goods, paper-hangings ascended to city shops. Many of these were owned by linen drapers and dry-goods merchants who catered to upmarket patrons.

Meanwhile, another localized trade took up newly fashionable paper-hangings – the upholders. Upholders (repairers) were buyers and sellers of wares such as curtains, drapes, and other domestic stuffs. One of their lines of work was steady, if a bit peculiar; undertaking. Caskets, palls, black drapes, pink'd shrouds – all were needed to suit the solemn day, and upholders gladly supplied them. In the early-eighteenth century they broadened their reach to the cities, but everything suggests that they struggled to carve out some space in the London shop environment. One scholar found that there was no indication of prosperous regular upholders' shops in London until around 1730.[86] It would seem that Thomas Bromwich's graduation into the world of business in 1737 came just in time.

From early on, paperstainers, too, faced challenges. Block-cutting was expensive. The product needed to be well made, yet affordable; and distinctive, yet familiar. These aims were met through the skilful selection of pattern. Designing wallpaper was like mining for precious metals, because makers needed to find and exploit a vein of public taste. Once stencils or blocks were created, a different and arguably more important phase began – that of adapting the design. Paperstainers enhanced their wares and shored up their investment by changing colours, adding or deleting motifs, and adding a few stripes or spangles. Designs could never be *outré*. Yet, if they were too tame, the public would grow weary. The profit in paper-hangings did not come from controlling the market, nor was that possible. Profit came from units sold – from enlarging the market.[87]

In Paris, most decorative papers were sold in the rue St. Jacques. The Sorbonne (university) was nearby, fuelling the demand for stationers' goods. The counterpart in England was around St Paul's Churchyard, where generations of leather gilders, stationers, and paperstainers set up shop. In Dublin, it was Temple Bar, near the south bank of the River Liffey. In North America, the stationery strongholds were Boston, Albany, New York, and Quebec. Once well-heeled consumers gained confidence in the capabilities of paperstainers, the bespoke (custom) market opened up. Although this specialty work was often solicited in ads it seems likely that most wallpaper would have been printed from existing blocks. It was far cheaper and easier to print with an existing block than to carve new ones.

In the paperstainer's workshop, a cycle of copying and creating was the norm. Paperstainers could add new patterns by adapting designs from ornament books; copying the latest paper-hangings from competitors; soliciting bespoke patterns; creating from scratch; or converting textile patterns to paper. For example, many black and white silk embroidery designs were popular in the first half of the seventeenth century. Interpretations in paper-hangings were also popular in the second half of the century. Copying gained in importance (and was probably easier to get away with) away from major cities.

In 1746 the Messink family of Dublin unashamedly advertised paper-hangings based on 'Patterns from London'. About ten years later the widow Ashworth 'supplied herself constantly with the newest Patterns in the English and Indian Strain'.[88] Fifty years later, paperstainers in the American colonies were just as frank about their appropriations. When they bothered to mention copying, it seems almost a point of pride. Although intellectual property rights didn't exist in the early modern period, there was sporadic protection for fabric and leather hangings designs. The same is rarely found for paper-hangings. In France the *privileges* were important, but were directed at processes rather than patterns. English patents, too, seem mainly concerned with processes: gilding, embossing, and the like.

The paper-hangings trade grew from humble origins, but it eventually broke through. Wallpaper had a measurable impact on the furnishings market in the 1720s and 1730s, when 'design' was being simultaneously invented by tradesmen and discovered by the buying public. One scholar attributes this rise to 'retailers' competition to provide variety and novelty to their customers' which resulted in 'the formation of specific retailing identities in the 1720s'.[89]

In the second quarter of the century, print rooms and papier-mâché emerged as respectable options for wall decoration. These successes must have lifted the spirits of wallpaper tradesmen and encouraged them to seek out new customers. Wallpaper consumers certainly deserved their attention. As the ever-quotable Daniel Defoe put it in *The Complete English Tradesman*: 'As buying is indeed the first, so selling is the last end of trade'.

# CHAPTER 6:

# Wallpaper Shopping

## 1699

*Of paper there are divers sorts finer and coarser, as also brown and blue paper, with divers that are printed for the hanging of rooms; and truly, they are very pretty, and make the houses of the more ordinary people look neat. At Ebbisham [Epsom] in Surrey, they call it paper tapestry, and if they be in all parts well pasted close to the wall or boards they are very durable; and it ought to be encouraged, because 'tis introductory to other hangings.*[90]

*A great deal of paper is now a-days so printed to be pasted on walls, to serve instead of hangings; and truly if all parts of the sheet be well and close pasted on, it is very pritty, clean, and will last with tolerable care a great while; but there are some other done by rolls in long sheets of a thick paper made for the purpose, whose sheets are pasted together to be so long as the height of a room; and they are managed like woolen hangings; and there is a great variety with curious cuts which are cheap and if kept from wet, very lasting.*[91]

The consumer press did not exist in wallpaper's infancy, but the journalist John Houghton spoke directly to farmers and small businessmen in these two articles. An appraisal of Houghton notes that 'it was not to the gentry or the scholars that he appealed; it was to a middle-class seeking edification, and interested in reading'.[92] Thus, Houghton's observations have great value: through them we see this new product as a contemporary consumer might have.

In this chapter wallpaper finds its commercial footing, as reflected in ads. Although the advertisements are repetitive, they can surprise us with intriguing details. One of these is the invention of 'mock flock' – wallpaper which had the nerve to imitate itself. Mock flocks were cheaper versions of flock wallpaper which substituted pigments for wool fibres. These and other types continually built up the variety of wares as the market expanded. There's no doubt that the 1712 wallpaper tax and royal patronage by 1725 were signs that wallpaper had arrived. Yet, expanding market or not, these developments by no means catapulted wallpaper into well-stocked upholstery shops. Stationers continued to dominate the trade.

It's fitting that Houghton's 1699 comments about 'the houses of the more ordinary people' lead off a discussion of the wallpaper market, because they strike a balance between

## First Interlude:
## Sending Wallpaper Across The Seas

In 1737 Thomas Hancock, stationer in Boston, sent a personal request to John Rowe, stationer in London. Hancock's letter shows how personal and finely tuned the acquisition of wallpaper could be; he even asks for it to be 'done by the same hand'.

### 1737

Sir – Inclosed you have the dimensions of a room for a shaded hanging to be done after the same pattern I have sent per Captain Tanner, who will deliver it to you. It's for my own house and entreat the favour of you to get it done for me to come early in the spring, or as soon as the nature of the thing will admitt.

The pattern is all was left of a room lately come over here, and it takes much in ye town and will be the only paper-hanging for sale wh. am of opinion may answer well. Therefore, desire you by all means to get mine well done and as cheap as possible, and if they can make it more beautiful by adding more birds flying here and there, with some landskips at the bottom, should like it well. Let the ground be the same colour of the pattern. At the top and bottom was a narrow border of about 2 inches wide wh. would have to mine. About three or four years ago, my friend Francis Wilks, Esq., had a hanging done in the same manner but much handsomer, sent over here from Mr Sam Waldon of this place, made by one Dunbar, in Aldermanbury. In other part of these hangings are great variety of different sorts of birds, peacocks, macoys, squirril, monkys, fruit, and flowers, &c.

But a greater variety in the above-mentioned of Mr Waldon's and should be fond of having mine done by the same hand if to be mett with. I design if this pleases me to have two rooms more done for myself. I think they are handsomer and better than painted hangings done in oyle, so I beg your particular care in procuring this for me, and that the patterns may be taken care off and return'd with my goods.[96]

the lower-class origins of wallpaper around 1650 and the slick commercial veneer it had obtained by 1750. Wallpaper started as a rural craft exporting to the city but over these hundred years the path reversed. Exchanges between high-born lady letter-writers prove that they relied on city fashion while decorating country homes. One of the results was that travelling installers sent out from city firms installed products that had not yet appeared in local markets.

French tradition holds that *dominotiers* produced and sold wallpaper. Across the channel, this was certainly true of Edward Butling in 1690 as he opened his shop doors in Southwark every day at the foot of London Bridge (see Texts: Butling). A few years later, on the opposite side of the bridge, stood the shop of James Brooke.[93] Butling's shop was called the Knave of Clubs, an allusion to the playing cards he stocked. The elevation of paper-hangings to higher social status by 1735 or so may have changed the rules of the game. As paper-hangings became more available in the high-rent districts, the need for customers to associate with street pedlars or small shops dwindled.

A half-dozen wallpapers from the late-seventeenth century have been identified with workshops (or perhaps a single workshop) near Epsom, Surrey. These papers were found in homes built by London merchants in Epsom, a spa town. In retrospect, it's no wonder that merchant homes like those in Epsom – prosperous and well cared for – have harboured and preserved some of the earliest wallpapers. At least one paper was found in modest circumstances in the South Street Cottages.[94] This local aspect may well have characterized early production and use. In France, the *dominotiers* sometimes sold their wares on a circuit – travelling, for example, on horseback to surrounding towns and villages. In fact, Jean-Michel goes to the trouble of showing a man on horseback in front of the Papillon workshop (figure 6) in one of his drawings. Prints were another product that depended on pedlars: 'This popular market for prints was sustained by the chapmen who travelled the country hawking miscellaneous wares'.[95]

Hancock's tasteful friend, Francis Wilks, came from the Austin Friars section of London. Wilks was a merchant and the agent of Massachusetts in England from 1728 to 1742. In view of his decorating tastes, it's interesting that he was a member of the East India Company. Few colonials were as well placed as Thomas Hancock for their wallpaper shopping needs. He inherited the shop of Daniel Henchman, the most prolific wallpaper trader in early America. Years later, many colonists bought wallpaper from Hancock himself, as we shall see.

# The Paperstainer's and Upholder's Shop

Lady Hertford (later Duchess of Somerset), lady-in-waiting to Queen Caroline, visited a paper warehouse in 1741 and left with some wallpaper. Certainly wealth had its prerogatives; she could have afforded to put anything she wanted on her walls. It's easy to imagine her strolling into a shop like the Golden Lyon on Ludgate Hill, almost continually occupied by upholders in the eighteenth century, including Thomas Bromwich. While there, she could have peeked in the back rooms at the bespoke patterns of others or ordered some for herself.

In theory, a bespoke product, including the template, belonged exclusively to the patron. Perhaps some patterns made for royalty were taken out of circulation. However, it's more likely that most bespoke patterns never left the paperstainer's cellar. In a few weeks or months another iteration could be printed up; strategies like adding a leaf or stripe could ease the way. Nevertheless, custom trade *was* important. It earned not only cash but also prestige.

Lady Hertford, nor anyone else, of course, could shop until businesses were established. Founding a business was always risky and expensive, but the stock required for an upholstery shop stretched resources to the breaking point. Trade guides say that between £10 and £500 were needed to set up as a paperstainer, but that setting up as an upholder could take twice as much. The need for capital continued in America: 'At the start of his career in 1728, Samuel Grant acquired goods costing over £600 to stock his shop. Like many young Boston tradesmen, Grant lacked the necessary capital to make such immense purchases outright and therefore drew on his ties within the community to receive goods on credit'. Yet, there were forty-four individuals recorded working as upholsterers in Boston between 1700 and 1775: 'The great majority came from well-established, local families of the middle and upper strata of society [...] Prominent Boston families clearly considered the upholstery trade a suitable profession for their children'.[97]

There were few upholstery shops in London around 1700 but they were not unknown. For example, The *Female Tatler* of 1709 described the drapers' shops on Ludgate Hill as 'perfect gilded theatres'.[98] In these shops columns were made of plaster instead of stone, and the interiors had a dramatic flair. Equally important was the role played by the proprietors of these theatres. According to Claire Walsh 'the upholder had to exhibit a knowledge of which objects, or combination of objects, were tasteful and an intuitive understanding of what might be considered tasteful in the near future'.[99]

As the market grew, the established shops were buffed and polished until they shone. By crowding their shops with mirrors and furniture, linen drapers and upholders created a 'domestic ambiance around their wares'.[100] William Marford's draper's shop, inventoried in 1721, included a 'pier glasse and 3 glass sconces, 4 leather stools, 2 chairs and cushions, a silk curtain and 10 indian pictures'.[101] Away from the shop, the personal refinement of the upholder, the interior decorator of his day, made up for deficiencies in the manner and appearance of his tradesmen.

Without question many samples of wallpaper must have been unfurled to advantage within the shop, where they would have been hoisted onto display boards and placed in windows. Because patterns of paper-hangings were wildly disparate, they could hardly be sold through advertising alone. And once shoppers arrived to pick out the wares, they quickly learned that wallpaper was by no means straightforward to use. Fitting it into important rooms was never easy, and fitting alongside of raised panelling, high dadoes, and fine window hangings was more challenging yet. These problems were solved by talking with a well-seasoned proprietor, someone who'd seen it all and could advise on best practice.

According to Walsh, 'the retail shop and the workshop of up-market retailers were always distinct and separate areas. The specialized activity of selling was kept away from the dirt and noise of manufacturing'.[102] Paperstainers' workplaces, which were often small, reeked of hide glue and had messy colouring materials strewn about, would have been particularly well segregated.

The recorded costs of early-eighteenth century wallpapers are few, yet they suggest that a range of prices was the norm. One scholar argues that 'it was the consumer market that mattered ultimately' for eighteenth-century trade, and that craft luxury goods were merely another form of consumer durable.[103] This certainly rings true for wallpaper, which appealed to peasants as well as to princes.

As we've seen, consumers very occasionally used decorative papers on walls. Sometimes, wallpaper was used off the wall. One strange instance was the 'touching and innocent custom' known as Maiden's Garlands. A ballad celebrates the practice as early as 1630. These paper flowers were inserted into woven baskets and hung high in church aisles to memorialise betrothed females who died before their wedding day. In *Hamlet* (1601) a priest chants at the burial of Ophelia in the churchyard:

> Yet here she is allowed her virgin crants,
> Her maiden strewments and the bringing home
> Of bell and burial.[104]

This particular folk use incorporating 'crants' (derived from German *Kranz* or Dutch *Krans*, meaning 'wreath' or 'chaplet') was widespread. There are around sixty-five churches in England with records or examples, and they have also been found in France and Germany.[105] Many of the paper flowers within the baskets were boldly coloured with reds, yellows and blues, and some of them were, in fact, decorative lining papers and wallpapers.

Quires of seventeenth-century wallpapers were stockpiled and used long into the next century to create these paper flowers. Some of these fragile paper bouquets were conserved some years ago. When examined by a paper conservator, 'the paper revealed a pattern of flowers in a vase and Tudor roses printed in black with green and white additions. Further investigation revealed that the black design was actually a woodblock print overlaid with green and white stencilling'.[106]

## Random Notes On Trading Customs

Though there were Irish paperstainers before 1750, it's not until the advent of the 'Donnybrook Papers [...] printed in the neatest manner' by Thomas Ashworth in 1754 that the seriousness of the Irish trade is evident. Ashworth operated out of the Blind Quay and petitioned the government for aid. He received £500 to expand his business. Unfortunately, he was robbed and murdered on the byways near town in December 1757. His widow carried on. She claimed some years later that they had sunk £2,000 into the shop.[107] It seems that the generosity of the authorities was prompted by the desire to sustain and expand home-grown businesses.

A Dublin ad from 1746 is interesting for its association with tapestry, the variety of the wares, and for the assertion that goods are both made and sold:

> [Bernard and James Messink] [...] do make and sell superfine Imbost shaded Paper Work, in imitation of Tapestry or Needlework, fit for hanging of Rooms, Skreens, Fire Skreens, Chimney Pieces and Door Pieces and make all sorts of common Imbost paper Work in imitation of Coffoy, or Green Damask, as also all other sorts of printed Paper with Variety of Colours and Patterns from London, which none in this Kingdom can exceed, nor execute equal to them.[108]

Samuel Dixon advertised 'large India Paper for Hangings' in 1754 in addition to his own 'special work' in 'basso relievo, etc.' at Capel Street.[109] 'Basso relievo' is Italian for low relief, an unmistakable reference to papier-mâché.

Contraband was another significant aspect of consumerism. Smuggled goods have a persistent if not exactly upright history among household acquisitions. For example, goods coming into New France were required to be produced in France, and a 1733 French law prohibited 'all shipowners and traders dealing in the American colonies' from sending 'fabrics and canvases of India, Persia, China and the Levant' into Quebec. 'Papers of India' faced stiff duties even when coming into France. But smuggling, aided by official complicity, was widespread. A sweeping search by the Quebec authorities in 1741 found that 449 out of 506 dwellings contained English contraband.[110]

Wallpaper was soon so prolific that product names became overwhelming. The fifth edition of the *Compleat Appraiser*, a London commercial guide, said in 1783 that 'To set down all the particular names that wall-paper is distinguished by would be endless: the following are the most general names the patterns are known by, viz. imbossed, stucco, chints, check'd, striped, mosaic, damask, common'. A 1752 magazine, Henry Fielding's *Covent-Garden Journal*, told how far paper hangings had spread:

> Of all our Manufactures, there is none at present in a more flourishing Condition, or which hath received more considerable Improvements of late Years, than the Manufacture of Paper. To such Perfection is this brought at present, that it almost promises to rival the great staple Commodity of this Kingdom [wool]. [...] Our painted Paper is scarce distinguishable from the finest Silk; and there is scarce a modern House, which hath not one or more Rooms lined with this Furniture.[111]

Meanwhile, across the channel, French artisans had been tardy in realizing the possibilities of roll paper. Finally, in 1750, stationers like J. P. Fournier, who traded at the sign of the 'Good Workman', rue Carrè St. Martin, began pasting sheets together to form rolls. The second half of the century was to be as full of French roll paper as the first half was bereft.[112]

## CHAPTER 7:

# 'where there is wall'

Figure 13: Planche 3.4.; patching walls.

## 1733

*I am told if yr walls are not thorough dry your paper will be quite spoyld, and if they are dry the best way is to put the paper to the walls without any liming, if the walls are only one ruff cote and not whited, but if they are whited, it will not do so [...] This is a good scheme to save expence, and I am ashured 'tis by much the best way where there is wall.*

Letter, Sarah Byng Osborn to her son, Danvers.[113]

Sarah wrote to her eighteen-year-old son about the renovations he was overseeing at the family seat. Overseeing, that is, when he was not in London staying up half the night! After hearing that young Danvers has 'kept very ill hours since he went down [to London]', she wrote to her sister asking her to convey advice from an anonymous friend that 'two o'cock in the morning is very improper hours'.

The plastering was being done in preparation for wallpaper at Chicksands in Bedfordshire, seat of the Osborn Baronetcy. Saving the expense of the final plaster coat, even at this early stage, was a selling point for paper-hangings. By 1733, the dangers of moisture striking through and wrecking paper-hangings were well-known. No doubt with the spread of wallpaper came a growing understanding of how it should be installed. In another letter to Danvers, Sarah wrote that 'the chimney wall in the little green room was not dry enough to put up the green paper'. Apparently all went well: 'I am persuaded you will be pleased with ye furniture of that room [the library], tho it is but paper'.

Wallpaper was easily adapted to the changes in wall surfaces. Certainly plaster was more hospitable than wood, which often split wallpaper asunder due to seasonal expansion and contraction. Wallpaper and plaster were a match made in heaven, so easily did the porosity of one work with the porosity of the other. Nevertheless, wooden walls had developed, by 1733, an entire vocabulary of constituent parts. These forerunners can be traced in today's walls, with their baseboard (plinth), wall surface (panel), chair rail (surbase) and crown mouldings (cornices).

## Defining A Wall

In England, wattle and daub (branches and mud) were used in countryside houses for hundreds of years. The insulating qualities of plaster and wood sheathing were recognized and integrated into vernacular framed buildings to defeat the problems of rain, drafts and rising damp. Over this same period, stone and masonry were the mainstays in the construction of more pretentious dwellings. It seems that most of the paper-hangings coming into use after 1650 or so were hammered into or pasted onto wood walls. A hundred years later, plaster was the rule for domestic walls, at least in the better dwellings.

*Sheathing* is the rudimentary type of flat panels that cover a void before something more elaborate is added. *Panelling* is a generalization to denote plain panels (usually vertical, but sometimes horizontal). These could be flush (butt seamed), tongue and groove, or slightly lipped. A raised decorative moulding at the edge of the panel was more attractive, but cost time, skill and money. C. F. Innocent depicts several of these interesting boarded partitions and comments: 'they show the inventiveness of the old carpenters within a very limited range'.[114] On American shores, this type was sometimes called *creased*.[115] *Wainscotting* is a full complement of stiles (vertical moulding), rails (horizontal moulding) and panels of various shapes and sizes. *Raised panelling* or *boiserie* denotes an elaborate formal approach. This type had to be completely resurfaced (battened and canvassed) to be made ready for wallpaper.

So much for definitions. Yet, the progress of wall surfaces in Western Europe is often contradictory. If a house had a raised panel interior in one generation, that was no guarantee that it would not be altered in the next generation, as may have happened at Chicksands. The situation was somewhat different in North America, where all housing was new. Nevertheless, it's difficult to plot a neat progression for wood and plaster in either location.

Joseph Moxon was a Restoration-era map and chart maker and is best remembered for his *Doctrine of Handy-Works*, in which he laid down contemporary rules for a variety of trades. His rules for panelling have surprising relevance because ever since, wall

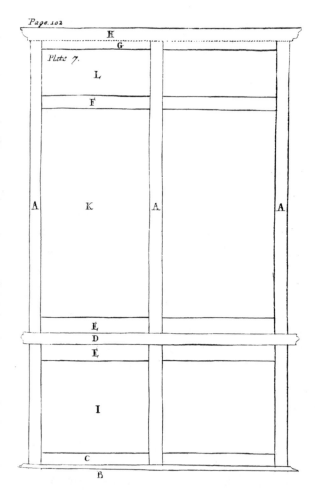

Page. 102

Plate 7.

decoration has tended to follow his neatly catalogued forms, as described below:

A. Stiles
B. Base
C. Lower Rail
D. Sur-base
E. Middle Rails
F. Frieze Rail
G. Upper Rail
H. Cornice
I. Lying Panel
K. Large Panel
L. Frieze Panel

The full wainscotting treatment included three types of panels and four types of rails. Although panelling followed certain conventions, there was always a need to adjust the size and number of panels. Moxon gives considerable latitude to the joiners:

Figure 14: Moxon's drawing of wainscot; Plate 7, p. 102 in *Mechanick Exercises.*

*In wainscoting of rooms there is, for the most part, but two heights of panels used; unless the room to be wainscoted be above ten foot high, as some are eleven or twelve foot high, and then three heights of panels are used: as: I. The Lying Panel, above the base; K. The Large Panel above the Middle Rail; and L. The Frieze Panel above the Frieze Rail.*

*The Frieze Rail is to have the same breadth the margent of the stile hath; the Middle Rail hath commonly two breadths of the margent of the Stile, viz. one breadth above the Sur-base, and the other below the Sur-base. And the Upper and Lower Rails have also each the same breadth with the margent of the stile.*

*Those moldings above the prickt line on the top, as H., are called the Cornice.*

*Sometimes (and especially in low rooms) there is no Base or Sur-base used, and then the Middle and Lower Rail need not be so broad: for the Middle Rail need not be above a third part more than the margent of the Rail: and the Lower Rail you may make of what breadth you see convenient. They are commonly about three inches and a half, or four inches broad, yet this is no rule: for sometimes workmen make only a flat plinth serve.*

*You may (if you will) adorn the outer edges of the stiles and rails with a small molding:*

*and you may (if you will) bevil away the outer edges of the panels, and leave a table in the middle of the panel.*[116]

Moxon advises that some of the lower parts should be narrowed in a low room, or even dispensed with. His hints about 'adorning' the outer edges of stiles and rails with mouldings were just the beginning: over time, panel mouldings became highly decorative, mirroring the evolution of wallpaper borders.

Despite more attention to the decoration of mouldings, mitring was not often done in joinery work – it wouldn't hold because of seasonal swelling and contraction. Instead, skirting boards and the like were scribed to overlap each other. In Moxon's guidebooks, mitring is hardly mentioned, other than for 'Picture Frames and Looking-Glass Frames'.[117] When wallpaper borderwork from around 1700 is overlapped rather than mitred, as seen in figure 1 (the Blew Paper Warehouse ad), it raises a question: could this overlap be a reflection of the joinery of the time?

In Moxon's rulebook, proportions are important and rise to almost decorative levels. He mentions that Rails are conventionally 3 ½" to 4" wide. Similarly, the major categories of timber were fixed by custom regulations. Boards less than 7" wide were considered *battens*. *Deals* were plain sawn boards up to 3 ¼" thick, and from 7" to 11" wide. Boards more than 11" wide were *planks*, on which the highest duty was paid.[118] In all probability, when full wainscotting started, the existing sheathing was covered, resulting in two layers of insulation. Medieval panels were beveled on the back side so that they could move with the seasons. When bevels began appearing on the front side, panels took on a whole new life. What had been functional was now appreciated for how it looked. Practicality ruled when plaster began replacing wood. Lath and plaster wall cavities aided insulation, for example. The dado rail/chair rail/wainscot cap was retained not for an architectural or a design reason but for a practical one. It prevented chair backs from slamming into walls and thus saved on upkeep.

When fixed fabric hangings and paper-hangings came along after 1660 or so, the decorative development of panelling was curbed. There was no need to paint or varnish something that would be covered by finer materials.[119] Late seventeenth- and early eighteenth-century panels of plain wood became substrates for tacked fabric hangings or supports for canvas underlayments to be followed by paper-hangings. Sometimes, canvas was stretched and nailed to grounds (studs in the corners). An alternate method was lining the perimeter with battens. These wood members were mainly softwoods. The appearance of softwoods in building interiors is somewhat taken for granted but one advantage is that they were much easier to hammer into.

In 1700, cedar planking from the South Carolina Colony was being exported to Bristol, England. Abundant North American pine and fir competed with Norwegian softwoods to furnish panels and sheathing for European rooms. All these types of wood could be stained, painted or varnished. They were even grained, counterintuitive as that may seem. In the hierarchy of costs, graining deal to look like cedar cost 10d. per sq yd (1694), whereas the cost for real cedar was 5s. per sq yd (1701). In contrast, a typical cost for paper-hangings was about 4d. per sq yd (1700).[120]

When plaster entered the wainscotted room, it filled the top twelve inches or so of the wall and was sometimes moulded into decorative relief. The next step was to lower the wainscot to a high dado. In succeeding years the wainscotting was reduced still further until it reached what is familiarly called the chair-rail height. The sand, animal hair and lime ingredients of plaster were often available locally, creating regional variations of surface texture and colour. A well-plastered wall, marble-like in its smoothness or left pleasingly rough without a finish coat, is a thing of beauty. It seems that many plaster walls were left undecorated for long stretches of time for this very reason. Half-plaster walls were replacing wainscot in fine homes like Chicksands before 1733, and eventually, plaster took over nearly completely. Plaster never reached the base, however, where practical housekeepers continued to demand tile or wood.[121]

The staircase was a special area. Like the bookcase it was encased in wood and made up by joiners. Leather gilders repeatedly advertised their ability to make up custom sets of gilt leather for staircases, indicating that special treatment for these odd shapes was advisable. The walls surrounding the staircase were some of the first areas simplified when wood and plaster replaced raised panelling.

Sketches of carefully arranged 'hangs' for picture collections exist in some eighteenth-century archives.[122] Planning for pictures was not only aesthetic; it included the strategic placement of studs and framing members. These wooden members were necessary for pictures in heavy frames; they supported fabric hangings, and paper-hangings as well.

# 24 June 1737

*Memorandum for Andrew Gardener anent several alterations intended to be done at the house of Buchanan [...] The blue damask bed which is in the bed chamber off the dining room at Buchanan must be put into Lord Graham's bed chamber. There must be washing boards put around the said room and painted chocolate colour. But in regard to the walls are all to be covered with a handsome blue figured paper in place of hangings, corresponding as much as may be to the colour of the bed. The joiner and the upholsterer must agree upon the proper method of placing the timber or laths for putting up the paper or hangings and there must be a moulding of wood round the room, painted chocolate colour, to answer the height of the backs of the chairs that they may not rest upon nor spoil the paper hangings. And Nota. this must be observed in the three other rooms which are to have paper hangings.*[123]

Buchanan Castle was owned by the Duke of Montrose; his family moved from Glasgow to Buchanan in the 1730s. The Duke's son was the Marquis of Graham, and Andrew Gardener was a retailer in Glasgow. In this instance, 'timber or laths' were placed with extra care. Instead of the paper being fit to the room, at Buchanan the room was being fit to the paper.

Did English and American building practices differ? As a general rule, according to

Abbot Cummings, 'Englishmen's lives and attitudes in the New World must be seen as a part of a continuum'.[124] He gives the example of the arrival before 1650 of John Emery, Francis Bushnell, William Carpenter Jr, Ralph Mason and John Roper. All were professed carpenters who brought their traditions, tools, and artisanry with them. The dwellings they created were no doubt modelled closely, even exactly, on those back home. Men with skills like these disprove the notion that sturdy yeomen became do-it-yourself timber-framers and joiners upon disembarking.

In America, plaster made from sea shells was common in the earliest settlements on the coast, but inland ports like Hartford lagged until lime was available nearby. Eventually, most major rooms had three plaster walls, while the fireplace wall was often sheathed or panelled. It was not simply a matter of evolution, because by 1725 a gentleman could have used plaster, soft furnishings over sheathing, paper-hangings, or raised panelling. All were possibilities, even if not easily available.

Raised panelling had begun to replace wainscot sheathing as early as 1700. This elaboration of plain panelling went on for decades, but after about 1750 or so, 'the decreasing use of panelling, in some of the finest houses, was closely related to the development of paper-hangings'.[125] After 1750 wall arrangements were simplified, and panelling was usually contained below the dado. Despite these developments, the colonial fireplace wall remained elaborately panelled in finer homes. This treatment can be seen throughout Schuyler Mansion near Albany, New York, built in the early 1760s. Eventually, the fireplace wall also succumbed to plaster.

Plaster was often painted in oil and distemper in England as well as America. But many of these painted walls gave way to paper as the eighteenth century wore on. One of the most spectacular changeovers occurred in 1735, when the scenic decoration painted by Verrio in Queen Anne's Drawing Room in Hampton Court was covered over in green flock paper. Verrio had painted the ceiling and walls around 1704 in jaw-dropping fashion in this room built by Wren in 1694. During renovations in around 1735 Queen Caroline had the walls battened and canvassed. These underlayments were followed by the flock, which served as a backdrop for the *Triumphs of Caesar* series of oil paintings by Mantegna. Over time the green flock was replaced with red, and the paintings were moved to other parts of the estate. The flock stayed in place for a very long time. An account of the renovation in 1899 says that:

> The battening, canvas and paper were stripped down, and the painted walls, hidden for a hundred and sixty-four years, were once more revealed to sight [...] The [painted] borders had been here and there injured by the cutting away of the plaster to insert the wooden frames on which the canvases were stretched, and by, literally, hundreds of holes, made by the nails to hang pictures on, driven in through the canvas all over the surface.[126]

Imagine if you will bowing to Queen Caroline and climbing hand over hand to the top of the scaffolding in a room twenty feet high with walls thirty-five feet wide. Your assignment is to grab a chisel and hammer and carve out great slices of exquisitely painted plaster for the placement of the battens. A job not for the faint of heart!

It's ironic that the newly-restored wall paintings, which included views of the 'British Fleet and Prince George of Denmark pointing to it; and the four parts of the world, shown by four figures' were surrounded by a frame painted to 'represent a large panel of tapestry, with a gold fringe and a wide border of flowers, flanked by pillars and pilasters of pink-coloured marble'.[127] Thus Verrio's tapestry-like painted walls were once again revealed after a 160–year hiatus during which they were covered completely with tapestry paper.

# CHAPTER 8:

# Paperhanging

John Schaw was 'the most employed upholsterer in Edinburgh', according to master builder William Adam, who recommended him to the 5th Duke of Hamilton in 1740.[128] Schaw put up flock at Holyrood Palace in 1742 for Lord Glenorchy. The flock wallpaper was chosen, among other reasons, for its cheapness relative to fabric. It was put in a dining room on the south side of the Palace. 'There is some art, though not much, in putting it up' Glenorchy remarked at the outset.[129] Seemingly, all went well. But he later asked Schaw if he had used canvas under the paper. Later still, he wrote from London that 'when we put up paper hangings here over deal, they always paste them on harn [canvas] because deals warp and tear the paper'.[130] This line of reasoning suggests that the flocks were not put up as artfully as necessary.

Canvas underlayments are a refinement over methods for putting up paperhangings that were fairly well-known by the 1730s:

## 1734

Please to observe the following method of putting up the said hangings in any room, viz., first, cut one edge of each piece or breadth, even to the work, then nail it with large tacks to the wall and paste the edge of the next breadth over the heads of the tacks and so from one to another, till the room be perfectly hung, observing to make ye flowers join. N.B. damp the paper before you put it up, and begin next the window and make stiff paste of the best flour and water.

From the instruction sheet of Robert Dunbar's 'Paper Warehouse'.[131]

## Dunbar's Advice

This appears to be the first recorded instance of a paperstainer printing a borrowed instruction sheet on a bill-head and stuffing it into a roll of wallpaper. The wording

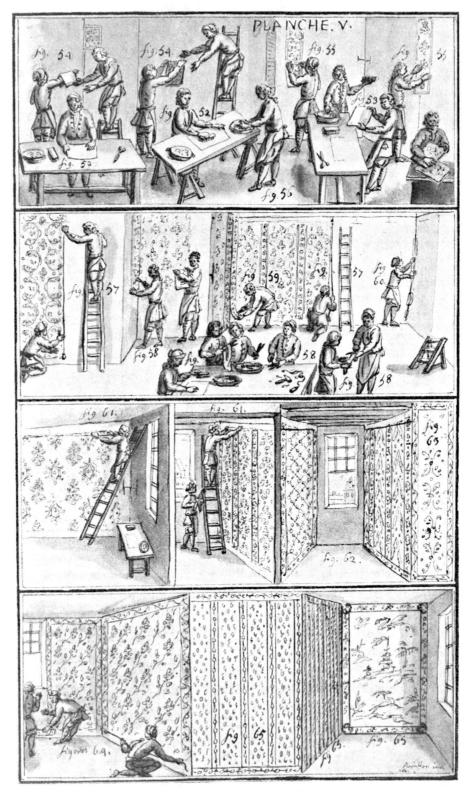

Figure 15: Planche 5; installation.

is practically identical to the thirty-year-old advice of the Blew Paper Warehouse (see figure 1). Plaster was gaining in fine homes but panelling was still common. One new recommendation in 1734 is paste – only tacks had been mentioned in the earlier instructions. Curiously, Dunbar mentions 'large tacks' while the earlier version had specified 'small tacks'. Dunbar also advises the following:

<u>cut one edge of each piece or breadth</u>: The full roll (piece) could be trimmed, or just one strip (breadth). By cutting <u>even to the work</u> Dunbar must mean 'cut to the pattern'. The other side of the strip retained the selvedge, which was covered on the wall by the trimmed and overlapping edge. The width of unprinted selvedge varied, but it was usually not less than a half-inch or so. Hand-trimming with shears left an edge that wavered slightly; yet, it was satisfactory for the time and place. Since the untrimmed edge was covered, it could retain a deckle (uneven) edge just as it came from the papermakers mould. Deckle edges are also found on the underlaps of joined sheets.

<u>nail it with large tacks</u>: This advice seems impossibly crude now. It's obvious (though not often brought out) that nails or tacks were ideal for hanging paper on wooden softwood panelling, high dadoes and surrounds.

<u>paste the edge of the next breadth over the heads of the tacks</u>: Only the first strip is tacked round its perimeter. Succeeding strips are tacked on three sides with the fourth side pasted over the tacked vertical edge of the first piece. Perhaps installers aligned the strip, anchored a single tack at centre top, tacked centre bottom, pasted the edge over, then finished the sheet by tacking the other three sides. Alternatively, they may have pasted the edge, taken the strip to the wall and aligned it, followed by tacking. Either way, plumb bobs would have been used for guidance. Most of the sheet appears to have been left floating. This would have allowed the paper to follow changes in relative humidity without buckling or tearing. During 1650–1750, there was no word for 'butted' – wallpaper was invariably overlapped.

<u>observing to make ye flowers join</u>: Researchers uncovering ancient decorative schemes are sometimes shocked to observe the degree to which 'ye flowers' *don't* join. Different cultural standards, different installation standards, and rudimentary production all worked against a perfect match.

<u>damp the paper before you put it up</u>: The similarity to fabric is brought out. When moisture infiltrates paper the fibres expand and relax. This improves the 'hand' or 'drape' of the material, which becomes easier to work with. The handmade paper of Dunbar's time was formed with a 'papermaker's shake' which resolved fibres into a criss-cross pattern. When relaxed by paste, the sheet expanded from the centre in all directions. This is the enduring magic of paper during installation, that it becomes fabric-like under the influence of moisture, and can be adapted to small discrepancies in the plane of plaster

walls or in the registration of printed patterns. Machine-made paper (common after 1840 or so) has a grain and therefore expands in only one direction – but it has many of the same virtues.

begin next the window: The installer hangs away from a window in either direction. This is perennial advice in trade manuals. If paper is hung toward the light, the overlapping edge causes a shadow. If paper is hung away from the light, the overlapping edge faces the light, eliminating a slight shadow.

## Tacks And Nails

Records of installations before 1750 are rare, but some were clearly tack jobs. Bills widely scattered by time and place show the use of tacks and nails (often rendered in the 'M', or per-thousand designation). In America, a 1741 job entailed 'New Tacking the paper hanging above in the chamber'.[132] This utilitarian tacking, which was covered by borders, is unlike that for finish upholstery, where the rich appearance of gilt nails and other decorative hardware is central to the work.

A 1740 bill from Robert Dunbar to Richard Hoare includes an entry for '1 M Tind Twopenny...0,1,6'. It's likely that they were used on the immediately preceding entries: '53 ½ yds 2 Green on Yellow Mantua' and '4 Dozen Frett Border'.[133] The border was almost certainly a papier-mâché or pressed paper substitute for a carved wooden cornice. At Traquair House (Scotland) in 1750, 'tinnd tacks' were used on a screen installation. They secured the wrapped canvas on a four-panel screen.

In the hierarchy of cost, simple black tacks for coarse underlayments were about 1s. per thousand, tinned tacks 1s. 6d. per thousand, and gilt nails for fabric could cost from 9s. per thousand and up. A 1736 bill shows a gilt nail cost of £1 per thousand.[134] Sometimes upholsterers put a 'red silk ferret' fabric tape under gilt nails to avoid rust. In a 1717 installation for the royal family Thomas Phill used 7,000 gilt nails at £2 per thousand for the upholstering of scarlet silk.[135]

## A Case In Point: A Bill from the Rose and Crown

Mrs Massingberd London April 24 1753
Bo't of Joseph Smith at the Rose & Crown
the corner of Angel Street St. Martins Le Grand

| | |
|---|---:|
| 13 ps & ½ of New Taby @ 2/ | 1.13.09 |
| 3 ps & ½ of New Stocko @ 3/- | 0.10.06 |
| for hanging 17 ps of Paper @ 1/- | 0.17.00 |
| Peast @ /2d @ ps | 0.02.10 |

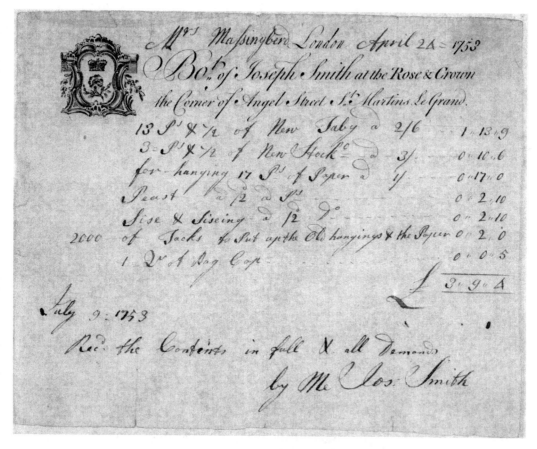

Figure 16: 'Bought of Joseph Smith at the Rose and Crown'.

| Sise & Siseing @ /2d do | 0.02.10 |
| 2000 of Tacks to put up the Old hangings & the Paper | 0.02.00 |
| 1 Qr of Bag Cap | 0.00.05 |
| | £3.09.04 |

The prices of the wallpaper seem toward the respectable lower end. 'New' often appears in bills with no further explanation. It may simply be a workshop designation, similar to run numbers, i.e. 'this is the New Stocko not to be confused with the previous Stocko, which we are nearly out of', thus helping to keep track of stock. 'Taby' paper-hangings were modelled after silks which were embossed with rollers to produce a watered or wavy pattern. Hanging charges at 17s. are about 33 percent of the material cost; this proportion is not uncommon.

This thorough bill suggests that Smith's shop was well established. Charges for paper, paste and size are included and an additional charge is made for the labour to apply the size to the wall. The foreman also puts in for 25 sheets of bag-cap, a cheap lining paper. These are so few sheets that they must have been used for wall repairs, or to line the edges of the canvas. The tack charges show that the old canvas was reused by pulling it taut and re-tacking; perhaps it was stripped of its old paper by others before Smith's crew arrived. 13 ½ pieces of New Taby would cover about 800 square feet, or a room 20 by 20 by 10 feet high. The amount of New Stocko is small in comparison. This amount of raised ornament could not have covered the ceiling; it was probably used as a border.

## Wheat Paste And Size

Starch pastes were commonly used for paperhanging. These were sometimes strengthened with glue, depending on the type of material to be hung. The wheat was cooked to a pudding-like consistency, and the glue warmed in a double-boiler (gluepot). Installers also *sized the wall*, spreading dilute glue onto plaster with large bristle brushes in order to reduce porosity and promote adhesion. These methods were the prerogatives of members of the Painter-Stainers' Company. To be sure, the technique known as marouflage (adhering painted cloth or textiles to a wall) required something stronger: 'Traditional mural adhesive recipes of the seventeenth and eighteenth centuries include Burgundian pitch, wax, resin and red ochre' as well as lead.[136] Paper, in contrast, was rather easily secured.

In 1699 Houghton noted that roll paper should be 'managed like woolen hangings'. It could just be that this manipulation involved tacking or nailing the paper, as opposed to pasting single sheets. When printed paper was 'well pasted close to the wall or boards', as he advised, the splitting of the paper from expansion of the wood must have soon prompted different methods of hanging.[137] Surprisingly, one of these was sewing. More surprising yet, this took place in Sweden, not a country that is often associated with early wallpaper, yet one that has its own well-studied traditions.

## Sewing

Swedish workmen used tacks and nails to fasten paper-hangings. On occasion, they also sewed the edges of the paper together prior to tacking and/or pasting. This was accomplished with large needles using thread with flax content. The rag and linen content of early paper gave it fibrous qualities unlike the paper of today. In a variation, the widths for an entire wall were sometimes sewn together. This large joined rectangle was nailed into place and finished with borders. This may have been how 'others after the mode of real tapistry' were installed, as stated in the text in figure 1.

A third Swedish method was blind tacking, called *Vändspikning*. It was common in the late-eighteenth century, but probably started many years earlier. After the first strip was nailed in place, the next strip was placed face-to-face on top of it. One side of the selvedge was nailed top to bottom to matching points and a cord was stretched tight between the nails. The strip on top was folded back to create a neat seam which would reinforce the installation.[138]

# Batten, Canvas, And Lining Paper

Linna Shaw, the imaginary little girl in the introduction, was annoyed with her brother for pulling a piece of canvas over her head, and with good reason. Canvas of this era was not like modern smooth cotton canvas, but more like biblical sackcloth, with scaly long fibres. Canvas supports had been used for leather installations long before 1600.[139] No doubt trial and error taught that paper adheres better and for a longer time to canvas than to wood. Best of all is a paper-to-paper interface, which explains the appeal of utilitarian lining paper (bag-cap, lumberhand or cartridge papers).

Canvas supports were pinned to the margins and sometimes shower-tacked all over a wooden substrate. Alternatively, an air space was created by nailing and stretching sewn canvas several inches from the substrate. The last step was to install the paper on the stretched canvas. As long as paper was not put directly on outside walls, it was safe from the transmission of moisture.

Stretched canvas was covered with *lining paper* for the better installations. Not to be confused with *decorative lining paper* for deed boxes or trunks, these lining papers buffered all kinds of installations. Liners absorbed paste from the finish paper so that moisture was less likely to strike through and affect inks. If no liners were available, newspapers or old court documents could be used. In all countries wallpaper was often hung directly over prior wallpaper, thus using the first wallpaper as an ad hoc lining paper.

Lining paper was especially recommended for large-figured flocks. The dyes and colours used for their backgrounds could be touchy, even if the wool itself was robust. Another reason for liner was that canvas's linen and hemp fibres (a byproduct of flax production) were rough. A London upholder explained to his patron in 1755 that 'your method of covering the walls with plain wood is certainly the best; and put up strong mearns Linen under the paper in Stead of canvas and paist a coat of writing paper upon it before the India paper is put up, otherwise you'll see all the threads of the linen thro' the India papr' (see Texts: The Duff/Mackay Correspondence).

Though canvas and lining paper improved the appearance and longevity of paper-hangings, these refinements were never in general use, even among the wealthy, who had a reputation for savings as well as extravagance. Nevertheless, such materials and methods must have been familiar to professed upholders like John Schaw and Thomas Phill, who were expected to make walls ready. Some walls had merely been furred out and hung with fabric, some were wainscotted with raised panels, and others had been panelled with plain deal. Batten and canvas frames fixed many of these situations.

# Borders

Tacks were needed to fasten wallpaper to wood, flat-headed nails were needed for piercing plaster, and both needed to be hidden. This need was met by the application of a small border.

Border methods were modelled on the book trade. Borders finished, decorated and

## HOW IT WORKS: HANGING PAPER ON CANVAS

Canvas was often used for underlayments, but the details were rarely written down. When paper is pasted to a strained canvas which had been stretched and nailed over an air space, the moisture from the paste saturated the fabric. Then, paper and canvas dried together, contracting all the while. In this way the surface became tight as a drum. Many, if not most, of the references to canvas underlayments probably followed this model. In a second method, the canvas was secured to the wall with paste, followed by layers of paper. A third method is shown in Papillon's drawings in Chapter 4 (figure 11, Planche 7.1.). A large piece of canvas is tacked directly to a wall. Paper and border are pasted to the canvas. When dry, the assembly is removed from the wall. The decorative paper panels are then tacked or pasted to rectangular wall spaces as needed. This last method was probably used the least because of potential damage to the decoration.

protected a wallpaper installation just as covers and marbled endpapers finished, decorated and protected a book. Paper-hangings borders often enclosed the perimeter of each wall, effectively creating a series of frames. In addition, each seam of the wallpaper was sometimes covered by a vertical border (see figure 1). A vestige of this practice is seen anytime an 'early pattern' of florals is subdivided by widely-spaced vertical borders. The effect mimics paned fabric on state beds common around 1717 where seams are covered with a narrow length of trim every 22" or so. The borders in the corners of figure 1 are unmindfully overlapped at 90 degrees; this, as opposed to the elegance of a mitred border. To be sure, borderwork of this period was far from fastidious. Instead of being inlaid directly against their sidewalls, borders were most often stuck on top of them. This overlapping technique was even used on flocks with a heavy pile. It may be tempting to dismiss some of this work as sloppy. And yet, it served the needs of the time.

Once the necessities were taken care of, decorative possibilities opened up, and borders bloomed with flowers, vines and a variety of architectural motifs. If a sidewall was trimmed right to the ceiling line, and a border placed on it, contraction from drying paper could pull both away from the wall. To avoid this, installers usually cut the tops of their sidewalls to extend just beyond the lower border line. This allowed the top half of the border to grab the wall as well as the sidewall. Following fabric conventions, vertical wallpaper borders were narrower than horizontal borders. Borderwork gained in importance when it was used to link up wall schemes for Chinese cabinets and print rooms.

Borders were often called dozens – another borrowing from the fabric trade. The highest grade of coarse, undyed woollen cloth among Yorkshire merchants was 24 yards long. The term 'double dozen' was sometimes used to describe the full piece, and 12 to 13 yards were called a 'dozen'.[140] Eventually, the term came to stand for a yard of borders. For example, an itemized bill from Robert Dunbar in 1741 included '40 ½ doz borders, 12d the dozen, 2.0.6.'.[141]

The term 'dozens' is sometimes confusing in a wallpaper bill, but here 'dozens' must mean 'yards'. It's worthwhile to follow this calculation to its logical conclusion. The borders in the example just cited were going into seven rooms. If '40 ½ doz borders' is taken to mean 40 ½ pieces of 12 yards, the result is nearly 5,000 linear yards of border – far too many for the seven rooms. But, if the figure of 40 ½ is taken to mean yards, this would produce about 1,200 yards. When this amount is divided by the seven rooms, the result is about 170 yards of border per room – a much more likely outcome.[142]

Borders were an ingenious solution for finishing a space. Quite apart from their decorative impact, they compensated for uneven walls and unsteady hands. In a nod to symmetry, they sometimes ran up each corner of all four walls, resulting in a double line in the corners. This corner treatment was grounded in practicality. If a sidewall pattern was centred on each wall, a mismatch at each corner was inevitable. This objection was partially answered by borders. Corner borders hid mismatches, or at least minimized them, while providing a frame. This problem solver turned into a style, though never one that was widely adopted. Double courses of border belonged to the high side of decorating. This treatment can be found into the early-nineteenth century, as seen in a request from a London firm to a prospective customer: 'you will be pleased to favor us with the dimensions of the room, as the border is usually put at the top and bottom, and up the four angles'.[143]

Batten and canvas nailing systems encouraged the use of three-dimensional fillets, which hid fasteners completely. Gilt borders in relief were popular because of the sparkly way they caught the light. In America, the noun 'bordering' became common, once again following conventions in the fabric trade: 'Sheets and blankets belonged to the class of goods that, when sold as yardage, had an 'ing' suffix added, as in 'sheeting'. Sheeting, which was mainly linen, was available in several widths and qualities, and could be seamed together at home'.[144]

However borders were used, it seems that they were almost always used. From the mid-seventeenth until well into the nineteenth century, wallpaper installations without them are rare.

CHAPTER 9:

# Installers

## 1742 [court testimony in Dublin]

*...Catharine M'Cormick says, she knew Lord and Lady Altham, when they lodged at Mrs Vices near Temple-Bar,, where Deponent was Servant in the Year before Queen Anne died, in or about the latter end of summer[1713]...*

*...Catharine M'Cormick: Being asked in what manner she got her livelihood? Says, by her honest industry, and that her employment is stamping or printing papers for rooms...*

*...thirty-third witness. Hannah Shaw, being asked if she knew one Catharine Mac Cormick; says, she knew one Catharine Mac Cormick that papers Rooms; that she came to the Deponent about a year before to paper a room...[145]*

The court case about Lord and Lady Altham is bizarre. It includes miscarriages, alienation of affection, a lost fortune, charges of murder, exile to America, and a return to Dublin. But for us, the testimony of Catharine Mac Cormick has special relevance: it proves that at least one lady installer/paperstainer was active in 1740s Dublin.

From Catharine's short resume, one gathers that she was a life-long member of the local working class. There must have been many female installers like her. Yet, these folks are truly lost to history. Whatever their gender, installers before 1750 did not operate stand-alone paperhanging businesses; they were not part of a painter/paperhanger alliance; they were not even called 'paperhangers'. That's why this chapter is about 'installers'.

Of course, there were reasons for Catharine's obscurity. In all countries, organized labour as we know it did not exist. Trade groups existed, but Catharine was probably not eligible to join them. Early modern craft groups espoused education, protection of the public from shoddy work, and constant improvement of skill levels. But on the contrary, the true intent of guilds and companies in the early-eighteenth century seems directed at securing trade within city limits – and denying it to others.[146] In England, the Painter-Stainers' Company sought to monopolize the creation and application of paint media.

The Worshipful Company of Upholder's had a more diverse bailiwick, a reflection of the buying and selling that was so congenial to its members.

Both operated to some extent as mutual-aid societies. They tried to look after their own, but their benefits could not compare with those of the major livery companies. A pension fund in the Worshipful Company was endowed in 1707 from a donation of £800. From it, twenty deserving members, or widows of deceased members, were given a yearly benefit of one pound sterling: 'In 1736, when Humphrey Skelton was taken ill, the Company gave him ten shillings and paid his landlady one guinea for looking after him. When he died a year later, the Company paid the funeral expenses which amounted to £4 10s.'.[147] One imagines an impressive display to mark Humphrey's passing, for he had been a member since 1698. But of what material were those black drapes made? Were they baize, or velvet? Was his shroud pink'd, or plain?

Two fraternities of artificers and installers, the Painter-Stainers' Company and the Worshipful Company of Upholders, are the main subject of this chapter. The Painter-Stainers', an ancient trade, are not to be confused with the *paperstainers*, who only emerged in around 1675. And this emphasis on groups should not lead to the conclusion that it was only, or even mostly, members of these groups who made wallpaper and carried out wallpaper installations. On the contrary, the evidence goes the other way: paperstainers and installers came from a variety of trades – and sometimes returned. Nevertheless, the story of these groups tells a lot about working conditions in the early modern period.

Both groups played important roles in handing down skills, whether hard-won or intuitively grasped. Apprentices were not ordinarily paid, though the master took care of most of their material needs. Future artisans started with the most menial tasks: grinding pigments and sewing underlayments. Only gradually were they allowed to touch more important work. Supposedly, during a traditional seven years apprenticeship, the artisan would receive a thorough grounding in the art or mystery at hand. At long last, administration – accounting, buying and selling, handling credit, and other front office work – was addressed, if not necessarily mastered. But apprenticeship (*servitude*) was only one way to join a company. Equally important was *redemption*, which meant buying your way in. Another way to qualify was through *patrimony*, which was limited to a son or daughter of a member. However entrance was achieved, the further step of obtaining the freedom of the company (graduation, in a sense) was essential. Self-directed and gainful employment became possible, even if the life of an artisan or a tradesman was hardly a gateway to prosperity.

## The Painter-Stainers' Company

For hundreds of years the exteriors of vernacular housing made do with wattle (branches) and daub (mud). Maintenance consisted in applying another layer of mud; amazingly, a layer of dung was not uncommon.[148] These coatings evolved into firmer and better looking materials which needed the protection of painting. Softwoods also came into use for interior and exterior walls, and these needed more protection than oaks and other hardwoods. From about 1200 or so, this 'house-painting with regards to maintenance would have been carried out by property owners on an ad-hoc basis'. On the other hand, decoration 'would have been undertaken by a professional'.[149] Starting with this early focus on decoration the painters added to their repertoire. By the fourteenth century the painters were well organized even if their numbers were small.

The Painters merged with the Stainers to form the Painter-Stainers' Company. The Company ordinances of 1582, Section 4, reserve the rights to gild and to lay or work colours in any medium such as oil, size, gum or varnish. The list of surfaces includes wood, stone, paper, parchment and plaster.[150] As early as 1626 the Company claimed 'flock-work' as one of their monopolies.

Throughout the seventeenth century, the Painter-Stainers' and the Plasterers' Company fought over who should paint what. The problem arose because by 1603 the Plasterers, in addition to occasionally painting on plaster with pigments in size or distemper, fell into painting with oil colours on surfaces other than plaster.[151] This was a clear encroachment on the rights of the Painter-Stainers'. In 1664 the Painter-Stainers' were self-described as 'in number above 400 householders within and about the City of London, besides their families; the greater part not attaining to the perfection of workmanship, have usually lived upon the grosser part of the science, as painting upon timber, stone, iron and suchlike, which the Plaisterers now intruding into the said science of Painting, have utterly taken away; but our Bill now exhibited is only to restrain them [the Plaisterers] from oil colours'.[152] The resolution of the dispute clarified the roles of the joined guild. The Painters were entrusted with painting upon 'timber, stone, iron and suchlike and the staynours for cloth, silk, and suchlike'.[153]

So it was that the Stainers and not the Painters had early command of the paperstainer's craft. This helps to explain why, throughout the eighteenth century, professional painters are more likely to be found glazing windows or painting coats of arms on carriages than fussing with paper-hangings. These guild rules may be archaic, but they always had a point. According to Patrick Baty,

> The Stainers' were employed in the production of stained or painted cloths, which were used instead of pictures on plaster walls [...] The quality of work produced was carefully controlled [...] no one was to produce work 'wrought with stencil or otherwise as painted [...] upon cloth, silk, leather or other things' [...] this was considered false and deceitful.[154]

Thus, moral aims could be served as well as economic ones. If there was any lingering shame attached to stencilling, this seems to have melted away by the time that paper-hangings began appearing in stationery shops. Although most of the recorded history deals with London, there are at least twenty-eight towns in England and Scotland that had a tradition of guildry, according to J. R. Kellett.[155] The Painter-Stainers' and other guilds naturally aspired to control their trade, but it was a losing battle. As early as

1614, the guilds had lost much. In a calamitous string of five cases decided by common law principles, it was evident that

> they could no longer be sure of their ability to enforce gild membership on unfreemen practising their craft or trade; nor could they compel the translation of men who could prove statutory apprenticeship with another company. Their powers of seizing goods during the search were in dispute and it was doubtful whether their ordinance prohibiting the sale by freemen of goods made under contract by unfree craftsmen would be upheld at law.[156]

By the last half of the seventeenth century, there were four groupings in the Company: Arms Painters, House Painters, Leather Gilders and Picture Makers.[157] By the time that paperstaining was well established, Companies and guilds were long past their prime. Nevertheless, the Painter-Stainers' Company remained the most important trade group for paperstainers and leather gilders, at least in London, for the rest of the eighteenth century.

## The Worshipful Company Of Upholders

The Worshipful Company were an equally venerable group, but not well defined. Their early modern history begins in 1626 with a charter from Charles I. They started as upholders (repairers) of household wares: 'The English tradesman who was responsible for upholstering chairs was the coffer-maker [...] the maker of the medieval traveling trunk, the trussing coffer, and the standard; and he applied fabric to chair-frames in the same manner as he applied leather to his coffers'.[158] Perhaps the disposal of leftover fabric and leather led the upholder into buying and selling generally. At first, they were loosely associated with the Skinners' Company. 'Frippery' seems appropriate to describe their wares, which may have been acquired in roundabout ways. From this unseemly start upholstery worked its way up. Yet even as upholders served royalty, they apparently never left behind the practical arts of creating and repairing soft furnishings.

After the Restoration of the monarchy in England, Scotland and Ireland in 1660, French goods and upholstery came into fashion, although of course English upholders did the bulk of the work. The Frenchman Francis Lapiere worked for Charles II (1660–85). Yet it was Robert Moore who claimed to be the official 'upholster in Extraordinary'.[159] Moore was moved to petition his monarch in graceful but persistent language because Charles had quickly racked up a debt of £9,800 and made good on only £600. The royal custom was to pay good artisans just enough to keep them engaged. This worked well until the day in 1677 that another renowned upholsterer, the Frenchman John Casbert Sr, was terminally disengaged. He went to his grave without the £1,464 he was owed by the English Crown.

The next monarch, James II (1685–88), liked French beds and upholstery no less than Charles and continued to employ Lapiere. Despite Lapiere's position, the official upholder around this time was the Englishman Richard Bealing. Frenchman Jean Poictevin, though he had no official status, supplied goods to the monarchy for decades, much like Lapiere. Throughout this time the ponderous Commonwealth style of joined furniture evolved. The sophisticated ideas brought to bear on the cabinet-maker's art reinvented upholstery of all types. State beds continued to offer the most lavish display, but windows and walls saw great changes, culminating in a fashion for fixed hangings.[160]

Despite this identification with great men and great furnishings, the Worshipful Company struggled. Karin Walton judged that 'the company was never an important one in the City's history'.[161] Adding injury to insult, the manuscripts of their early history were incinerated along with their Hall in the Great Fire of 1666. After that twin disaster, it seems that the Worshipful Company was perpetually broke. The loss of the Hall caused the members to meet for years at Paul's Head Tavern in Cateaton Street.[162]

Eighteenth-century diarists sometimes note the arrival of 'Bromwich's men' or 'Elwick's men', to carry on house renovating. Clearly, the travelling installers were sent out from headquarters. It's a reminder that installation usually involved hundreds and often thousands of square feet. These crews even received travelling money, though not without resistance. In 1751 William Windham complained that it cost 'a cursed deal' to bring a London shop outworker to install Chinese paper at Felbrigg Hall, his stately home in North Norfolk.[163] The charges included 3s. 6d. a day for labour, plus 6d. per mile traveling charges. No doubt William was relieved to bid his travelling paperhanger farewell as the paperhanger headed back to London.

Nor was William the only complainer. We've already seen that Charles II short-changed John Casbert Sr. Another troublesome client was the First Duke of Devonshire, who died deep in debt in 1707. John Mackey wrote in his memoirs that the Duke was of 'nice honour in everything but the paying his tradesmen'.[164] The Duke had built glorious Chatsworth – or rather, got others to build it. Thomas Chippendale begged Sir Edward Knatchbull to pay his overdue bills, but Knatchbull had a unique defence: 'As to what you sent last I have your Estimate of what it was to amount unto–& as I receive my rents once a year, so I pay my Tradesmens Bills once a year wch is not reckoned very bad pay as ye world goes; so that when the time comes round that shall be pd also'.[165]

How does the daily rate that Windham paid his traveling installer (3s. 6d. per day for labour, 6d. per mile for travel) compare to others? In 1753 an installer from the paperstaining company of Crompton & Spinnage was also paid 6d. per mile.[166] These travellers were proxies for a busy paperstainer or upholder-in-chief who was back in the shop drawing up contracts, corresponding with clients, buying supplies, and getting new work fitted up. But most local paperhanging must have been done by local installers. It is unknown who these counterparts to Catharine Mac Cormick were, or what their wages were like. On one occasion, John Blickley of London employed two other installers in 1756 and charged out their labour, and his own, at a daily rate of 1s. 10d. This was far less than William Windham's installer received.[167] Yet, just as there were different qualities in the merchandise, there must have been different qualifications in the work force. The anonymous author of *A General Description of All Trades* cites a daily rate of 2s. 6d. for a working upholder in 1747, thus neatly splitting the difference of the two wages cited above. Inevitably, the better-known installers operated at the upper reaches of society.

John Schaw, already encountered, was 'the most recommended upholsterer in Edinburgh'.[168] Another paragon was Thomas Phill, who supplied goods and services to royal households in England. Accomplished professionals like these installed fabric, leather and wool hangings. Adding the newly fashionable paper-hangings to their repertoire was a natural progression. Even French upholsterers specializing in state beds worked on walls: 'Francis Lapiere was a leading exponent of the 'upholstered room'.[169] 'Patronage' is perhaps too strong a word to describe the relationship these installers had with their clients, but it was not far from that.

Phill was apprenticed in the late-seventeenth century to 'Master Taylor' James Sims and was admitted to the Worshipful Company by redemption on 23 April 1700. He and Jeremiah Fletcher provided upholstery for the coronation of George I in October 1714. He sewed and nailed up the Crimson Damask hangings in the Great Gallery at Kensington Palace in 1727. Like John Schaw, Phill profited by selling materials as well as installing them. The *Daily Post* of 1 May 1728 carried an auction notice for the earthly belongings of Thomas Phill, deceased. The lots included 'above 100 carpets of all sizes'.[170]

The organized upholstery trade was just one stream contributing to a pool of installers. There is no reason to believe that longstanding trade practices like the underground economy, exploitative wages, kickbacks, and arbitrary dismissals were not common in the early period. Paperhanging takes a reasonable amount of skill; planning and attention to detail are important. But, many of these qualities can be gained through on-the-job training. When work got slack (an inevitability in the decorating trades) no doubt many simply moved on.

## 1725–50: A Time Of Change

So much for the guilds and companies. Some few of these professed artisans came to North America. Thomas Child, member of the Painter-Stainers' Company, was in Boston by 1685, and Job Adams, a member of the Worshipful Company, had 'lately arriv'd from London' to Philadelphia in 1732.[171] On the French side, there are seven upholsterers recorded in Quebec between 1668 and 1699, though it's not known how actively they pursued their trade in their new surroundings.[172]

The years around 1725 were tumultuous for the upholders and painters of London. One reason was the proliferation of new artisans and industries. There was more painting work to be done, but due to licensing battles, which did not often resolve to the Painter-Stainers' advantage, more unlicensed workers to do it. Many upholders were opening up storefronts and competing with linen drapers, leather gilders and, especially, cabinet-makers. The cabinet-maker has been portrayed as the 'right-hand man' of the upholder (by R. Campbell) but any supposed alliance seems to have turned into all-out rivalry by the 1720s. James Moore was the royal cabinet-maker, yet he seems to have been part of a clique called the Company of Upholders who sought the high-end funeral trade. Moore was clerk-of-the-works at Blenheim and parlayed this connection into royal patronage, a role which his apprentice Benjamin Goodison inherited. Though a professed cabinet-maker himself, Goodison had a variety of skills. He gilded doorways and hung fabric and wallpaper. Whether cabinet-makers or upholders, all these people were vying to supply fine furnishings for fine people paying fine rates.

Another change was the maturation of the paperstaining trade. What had been a sideline of leather-gilders or a field dominated by entrepreneurs like Abraham Price and Robert Dunbar was growing. Still, these new companies existed mainly at the subcontracting level and therefore under the radar. It was not until well after 1750 that numbers of paperstainers were selling to the public under their own name.

These changes affected the professional groups differently. The Painter-Stainers' were traditionalists and most of them actually worked in the trade. In 1761, out of the total membership of 112, the trade was practiced by 95.[173] The Upholders did not, by and large, work in their trade, but rather bought and sold wares. Plus, they were already on a downward trajectory. Essentially, all of the guilds were the victims, over time, of benign neglect: they were expected to enforce Company laws, which were feeble to start with, on their own. The London government (known as the Corporation) did not help.

Most of the small shopkeepers whose livelihoods sprang up in the 1720s and 1730s, such as the lace and mantua makers, joined the twelve large Livery guilds. These offered the trappings of legality without much interference. Whatever the size or style of the new companies or the struggles of the older ones, there were longstanding problems within the guild system. Participation from freemen had plummeted: 'From an intake of over 2,100 freemen per year in the late 1670s the figure had fallen to 1,900 per year in the first five years of the eighteenth century; between 1710 and 1720 the average was 1,700, and by 1745 the figure had fallen to 1,250 per year'.[174] The Painter-Stainers' average annual enrolment was equally dismal. From 1700 to 1710 enrolment was forty per year, and by 1740–50 it was thirteen per year.[175] When Thomas Bromwich became Master of the Painter-Stainers' Company in 1761 it appears that he took charge of a dying (or at least a radically changing) institution.

The Worshipful Company staked their hope on legislation. The Upholder's Bill, crafted in the second quarter of the century, was supposed to guarantee them control over their trade. Alas, the Bill was passed in 1750 yet led nowhere. As Karin Walton put it, 'the 1750 Act appears as little more than a last desperate attempt by the Company to win a degree of power which it had never yet managed to achieve'.[176]

## Thomas Chippendale: Cabinet-Maker, Upholder...Or Tradesman?

The main business of the upholders, buying and selling, was difficult to control. That may explain why they gravitated toward managing. By 1747, the upholders were called 'the absolute necessary tradesmen' for furnishing a house in London (see Texts: *A General Description* and *The London Tradesman*). The catalogue of duties for overseeing the work listed by R. Campbell is dizzying. But, it was just this aspect that was important – the trade had divided between hands-on craftsmen and supervisors like Thomas Chippendale. Thomas had trained as a journeyman cabinet-maker, but that was merely a launching pad for his career.

Campbell said that 'a master cabinet-maker is a very profitable trade; especially, if he works for and serves the quality himself; but if he must serve them through the chanel of the upholder, his profits are not very considerable'.[177] This explains a great deal. Around 1725, there was fierce rivalry between the upholders and cabinet makers for the ear of the client. From Campbell's description, the cabinet-maker is an architect of wood: his skilful choice of woods and design ensure that the finished products are elegant rather than strong; the skills of drawing and designing are not just advisable, they are paramount. They lead to new fashions which are as exciting to the consumer as they are profitable to the artificers. Thomas seems to have taken these skills to a high pitch. His obituary listed him as 'upholder', yet in his working life he used the trade of cabinet-making to sharpen his entrepreneurial skills and push through to higher levels – almost exactly as summarized by Campbell.

## Types Of Installers

Some installers, like Phill and Schaw and Lapiere, rose to the top. Some were like William Reid, Mr Brewer, and Mr James, outworkers for Chippendale's company at Harewood House. They carried out wallpaper and fabric installations as part of a team, often for many months at a time.[178] Some installers were from a related trade: Benjamin Goodison, cabinet-maker, was pressed into service pasting eighty-eight Chinese pictures onto Lord Cardigan's walls in 1737. And, of course, some were like Catharine Mac Cormick who found employment where they could. One poignant notation in the daybook of Samuel Grant, an early American upholsterer, shows that half the cost of a boy's board for the year was charged to the shop. Colonial money in the amount of £1. 11s. 3d. was paid 'for board of a negro boy named Devonshire'.[179] Perhaps he was an apprentice, or worked as a paid servant for the upholsterer.

Owner/installers like Thomas Bromwich differed from those who worked under them. The shop owners amassed capital whereas the workers received day-rates or piece-rates. Another way to express the difference would be master/journeyman. Many women laboured in the underworld of the upholder, but were disparaged rather than praised for their work: 'All this part of the work [sewing and cutting] is performed by women, who never served an apprenticeship to the mystery [...] the women, if good for any thing, get a Shilling a day' (as opposed to a man's 12 to 15 shillings a week).[180]

Women artisans seem to have fared no better in the colonies, and are certainly less remembered than their European counterparts: 'The literature on European women in the crafts [...] is far more extensive than the literature on early American craftswomen [...] The study of artisans in early America, begun with the publication of Carl Bridenbaugh's *The Colonial Craftsman*, has considered precisely that – crafts*men*'.[181] Without question, woman artisans were more active during 1650–1750 than has been suspected. Exactly how active remains unclear, but studies of the daybooks, diaries, and other personal documentation of women artisans are beginning to surface.

## New France

In New France, immigrant upholsterers are documented as early as 1668. There are twelve upholsterers recorded in Quebec between 1668 and 1757. Henri Arnaud, for example, lived on rue Couillard from 1739 to 1757. Arnaud and others served a population of about 8,000 people in 1750. It's possible that some of these men worked at the trade before a passage to New France yet were not gainfully employed in the New World. For example, Jean Leduc is recorded as 'master upholsterer and valet'.[182] Nevertheless, should costly paper need to be hung from time to time (as seems likely) trained people like Arnaud were available. In one instance in Quebec in the 1770s (the Estèbe installation), wallpaper was pasted on canvas, the canvas having been stretched on a frame covering interior walls – exactly the technique one would expect from a European installer.

## The St. Luke's Guild

Considering that English customs and language were mandated in the area around Dublin beginning in the sixteenth century, it's not too surprising that in 1670 a group modelled after the Painter-Stainers' Company was formed. The St. Luke's Guild of Cutlers, Painter-Stainers and Stationers was a disparate company, yet it lasted well into the nineteenth century.[183] It was formed by eight cutlers (the most important of the three trades), three stationers, and three painters-stainers.[184] As we've seen, the painters in England worked with oil on hard objects and the stainers worked on fabric, paper and other porous surfaces. It's likely that the stainers in the St. Luke's Guild worked with paper-hangings. When block printing was taken up in Ireland, it was dubbed 'stamping' and the term stuck. Catharine Mac Cormick's name was also rendered M'Cormick. The widow McCormick ran a paperstaining shop in Dublin from 1762 to 1780. It would not be surprising to learn that the two were related.

When paper-stampers lacked work, some switched to hanging, like Catharine. By the same token, many installers probably worked at stamping. In Ireland, the trades of house painters, paperstainers and paperhangers seem much more closely aligned than in England. The same is true in Scotland, where Charles Esplin was a limner, a printer and a print-seller, as well as a paperstainer. Could it be a reflection of a smaller market, overall? The Irish may have imported a generalist approach to Philadelphia and other North American cities. In late-eighteenth century Philadelphia a paperstainer from Dublin, Edward Ryves, worked as a stainer or hanger, depending on demand.[185]

It is nearly impossible to know how many installers were like Catharine Mac Cormick, and how many were like Thomas Phill. No doubt the higher the cost of the material and the prestige of the clients, the more likely it is that a trained professional like Phill was entrusted with the work.

# CHAPTER 10:
# Leather Hangings

Gilt-embossed leather is more exotic and generally more expensive than wallpaper. Yet the methods, craftsmen, shops, and patrons of these two materials in the mid-seventeenth to mid-eighteenth centuries were surprisingly sympathetic. The trail left by leather workers throws a welcome light.

Leather skins and paper sheets are blank slates well suited to carrying decorative designs. Both are flexible, porous and react to moisture; easily joined together to form hangings; sometimes hung with a canvas underlayment; often nailed in place; and usually bordered. Even the size of the skins (20" by 27") was similar to the elephant size of paper (22" by 25 ½") coming into wider use for wallpaper in the mid-1700s. An unbroken line connects the 1637 birth of Henry Asgill, the first English leather gilder in the early modern period, to the death of Thomas Bromwich in 1787. In the middle of this line, John Rowland is found; his career and methods show the continuity of craft. Rowland began training in 1679 and rose to become Master of the Painter-Stainers' Company. He had trained about a dozen apprentices by the time he wrote the following letter to Admiral van Wassenaer in the Netherlands:

## 27 March 1722

> *My Lord*
> *the Gilt Leather Hangings are now compleated and I only expect your Lordship orders to send them for Holland a damp wet day is the most proper to put them up in and if there was some course canvas first nailed up very smooth & tight it would be better for the Hangings to be fixt over the canvas.*[186]

John Rowland sent to Holland a 'suit of guilt leather hangings painted with India birds & flowers containing one hundred thirty seven skins & a half', but this was almost like sending coals to Newcastle. By this time, the workshops of the Netherlands had long produced gilded leather. Spanish leather had earned a glorious reputation in the Middle Ages, one that has overshadowed artisans in other countries ever since. However, by around 1500, the discipline had spread: the English, the Dutch, and the Italians were gilding, block printing, varnishing and tooling leather skins. They were also making them into hangings. The first step in the process was to tan the hide, which consisted of a flesh side (underneath) and a grain side (top). Almost invariably, a silver metal leaf followed. This was coated with yellowish colours to give a distinctive 'golden' undertone. Decorative patterns were punched into the grain side with bookbinder's or similar tools and embossed from the flesh side with wooden moulds. This was followed by glazing and other hand-colouring. Skins used for gilt leather in the sixteenth century were often 20" by 24".[187]

A cheaper substitute emerged known as *scorched* or damask leather. Many scorched leather pieces covered globes, musical instruments, and chairs. These could also be joined into hangings, as explained by an Italian manuscript of 1520: 'After polishing with the ball sew the pieces together so that you will get hangings or other objects which one needs to decorate the houses'.[188]

All these types were stitched together on the flesh side, taking care to join the patterns on the grain side. However, when large painted images were involved, visible seams could work against the illusion of the painted image. All edges of the leather skins were therefore feathered, interlocked, and adhered prior to painting. Painted leathers of this description are still hanging at Dunster Castle in Somerset, England. Hans Huth explained an important distinction between smooth and sewn types: the sewing method 'was adopted in the case of goods made for export, so that they could be finished later and in the size required [...] thus, shipping and handling was expedited for the modular types'.[189]

By 1588, twenty-eight sets of painted leather hangings had accumulated at Kenilworth Palace in Warwickshire, England. Many had ecclesiastical themes and probably came from the Netherlands, according to leather historian John Waterer. Most were mounted on canvas. Waterer concluded that the use of such underlayments was a 'wise and fairly general practice'.[190] Canvas has been found contiguous with leather panels (glued to the back side). Canvas has also been found a few inches from the leather panels, creating an air space. The reasons for this air space were associated with housekeeping: dust, drafts and moisture were less likely to affect the leather panels. Air spaces of this type have also been found in fabric installations.

Around 1630 a revolutionary change came to gilded leather – plate embossing. Metal plates replaced wooden moulds and popularity soared. By 1645 there were eleven workshops in the northern Netherlands alone. Design samples printed on paper were another innovation in the field some forty years later. At least two producers used this distinctly early modern marketing method to send samples far and wide during the 1670s.[191] One of the engraved samples from Martinus van den Heuvel, a manufacturer from Amsterdam, is signed on the back and includes a testimonial that his leathers were made 'from Dutch and Frisian calf-skins'. By comparing his printed samples to contemporary leather *in situ* it's known that the 'Bacchus and Ceres' pattern from the Rijsende Son factory was hung in the vestibule of Dyrham Park, England, in the room now known as the East Hall. The pattern was designed by Willem van den Heuvel,

Martinus's uncle. The size of the individual skins is about 33 ½" by 27" and the design is polychrome.[192]

The leather at Dyrham Park was hung by an outworker sent by upholder Humphrey Skelton in 1702. William Blathwayt, a member of Parliament, was informed by his cousin Charles Watkins that 'as soon as Mr Skelton's man comes he shall take the first opportunity of Moist Weather for putting up ye Gilt Leather wch is thought most proper for that work'.[193] The 'Great Roome above stairs' was also hung with 'one hundred less seaven skins of Gilt Leather', but this installation didn't go so well. A memorandum states that: 'The Gilt leather in the Great Parlor very ill putt up and must be stretcht which can be done only in Wett Weather'.[194]

## HOW IT WORKS: HANGING LEATHER

Leather, like paper, reacts to moisture. Large leather panels pieced together from many skins are stretched and hung on rainy days because the moisture causes them to fully expand. As the materials dry, they contract, and the framed leather becomes tight as a drum. Canvas, leather, and paper can be expected to sag from age as well as from a moist environment. There are many references to 're-straining' leather and paper-hangings put on canvas.

Gilt leather was used in high style interiors up to about 1730, then made way for other wall decoration, including the more elaborate sorts of paper. Yet demand for gilt leather remained strong in the Netherlands. An English visitor in 1756 commented that the Dutch 'have not yet come into the taste of paper in their houses, the guilt leather, silks and tapestry is the only thing used'.[195] In colonial America a proposal was floated in 1710 to decorate the walls and sixteen chairs of the Great Room at the royal governor's residence under construction in Williamsburg, Virginia.[196] There must have been other instances in colonial America, even if the historic record is slim.

What about that direct line between Henry Asgill and Thomas Bromwich? Henry Asgill, citizen of London, was born in 1637 to John Asgill, painter-stainer, in Aldersgate. Henry trained at the Merchant Taylors' School, 1648–53, and joined the Painter-Stainers' Company, becoming Warden in 1680 and Master in 1688. In 1679 he accepted John Rowland, the earliest of his eight known apprentices.[197] Rowland gained his freedom in 1687 and succeeded to Master of the Company. One of his apprentices, Samuel Williams, gained his freedom in 1705, and became Master. Finally, one of Williams' apprentices, Thomas Bromwich, gained his freedom in 1737 and repeated the tradition, becoming Master in 1761.[198]

This section started with quotes from John Rowland's letter to a customer. His methods and charges bear a closer look. That Rowland was creating this 'suit' of leather at some distance explains why he needed to distinguish between the English and the Flemish methods of measurement. As fellow leather craftsman John Hutton would write some years later: 'The Raynland foot measure is one Quarter of an Inch Longer than the English foott measure as I find by ye paper scale you sent. There is no hangings for rooms ready made, butt wee always make them after bespoke, and according to ye modell whicth is sent to me'.[199] This explains why Rowland insists in his letter (see Texts) that van Wassenaer use red tape to get the exact height and width of the walls. The pieces of tape have 'a writing to each peice to distinguish them'.[200]

Rowland charged Admiral Wassenaer for 137 ½ skins, '60 yards of stampt bordering', '1500 of gilt nailes', and '1000 of black tax'. This list suggests that the recommended canvas and leather hangings were tacked up by local workers and followed by the border which was fastened with the decorative nails. An alternate method was to sew large borders to the hangings and tack the whole to a frame with decorative nails. The 137 ½ leather skins at 27" by 20" would have yielded around 500 square feet – roughly 125 square feet each, if there were four walls. If bordered around the perimeter, this amount of square footage would have required 180 linear feet of border or less, depending on how the corners were treated; the 60 yards of border estimated by Rowland makes perfect sense.

## Hutton's Letters

Ten years after Rowland's letters, some letters from a former apprentice to him, John Hutton, were also sent to Holland. While writing to a potential customer, Hutton makes a reference to the same satisfied customer (Sir Matthew Decker) mentioned in Rowland's letter – and adds Admiral van Wassenaer. Clearly, Hutton had a business connection to Rowland as well as a familial one (he was Rowland's nephew). He offers skins measuring 27" by 20" at 6 shillings a skin, and promises to complete the work within four weeks. This is exactly how Rowland worked. In an interesting bit of gamesmanship, his potential client suggests that he lower his price from 6s. to 5s. per skin. Hutton agrees, but with one stipulation: the quality will be cheapened. The price is immediately restored to 6s. per skin, and the work proceeds.

Hutton's skins were not sewn, but glued. Hutton promised that the hangings would fit the space, and that if they didn't, he would buy them back. Some time after the installation in Holland, the hangings started coming undone. Apparently, although a moist environment was helpful for the initial hanging, a persistently damp environment was harmful. Hutton advised that the room should be carefully dried out. He gives a formula for re-adhering the skins: three tablespoons of flour should be mixed into a pint of ale, and boiled down over moderate heat to a thick paste. Hutton states that this paste will do the job and dry out within twenty-four hours.[201]

Gilt leather costs certainly varied from time to time, but these exchanges suggest great stability. In 1722, Rowland offered skins to the Admiral at 6 shillings. He states that his prices are wholesale: 'I have charged the very lowest prices which I have of merchants &

those that make their advantage of them again'.[202] But whether wholesale or not, these seem his standard rates. The same rate is confirmed by Hutton ten years later. As late as 1756, a remarkable span of thirty-five years, Hutton is charging 5s. per skin for the small modular diaper pattern still hanging at Ham House, England.[203]

Paper-hangings, because they offered many more styles and types, were on a different footing than gilt leather hangings. Yet, the sheer variety of paper-hangings suggests an advantage. While a gentleman could count on gilt leather to impart style to his dwelling, the bar was high, and there was little opportunity for economizing, as Hutton's inquisitive customer soon discovered. The same cannot be said for the paper-hangings trade. Apparently, wallpaper could furnish economy as well as style.

# CHAPTER 11:
# Chinese Scenics And Flock Damasks

Chinese scenics and flock damasks probably amounted to a small fraction of early modern wallpaper installations, but their impact was, and remains, large. Large-figured flocks were well-made and costly, and therefore put up carefully. Anthony Wells-Cole has observed that 'country house owners were probably surprised and to some extent dismayed by the durability of their flock paper hangings well after the height of their fashion had passed'.[204] Chinese scenics, too, were long-lived: anecdotal evidence suggests that there could easily be a hundred sets of them preserved in England alone. Paper-hangings were spawned in the early modern period by the mingling of technology and design. For technology, we've already seen how the lack of domestic paper hindered development in Europe, especially England.

The technology in China was very different. Around the middle of the seventeenth century, Jesuits missionaries discovered eye-opening amounts of paper applied to the walls of domestic interiors. As Father J. B. Du Halde wrote in his collection of missionary accounts: 'It is inconceivable how much is consumed in private homes [...] the workmen of this country have the art of pasting it very neatly, and the Chinese take care to renew it every year'.[205] Father Louis Le Comte, who arrived in China in 1688, was a witness. He reported that 'there are sheets of ten and twelve feet long [...] much whiter & plainer than our own'.[206] French Jesuits like these played a small part, but the influx was significant – some 920 missionaries visited China before 1800.[207]

Meanwhile, in Europe the medieval tradition of illustrating books had advanced due to the printing press. Long dominant at church and court, printed illustrations of all types were increasingly being adopted in the home. One stream of design that influenced the young industry was the figurative tradition as expressed during the Baroque period by northern European countries such as Germany, Holland, and France. Ornamental elaboration pervaded the decoration of courtly culture and was common in folk culture as well. The other stream of design came from small-scale English and Irish architectural detailing, which especially influenced border design. The resulting framework was often tame. Yet, figure and frame worked well on the wall. Movement and repose, passion and action, came together.

Significantly, wallpaper production does not encourage freehand design; the whole idea of a template (whether it is a stencil or a block) is repetition. As wallpaper developed, figures rarely stood alone; instead, complementary figures alternated, or, secondary design would fill the space between dominant figures. The now-familiar arrangement of wallpaper design into rows and columns with alternating motifs was the result. While wallpaper is not traditionally viewed as folk art, its dependence on symmetry and repetition suggests the maxims of Henry Glassie: 'Folk art is characterized by forms that are composed of repeated motifs, by over-all symmetry [...] repetition proves the absence of mistake and presence of control, control over concept, technique, and material'.[208]

Chinese wallpaper came from entirely different traditions. Private painted scrolls were the physical prototype, and inspired scroll-like forms that covered windows and doors to a limited degree.[209] Tree of life and chintz designs had long been imported from India into China. Ironically, many of the Chinese papers really were 'India' papers, at least in derivation, though that misnomer came from their association with the East India Company.[210]

The dangers of pasting papers to wood were well known in China. *The Mustard Seed Garden*, published by Li Yu in 1679, tells how frames were used with pictorial scrolls to decorate interior walls. His book is about fine art, not export paper-hangings, but similar problems are involved. The book described two problems: pasting directly to wood would inevitably 'tear the picture to pieces' as the wood expanded and contracted with seasonal change.[211] But tacking them to the wall was no better. Scrolls were made with rollers at top and bottom. If the scrolls were tacked on top, the lower roller would bang around in the breeze. The solution was to prepare a wooden frame with lining paper, then mount the papers and secure the frame to the wall. The air space behind the paper allowed the paper to breathe while the frame anchored it to the wall surface. This framing method, with some modifications, became popular in Western Europe for hanging many types of wallpaper.

Aside from this technological background, the figurative motifs on Chinese papers unsettled the young field of wallpaper design. Such sprawling designs were not easily tamed. Each of the large panels of Chinese design connected, but the design never resolved into a repeat, either within the sheet, or from sheet to sheet. In their mature form, Chinese scenic panels measured 45 or 48 inches wide, reached as high as 12 or 14 feet, and came in sets of 24 or more – an enormous amount of paper. Imagine the bewildered expressions of installers, trained on much narrower widths, as they grappled with these for the first time!

It's important to remember that Chinese wallpaper was not a hugely traded item; it was brought in by the captain or supercargo as an extracurricular activity (not black market, just limited in scope). The main articles of the China trade were woven silks, chinaware, cotton textiles, and tea.[212] The India pictures, smaller and more numerous, posed the same problem as the scenics, namely: how could these extravagant figures be fit into Western-style repeats? The task was a little easier when large numbers of them were arranged on walls, because a coherent design could be made by linking them up with secondary ornament.

From a design standpoint, the results could be ungainly when these sprawling 'Indian' motifs were crammed into narrow widths and Western repeats. See for example the Indian-style designs on the Edward Butling trade card of about 1690.[213] They're a startling contrast to the conventional black and white borders on the same card. One of these Indian designs is similar to the crowded chinoiserie in the wallpaper found at Ord House (Berwick-on-Tweed, Northumberland). In this black-grounded wallpaper of around 1700, gigantic English red squirrels are poised to scurry out of the frame.[214] Another example of the fusion, which can be charming, is seen in figure 1 (the Blew Paper ad) of this volume. The creator of the sidewall design couldn't decide between Eastern or Western conventions.

It's time to address the so-called lack of perspective in Chinese wallpapers. More important than perspective in paper-hangings are balance and shading. Shading must be carefully rendered, because if the pattern leans, the viewer feels that the room leans, and the floor starts falling away. Far Eastern patterns were not always shaded to Western expectations, but they were always balanced. Still, the critics had their say, and among them was John Baptist Jackson.

John Baptist Jackson was considered a major figure in wallpaper history until the reevaluation forced by the publication of Edna Donnell's article in 1932. His early career included a contentious residency at Jean-Michel Papillon's workshop. Jacob Kainen has explained how Jackson succeeded at mastering the colour woodcut yet failed at wallpaper production: 'As soon as he arrived in England he was invited to work in a calico establishment, where he remained about six years. But making drawings to be printed on cloth failed to give him the scope he required. At the back of his mind was the passion to work with woodblocks in color. This led him to take a bold and hazardous step – to leave his position and attempt, obviously with little capital, the manufacture of wallpaper, not to please an established taste but to educate the public to a new type of product'.[219] This step proved disastrous. The public got no more educated and John Baptist slid further into penury.

He published two pamphlets. Though self-serving, these were eminently quotable and provided a neat explanation for the startlingly different landscape papers of mid-century. These showed hand-painted Roman ruins in elaborate frames, several sets of which have survived. In the absence of better documentation, he was long-credited with almost single-handedly defining that genre of wallpaper.

In his *Essay*, John Baptist explained that his designs avoided 'lions leaping from bough to bough like cats, houses in the air, clouds and sky upon the ground, a thorough confusion of all the elements [...] men and women, with every other animal, turn'd monsters, like the figures in the Chinese paper'. How unfair! Despite a profusion of ornament, figures and buildings, Chinese artisans had long since worked out the problems of display. Papers of Jackson's description did exist. But, they were first generation English-made imitations of the Chinese style. These chinoiserie designs forced outlandish figures into the narrow widths of domestic paper-hangings, like the design of the Ord paper with the mammoth squirrels previously mentioned. English paperstainers had certainly made

## SECOND INTERLUDE:
## SENDING WALLPAPER ACROSS THE SEAS

Figure 17: Chinoiserie paper at Estèbe House.

This wonderful wallpaper decoration was unknown to historians until 1946 – it was discovered by workers hired to remove some *boiserie*.[215] The chinoiserie paper was found pasted to canvas which had been hung on frames on the three interior walls of the room. The house was built in central Quebec 1751–52 for William Estèbe but the original wall treatments are unknown. The panelling was put in place around 1780. All things considered, the paper installation seems to date from the decade of the 1770s.

The motifs are the familiar ones: fences, vases and a conspicuously gnarled tree trunk in the foreground; further back are birds, flowers, and people. Two large motifs (dominated by people in small groups) alternate with two smaller bird and flower designs. The wallpaper appears to be put up in the usual 22" width, but each of the four motifs are on paper sheets which are around 36" high.

A vertical overlap of about an inch on all strips is visible in photos. The gnarled tree trunk is similar to one on a single chinoiserie sheet in the collections of the Victoria and Albert Museum.[216] The sheet in the museum is about 36" high by 32" wide. Curiously, the museum paper has a notation which appears to read '18d.' in the lower right hand corner. Documents in the Public Archive of Canada record '80 sheets India paper' which also cost 18d. per sheet.[217] These were put up in a governmental building in the 1770s. It seems that the Estèbe paper was printed and joined in a Western European workshop in an interesting melange of Eastern design and Western repeats.

The paper appears to have been hung, wrongly, as a drop match. Drop matches are a traditional method to introduce variety; this type of pattern drops a design element half the distance of the repeat on alternating sheets, yielding an A-B-A-B rotation. However, the construction of the Estèbe paper reveals it to be a four-part multiple drop. Multiple drops can use any number of motifs; the key is that each strip drops by a single motif, until the original motif once again appears at the top. In the case of the Estèbe wallpaper, each sheet should drop by one motif, and sheets one and five should be identical. It may seem surprising to encounter such a sophisticated design so early in the history of wallpaper, but it is not the only one. Another multiple drop match pattern was found in Lambeth, England and dates from around 1700.[218]

The result of hanging the Estèbe wallpaper as a drop match is that the two major motifs wound up in a straight row across the wall, lending a cramped look to the installation. This wallpaper, now in the collections of the Fine Arts Museum of Montreal, is quite unusual: it is a botched installation of a Western European adaptation of a Chinese design hung in a French colony in North America.

substantial progress in taming these motifs by 1755, so Jackson's criticism managed to insult both Chinese and Western wallpaper manufacturers equally.

Incoherent as Chinese paper-hangings may have appeared to Jackson, they were the culmination of a style perfectly suited to the display of unique design over an entire room, where there could be no shading because of the necessity of treating each wall alike without regard to the time of day or placement of windows.

In *The History of the Royal Residences*,[220] William Pyne described the redecoration of a room at Kensington Palace in 1725:

> It was on the walls of this drawing-room that the then new art of paper-hangings, in imitation of the old velvet flock, was displayed, with an effect that soon led to the adoption of so cheap and elegant a manufacture, in preference to the original rich material from which it was copied.

The planning of the redecoration is credited to William Kent. The hanging may have been done by Thomas Phill of the Worshipful Company, who supplied upholstery goods and services to the Royal Apartments at Kensington 1717–27.[221] At a different palace ten years later, the elaborate painted murals of Queen Anne's Drawing Room at Hampton Court were covered by flock damasks. The installations in these royal rooms mark the triumph of flock paper-hangings.

Yet flock, refuse from spinning and weaving operations, was an ancient and humble material. At first, it was stuffed into mattresses and pillow cases by village upholders. It was too useful to throw away yet not beautiful enough to decorate anything, until someone thought to dye it and apply it to fabric in imitation of finer stuffs. When strong paper became readily available, paper flocks were born, and flock was soon decorating a multitude of patterns. It's somewhat ironic that flock as a *pattern* has come to stand for high-style damasks, while flock the *material* is intrinsically lowly – the refuse from spinning already referred to. The resulting pile gave flock wallpapers great depth. It put them several steps above common papers, and, as Pyne noted, not far from textiles.

The relatively quick rise of flock from stuffed pillowcases to the walls of royalty was impressive. What was spreading was not just flock damasks, but, more fundamentally, roll paper. This could not have happened without paper-making, joining, grounding, flocking and printing – the work of many hands. It remains puzzling that craftsmen in France did not respond in kind for the first half of the eighteenth century.

Yet the very durability and prominence of flocks in great houses has led to a stereotypical view that from their inception flocks were intended only for the well-to-do. Ada K. Longfield, the astute Irish historian, saw things differently. She claimed that the flocks from the era 1660–70 were not necessarily expensive, and had limitations: 'they might not be very lasting – obviously, they would rub easily – and the designs were mere imitations of the textile patterns then in vogue, but they were relatively cheap, and so helped to increase the popularity of wall-papers in general'.[222]

There is no further record of the flocks created for Hampton Court and Kensington Palace, but it's quite possible that they were custom-made, considering the customers. Records of bespoke fabric from just this time show some of the conventions of the trade. Around 1708 the Earl of Manchester, ambassador to Venice, helped Sarah, Duchess of Marlborough, furnish Blenheim. She expressed a preference for plain colours:

*Your Lordship says scarlet is the more difficult, and seems to think they [in Venice] do not dye that so well as we do; but I think that what you sent me was the most beautiful colour [...] The figured velvets of general colours are not much liked, though the fashion; but I should like mightily scarlet-figured velvet, without any mixture of colours, and blue and green of the same.*[223]

The Earl advised her to send measurements of the height and width of each room along with a drawing of the patterns in colour. Once the weavers in Venice knew how many full drops were needed for each room, they could make the correct amount of running feet and put them up into bolts. This would avoid unnecessary waste when the hangings were made up back in England. Much of the early bespoke work in paper must have taken just this approach. That is the *how* of it. *Why* did damask patterns make this leap from fabric to paper? And why did large-figured paper flocks suddenly appear in the first quarter of the eighteenth century?

One advantage of plain fabrics in rich colours was that they made excellent backgrounds for gilt picture frames. But, they could be monotonous if used throughout the interior. Another problem was that few families owned pictures other than family portraits.[224] These concerns help explain why wall-hangings with more design impact and variety came into use. Among these were fabric hangings with large patterns. Paper flocks benefited from the trend.

Paper-hangings and fabrics were very different from wainscotting and tapestry because they were far lighter. By 1700, according to historian Audrey Douglas,

> most cotton fabrics could also be used in furnishings and supplied hangings, curtains, counterpanes, and upholstery. Their use [...] coincided with architectural changes that affected the type and volume of textile consumption [...] the large chimney piece was eventually to give way to the elegant mantel, accompanied by the substitution of hangings or wallpaper for the insulating warmth of panelling. The result was an emphasis, as in clothing, on the trend to lightweight fabrics.[225]

These 'new draperies' were quite different from the 'old draperies' – those made of wool.

Edward Butling advertised flock-work on paper around 1690 (see Texts). It's not clear what many of these looked like and it's another reminder that flock was a material, not a style, even if it became shorthand for large centralized patterns adapted from Italian cut velvets, like the Duchess of Marlborough's. The cost of most small flock patterns could not have been anywhere near that of these high style flocks.[226] Large-figured flocks were ideally suited for the many discrete rectangles of Georgian interiors. The key to their usefulness is that modular patterns radiate out. If damask patterns are centred, their perimeters are inevitably symmetrical. For this reason, they were often hung in the middle of the walls (or sections of walls). This was also true for the everyday tapestry paper hung by Papillon's men. It would be more than a hundred years before walls would be drowned in a 'flood of pattern' as one late-nineteenth century tastemaker put it.[227]

When large-figured paper flocks were first used on walls, the designs were contained within the strip. Later, they sprouted side-to-side matches. These matches improved the flow of the design and helped avoid negative space at the seams, which can cause apparent 'holes'. Large patterns and fuzzy surface texture helped paper-hangings achieve the necessary weight for genteel surroundings. This *gravitas* came a bit easier for hangings made of fabric, which allowed more play on the wall. It's interesting to compare almost any extant large-figured paper flock with the cut velvet hangings installed in 1743 at Longford Castle.[228]

Some repeats were outrageously large. Over the nineteenth century, large-figured flocks calmed down; their repeats dwindled from six or seven feet down to 36" and even 27". Chinese scenics, too, got smaller. Strips as wide as 44" and 48" narrowed to 39", and then to 36". The heights of wall panelling dropped from three panels to two, following wall heights in general. In the early-eighteenth century, large-figured flocks were hung straight across, resulting in a somewhat mannered appearance. Drop matches broke up this static quality by dropping the repeat half the distance on alternate strips. Another way for the paperstainer to produce variety was to split a motif, putting half on each edge of the paper. This half-motif could alternate with a neighbouring whole motif, or, the whole motif could end up in the next row.

Rounding a corner presented problems for these large patterns. The corners introduced a break in the pattern; worse, they were asymmetrical breaks. Well-planned interiors solved these problems architecturally. Pillars and pilasters were introduced, and whether the spaces between them were left plain or got fabric and wallpaper treatments, they broke up and defined the interior space. As these architectural interventions changed and wall spaces grew monolithic, wallpaper repeats changed with them. With less need for centring, repeats became smaller and less dramatic.

Hanging problems with large-figured flocks were not limited to corners. One interesting example can still be seen in Portsmouth, New Hampshire, from an installation before 1770. The low-ceilinged room created a wall space of about ten inches above a wide door. This was too much space for a border to fill. Yet arbitrarily continuing the sidewall pattern across the top of the door would have thrown the pattern off on either side of the door. Faced with this challenge, the installers started hanging paper from each side of the door. They then appropriated the central part of the sidewall design and hung it upside down to fill the space over the door, butting the pattern to the sidewall paper at the edge of the doorway. Though unconventional, this ad hoc 'overdoor' is centred, complements the flow of the sidewall and most important, looks like it belongs there. This pleasing result suggests that such solutions were neither impulsive nor rare.[229]

Bespoke wallpaper could be designed for a special room, which may have happened at Kensington Palace and Hampton Court. Or, an existing paper-hangings pattern could have been customized for such a room. That was still an expensive proposition, because even small adjustments required new blocks. It's likely that most customers chose an alternative that was cheaper yet – simply using an existing pattern. The second- and third-hand users of a custom-made template were lucky if the pattern fit their room perfectly. No doubt in many cases it did not, with attendant waste and foreshortening of the design. But these discrepancies can be subtle.

The one who decided whether a pattern should be custom or 'off the rack' in this period was increasingly not the client, but the upholder: 'He is the man upon whose judgement I rely in the choice of goods; and I suppose he has not only judgement in the materials, but taste in the fashions'.[230] The delegation of pattern choice to the upholder left plenty of room for the conceit that the paper was made for the room. Indeed the paper *was* made for the room – among many others. As the number of custom designs declined, there would be less and less justification for such a claim. Thus, flock damasks filled many needs: their large figures helped fill up the wall; they were a superior complement for artwork; suitably pretentious; and far cheaper than fabric.

All these trends converged when flocks were installed around 1735 over a dado of wood panelling in a Scottish residence called Quarrell. The homeowner, John Drummond, wanted to change the house from 'echoes of ruines' into 'a convenient little habitation [...] done frugally and effectively'. Fashion would be balanced with economy.[231] According to John:

*I shall wainscot or line the drawing room 4 feet high and then put upon the plaister from that to the cornice a plain green or red stuff or the new sort of paper printed like a green damask to hang my pictures on which will have almost all gilded frames.*[232]

Once established, this particular high style grew like wildfire among a certain clientele who valued special effects and outlandish proportions. The mid-1730s in England seem to have been the turning point. According to Wells-Cole, one iconic flock damask with a seven-foot repeat 'probably derives from a Genoese silk damask of c. 1730 and is also found in velvet at Holkham Hall, which was built and furnished in the mid 1730s. A two-colour flock paper of this design was hung in the offices of the Privy Council around 1735, and there is scarcely a great house that is without an example, either as damask or flock [eight houses are listed] the list could certainly be extended without much difficulty'.[233]

The fashion spread to France, Ireland and the American colonies by the 1750s.[234] In 1747 R. Campbell described methods of printing flocks in several colours: 'I have seen Hangings of this Sort performed in Ireland, whereon were represented Flowers in all their natural Colours and Proportions, with as much Delicacy as if they had been done with the Pencil'.[235]

Chinese scenics, India pictures, landscape papers, and large-figured flocks may have been supremely stylish and overpowering, yet those very qualities can cast a spell on our understanding. One peculiarity might be mentioned. Tour guides in historic homes which contain examples of these extravagant wallpapers sometimes claim that 'the paper was custom made to fit the room'. Yet when the record is examined the claims turn out to just as extravagant as the wallpapers. While there are documented instances of custom creation, notable the landscape papers ordered by Stephen Van Rensselaer II of Albany, New York, and Jeremiah Lee of Marblehead, Massachusetts, evidence for the custom creation of flock damasks and Chinese scenics to fit a specific room is extremely rare. This should not be read as a failure of documentation, but instead as a tribute to workshop artisans and installers, for it was their combined skills that customized a factory-made product to fit a particular room so convincingly.

## CHAPTER 12:
# Papier-mâché, Early Print Rooms, Screens

## 1750

*Moore[236] (who has lately been at London) talks to me of a sort of stucco-paper, which I had never heard of; and says Lord Foley has done his Chapel in Worcestershire with it (the ceiling at least). By his description, the paper is stamped so deep as to project considerable and is very thick and strong; and the ornaments are all detached, and put on separately. As suppose for example, it were the pattern of a common stucco-paper, which is generally a mosaic formed by a rose in a kind of octagon, it seems in this new way one of the roses is to be bought single; so you have as many in number as the place requires, which are pasted up separately, and then gilt [...] The ornaments of the cornices are likewise in separate pieces, and, when finished, cannot, I suppose, be known from fretwork. The difficulty and consequently the expense, must be in putting up these ornaments, which, as I understand, must be done by a man whom the Paper-seller sends on purpose from London: but perhaps your ingenuity might avoid that, if you could see any finished.*

Letter, Henrietta Knight (later Lady Luxborough) to William Shenstone.[237]

Shenstone sent back samples of Thomas Bromwich's wares. It's difficult to know if Henrietta avoided the cost of his travelling installers. But her letter shows that papier-mâché was being used in new ways. Not only were single 'roses' being put up to fit the space, but they were gilded in place; it all sounds quite new. She writes later that 'no person hereabouts has the smallest idea of it'. The same could be said of the methods of pasting engraved prints to walls, which resulted in so-called print rooms. Another destination for wallpaper was folding screens. These handy devices were the second-most popular destination for paper-hangings in the eighteenth century after walls and ceilings. They shielded occupants from the heat of the fireplace as well as from drafts. Screens could be finely wrought, but their main virtue was their usefulness.

Papier-mâché schemes depended on complementary ornaments such as centre medallions, fillets and swags. Illustrations of the large rooms of Hartlebury Castle show papier-mâché functioning like prints or small Chinese pictures – their distribution was matched to the proportions of the room.[238] While papier-mâché designs were diverse, print rooms were unique. Ground, imagery and ornament were important. More important still for both prints and papier-mâché was the sense of proportion needed to bring everything together. By the mid-1700s the gentry were accepting custom paper schemes of papier-mâché, Indian pictures and prints. That took a leap of faith. No doubt this leap was preceded by many small successes in closets and boudoirs.

## Papier-mâché

Papier-mâché had been used in ancient Egypt and the Far East long before the seventeenth century, but forming paper to imitate plasterwork seems to have started in the early-eighteenth century. As Henrietta described the process, 'the paper is boiled to mash and pounded a vast while, then it is put into moulds of any form. But further I know not; only that when it is tacked up, you either paint it white, or gild it, as you would do wood'.[239] Henrietta indicates that roll stucco paper preceded the modular types; both seem relatively easy to handle. The ease of handling is one of the virtues touted by the upholder Mackay in his letters to a Scottish patron.[240] Another virtue was the deep, bold relief. A reference book published in 1751 underlines this quality: 'There is also printed raised and embossed paper wherewith to hang rooms and wherein there is large consumption'.[241]

Papier-mâché was well established in London by the 1740s. William Wilton, an English decorative plasterer, is credited with founding a papier-mâché factory staffed by French workers. The product was later advertised by French artisans such as Peter Babel and Rene Duffour who probably worked at Wilton's factory. Mary Delany, the prolific memoirist and collage artist, referred to Duffour in 1749 as 'the famous man for paper ornaments like stucco'.[242]

Figure 18: Frontispiece from *One Hundred and Fifty New Designs* [detail].

Babel presented himself in Mortimer's *Universal Director* of 1763 as 'one of the first Improvers of Papier Mache ornaments for ceilings, chimney-pieces, picture-frames etc. an invention of modern date imported by us from France and now brought to great perfection'. Papier-mâché ornaments were frank imitations. There is nothing ironic about their attempts to fool the eye, which were often successful. Plasterwork had long been produced in modular form, and artisans were adept at running moulds along cornices in place – the difference now was the switch in materials and techniques which led to lower prices. This helps to explain why papier-mâché ornamentation was popular. It also explains why it was burned in effigy by outraged wood and plaster artisans. In the frontispiece of English wood carver Thomas Johnson's *One Hundred and Fifty New Designs* (1761) a patriotic shield emblazoned with 'For Our Country' is shown just below a putto setting 'French paper machee' ablaze.

Others blamed wallpaper in general for displacing plaster ornament. Isaac Ware complained in *A Complete Body of Architecture* (1756) that 'paper has in great measure taken the place of sculpture [plaster] [...] and the hand of art is banished from a part of the house in which it used to display itself very happily'. This may have been an overstatement, but it shows that wallpaper had a certain reputation. Ware was right that the tide was shifting. In 1752 Mary Delany, after hearing that her sister was about to have her parlour stuccoed, urged that she 'should rather hang it with stucco paper [and] must have plugs of wood [...] to hang pictures to fix nails in'.[243]

In Dublin, Thomas Fuller, John Gordon and John Rivett all made 'raised paper Stoco' and 'Paper mache' around mid-century. Their techniques may have been original, although a Frenchman in competition with them, Augustine Berville, was convinced otherwise.[244] In 1754, Berville advertised 'Pasteboard Stucco'. He said that he could 'finish in three or four Days, with as much Boldness, Relief and Beauty, as that of any other Stuccoe, the fullest and richest Design or Ornament for a Cieling [...] without sullying or hurting the furniture or lumbering the Room'.[245]

## HOW IT WAS DONE: RESTORING PAPIER-MÂCHÉ

It's bracing to hear from a present day practitioner, paper conservator Jonathan Thornton. He was called on to analyse, reproduce and install papier-mâché at the Miles Brewton House in Charleston, South Carolina, one of the very few North American residences with surviving eighteenth-century fragments. Jonathan comments that 'reproducing this material allowed me to appreciate its properties when new; it is tough, flexible, capable of fine detail, and, due to its absorptive nature, somewhat easier to gild and burnish than gessoed wood. To hold a strip of border that looks like polished gold yet weighs next to nothing tricks the senses'.[246]

## Print Rooms

'Print rooms' today stands for monotone-papered rooms decorated with black and white engraved prints surrounded by borders and often linked with other paper ornaments. Classic examples from the second half of the eighteenth century are at Woodhall in England and Castletown in Ireland. The fashion was widespread: around thirty-six print rooms in England before 1820 survive or were recorded. No doubt they are a fraction of those installed.

While decorating Strawberry Hill in 1753, Horace Walpole wrote to Sir Horace Mann that

> *the room on the ground floor nearest to you is a bedchamber hung with yellow paper and prints framed in a new manner invented by Lord Cardigan, that is, with black and white borders printed; over this is Mr Chute's bedchamber, hung with red in the same manner.*[247]

Walpole's rooms sound familiar, down to the black and white borders, yet it's hard to know why he ascribed the invention to the Cardigan installation. When Lady Cardigan hired the pious cabinet-maker Benjamin Goodison to hang eighty-eight 'Indian pictures' in 1742, Benjamin was almost certainly working with coloured pictures, not black and white prints.[248] If there was innovation, perhaps it consisted in more elaborate frames or more intermediate ornamentation than had been customary. Or maybe the choice of a dining room was a departure. If nothing else, the Cardigan/Goodison room may have been memorable for the scale – eighty-eight is a huge number of pictures. Goodison's job was to 'paste them all over the walls of a dining room', and to 'make good the Figures over the joining of the pictures'.[249] The latter comment is vague, but suggests that ornaments (masks?), festoons, or borders were added to link everything up. 'Make good'; could this mean improve the seams, as was sometimes done to the seams of Chinese scenics by adding twigs and leaves? With so many prints in a single room, the individual scenes could not have been large. Perhaps they needed a superstructure.

Goodison's handiwork must have looked different from the mature print rooms. The effect may have resembled that of the Small Chinese Room at Erddig (figure 19), concocted as a 'Chinese cabinet' around 1775. The illustration shows a corner of the room, in which around ten mid-sized Chinese genre pictures with two- to three-inch block printed borders sit on a yellow ground. Roundels dominate, with a few rectangles added for balance. Borders run around the perimeter of the room. The small Chinese scenes in the Cardigan/Goodison installation may have had similar borders. This rather free-wheeling type preceded the classic print room by many years. One decorative authority believes that prints were used on walls in England as early as the 1720s: 'There was clearly a substantial market for wood cuts and cheap engravings which could be pinned or pasted to the wall'.[250]

Figure 19: The Small Chinese Room at Erddig.

Earlier yet, 'hand-printed wallpapers and paintings on paper that could be pasted on a wall' were part of the cargo of the *Amphitrite* which travelled from Canton and docked at Port Louis, France, on 3 August 1700. Records of the East India Company show that 'paper pictures' to the value of several hundred pounds were ordered from Canton between 1699 and 1702.[251] Nevertheless, as already noted, they were not a commonly shipped item.

This trade, limited though it was, explains how shopkeepers in London were able to advertise brightly coloured India pictures as early as 1700. These single sheets, Oriental style, were tacked or pasted to a variety of spaces. The pictures were soon copied by English artisans using opaque watercolours. The artwork was rendered in a heavier and sometimes confused style, as opposed to the light touch and translucent brushwork of the originals. Some few chinoiserie sidewalls were created at 21" widths by putting Eastern motifs into alternating rows, as discussed earlier – a distinctly Western method.

Whether these single-sheet India pictures were original or imitations, borders were certainly used with them. Custom borders were needed for unusual shapes. It's likely that most custom border designs were done in freehand or with stencils, since block printing was still developing. 'Fitted up to the greatest exactitude' and 'match'd in paper' describe these bespoke services perfectly. Chinese scenics and India prints were evidently very rarely used in early America. Some of the latter were glazed (put under glass). In 1744, the Charleston merchant Robert Pringle sent to London for a set of 'India Pictures [...] about a foot square in frames glazed'.[252] However, these frames were probably fabricated in England.

A 1726 French reference to the 'new passion for cutting up coloured engravings' demonstrates the reach of the fashion.[253] Unlike the India pictures, these prints were cut out of costly books. They were apparently glued to pasteboard and varnished before being installed on walls or screens. In contrast, the mainstream approach was to paste commercial runs of engraved prints directly to walls. Mary Delany, the paper collage artist already mentioned, wrote to her brother in 1751 about her methods of 1) pasting prints on a wooden frame (a chimney board or the like); 2) pasting them to a wall; or 3) putting them under glass and then hung on a wall. Apparently the borders made by Vivares starting in 1753 or so were used for all three methods.[254]

Print rooms were quite different from the 'paper mosaics' which Mary created between 1774 and 1787. Those remarkable art objects were pasted into an album, not to a wall (though Mary, always busy, was one of the few amateurs fearless enough to try her hand at genuine print rooms). She shared her passion for handiwork with Miss Hamilton, who visited her at Bulstrode, home of the Duchess of Portland, for a month in 1784. Miss Hamilton later wrote about a chimney board composed by Mary from 'color'd paper, vases, antiques figures, &c...'.[255]

Professional artisans were no doubt the driving force behind the arrangement and installation of most print rooms, even if the ladies and gentlemen of the house chose the ornaments. An analogy could be made to upholstery, where the client picked out the materials and the working upholder did the stuffing, sewing, trimming and nailing. By doing this work, the artisan staked a claim on taste, gaining recognition from patrons and observers:

> *The dressing room [...] is prettier than 'tis possible to imagine, the most curious India paper has birds, flowers etc. put up as different pictures in frames of the same with festoons, India baskets, figures etc. on a pea-green paper, Mr Bromwich having again display'd his taste as in the billiard room below, and both have an effect wonderfully pleasing.*[256]

This quote from 1771 shows the continued vitality long past 1750 of joining up India pictures. Meanwhile, installations of the larger scenic panels continued. Maybe the (small?) size of this dressing room had something to do with choosing pictures as opposed to a full-blown scenic. As a contemporaneous ad put it, dealers offered 'a variety of India landscapes, both for ornamenting rooms by way of pictures, or hanging them entirely'.[257]

Between 1750 and 1775, the printed borders that accompanied print rooms, though skilfully made, began to lapse into a certain sameness. Illustrations of examples by Vivares show that the corners were not set up to be mitred in place, as with a proper picture frame. Instead, the mitres are pre-established, leaving the framing borders to join with the corners by chance.[258]

## Screens

Prints and papier-mâché ornament were adapted to walls, but custom-made screens went a step further; they were virtual walls. They could easily be made from scratch to answer the occasion. It's surprising how many small sets of leather have been preserved on these screens, which were often cheaply made. Paper-hangings with large figures were often placed dead centre in the panels. The chance that the screen is custom-made increases when a large centralized wallpaper pattern fits the screen exactly.

As with print rooms, a custom screen installation could display the taste of the installer. Although the high tide of print rooms dates from well after 1750, it's interesting that prints were used on an important folding screen in Scotland in 1746, thus combining the two ideas. No less interesting are the materials. Two screens were created on the Traquair estate about thirty miles from Edinburgh; one survives. The four-fold screen frames were built by estate carpenter John Paterson in 1746. After construction they were covered in '9 yds unbleached straiken [linen]' and then decorated with cheap bluish lining paper, marbled paper (on the edges), custom-cut pillars in various designs, prints and borders. The materials cost nearly £35.[259]

These prints were almost certainly purchased from Charles Esplin, who supplied paint and dozens of pieces of paper and border to the house in this period. The list of materials for the screen includes: '4 books of flowers and birds, 2 quair of blew paper, 1 quair marble paper, lumber paper, gilt paper for the screen panel and cupolo'. Esplin supplied additional prints and coloured papers for the screen in 1749. The 'cupolo' must refer to the two that surmount the end panels of the screen. The prints used were exceptional. One original pen and ink landscape drawing is dated 1718, and several seventeenth-century prints were used. Transcriptions from the latter show that one was probably purchased on rue St. Jacques, Paris. One of the prints shows the French politician Jean-Baptiste Colbert.

A large temple repeats on all four panels. The temple design retains embossed trade names and a slight metallic sheen. It was cut from sheets of French gilt paper and enhanced with Ionic columns drawn in pen and Indian ink. The panel edgings are finished with a bold marbled paper, rather worn on front and intact on the reverse. One of the brocade papers has the embossed inscription C P S C M Simon Heicheli (*cum privilegio sacrae Caesaris Maiestatis*). This signifies that the paper was protected by copyright within the jurisdiction of the Holy Roman Emperor and created by Simon Haichele of Augsburg.

The screen is a magnificent example of how to marry decorative papers, supports and backgrounds with a functional piece of furniture to create a unique object. Who created this marvel? Charles Esplin supplied many houses with paint and paper-hangings, and was an importer as well. His brother John was a partner before they went their separate ways. Charles Esplin supplied '7 pieces of cloth paper' for the drawing room at 8s. per piece in 1750. Estate records, however, never note charges for his labour. Charles may have installed, or prepared installations for others. He was paid £1 4s. for putting the 'Plans of The New Court of Offices on canvas' in 1749 at Buchanan House, a place we've visited.[260]

The upholsterer John Schaw worked at Traquair between 1739 and 1756. He supplied two pieces of 'superior fine two blue cloath paper on yellow ground' at 8s. each, 4 yards yellow ground common paper, and 22 yards border in 1748. The trade practice of providing materials was common among upholders such as Thomas Phill, but Schaw seems to have taken it to a high pitch. He also supplied a state bed, French carpeting and Blois paper for the Duchess of Hamilton's bedroom at Holyrood. Schaw profited as well by charging a shilling a day for '15 working days of my lad' at Traquair during August 1750.

Mr Thorburn, another artisan at the estate, made far less money than Schaw. He charged 6 pennies a day, on average, for his services, which included papering, but also 'transporting of beds', and 'taking the whitening off the passages'; thus, the services of a handyman.

Lucy and Ann Stuart, sisters of the owner of Traquair, may have helped in some way. Lord Charles Linton became 5th Earl of Traquair upon his father's death in 1741. The screens were created around five years later, near his fiftieth birthday. The sisters were educated at the Ursuline convent in Paris and became accomplished crafters. They had returned to Traquair by the time the screen was made. Charming examples of a silk purse made by Lucy as well as silk-on-paper colifichet needlework ('colyfishes') worked by Ann and Lucy survive.[261] Could they have helped choose the ornaments and arrangements? It's not hard to imagine that these two unmarried daughters would have enjoyed such a diversion. Although it's impossible to be sure, the complexity of the cutting along with the boldness of the execution argue for a practiced hand. It's hard to believe that it is not the hand of John Schaw.

The continued availability of small Chinese or chinoiserie pictures, the spread of commercial engraved prints, and the acceptance of paper decoration as a worthy addition to the upholder's repertoire all combined to encourage novel uses of paper on walls in the second quarter of the eighteenth century. These novelties led inexorably to the type of print rooms mounted at Strawberry Hill in 1753. Over the same period, the spread of papier-mâché ornament in fillets, rolls and modular forms encroached on the domain of plasterwork. Whether put on harn, screen or wall, and whether they were papier-mâché, flocked, 'printed, painted, or stained', paper-hangings had found a secure place in the Old World. Considering their early introduction and popularity in Europe, it's strange that we have so few examples of papier-mâché in the New World, and that not a single print room has been found.

Figure 20: Traquair House screen, front.

Figure 21: Traquair House screen, back.

# CHAPTER 13:
# Pounds, Shillings, Pence

## 1741

*Yesterday I was busy in buying paper, to furnish a little closet in that house, where I spend the greatest part of my time when I am within doors; and, what will seem more strange, bespeaking a paper ceiling for a room which my lord has built in one of the woods. The perfection which the manufacture of that commodity is arrived at, in the last few years, is surprising: the master of the warehouse told me that he is to make some paper at the price of twelve and thirteen shillings a yard, for two different gentlemen. I saw some at four shillings, but contented myself with that of only eleven-pence: which I think is enough to have it very pretty; and I have no idea of paper furniture being rich.*[262]

Letter, Lady Hertford to the Countess of Pomfret.

Frances Seymour, Lady Hertford, was the wife of Algernon Seymour, styled Earl of Hertford until 1748. Her letter introduces, at long last, the critical question of cost. Much earlier, an ad from 1693 had offered 'strong Paper-Hangings, with fine India-Figures' at 2s. to 3s. per piece. Around 1700, the Blue Paper Warehouse offered the 'true sorts of Japan and Indian figured hangings' for 2s. 6d. per piece.[263] These sound like substantial papers, yet there's little context. Once paper-hangings gain a foothold, people start talking and writing about them: Henrietta Knight, for example, and Sarah Osborn, Mary Delany, and Fanny Boscawen, who considered many wallpapers exorbitantly priced.

Lady Hertford considered some at 4 shillings per yard, and bought paper at 11 pennies per yard (11s. per piece), disclaiming any need for 'rich' paper. She considered her 11s. per piece paper very pretty and suitable for what sounds like her favourite sitting room. But, how does 11s. per piece compare to other prices?

Henrietta, who had written to William Shenstone about 'stucco paper', wrote to him again: 'good carving is too fine for my humble roof. The room, consider, is only hung with sixpenny paper, and is so low that I have but five inches between Pope's Head and the Motto over it'.[264] Henrietta downplays paper at only six pennies a yard, or 6s. per piece. Could *this* be the going rate in the mid-eighteenth century?

Three bills from Robert Dunbar's Paper Warehouse help address the question of cost. Dunbar was known for supplying paper-hangings to the gentry, including Francis Wilks, Esq., Lord Cardigan, and Sir Richard Hoare, Alderman.[265] One of Dunbar's bills from 1740 includes charges for '51 ½ yds 2 Green on Yellow Mantua, at 11d yd.'. Another from 1741 includes a charge for '50 yards yellow on yellow mantua, 10d yd, Grissies room'. The descriptions are vague, but they sound like figured papers of few colours.[266] The cost of these papers at 10 or 11d. per yard are comparable to Lady Hertford's, and suggest what sort of patterns were available.

The bill from Dunbar from 1741 just mentioned offers an extended look at pricing. It was made out to the Mellerstain estate in the Scotland borders region.

## The Mellerstain Bill

31 December 1741
To Robert Dunbar for Stampt Paper Hangings vis:

| | |
|---|---|
| 10 pices octogon for Hall 7 pices dit for Diningroom, 4d per yd | 3.08.00 |
| 56 yeards Blew on yellow revils, 9d yd, for Parlour | 2.02.00 |
| 50 yards yellow on yellow Mantua, 10d yd, Grissies room | 2.01.08 |
| 10 piece rid & white Sprige & Shel, 4d yd, tent room | 2.00.00 |
| 4 ½ piece Green & white, dit, Lady Binnings room | 0.18.00 |
| 8 ½ piece green vernish'd feather, Green room | 1.14.00 |
| 6 [½] piece blew & white Roket, 3d yd, table room | 0.19.06 |
| 40 ½ doz borders, 12d the dozen | 2. 00.06 |
| a box 3s warfage, 6d of dit | 0. 03.06 |
| | £15. 07.02 |

It's interesting to see that 'Lady Binnings' room was outfitted with paper costing only 4s. per piece, and that paper could go as low as 3s. per piece (the 'blew & white Roket'). The cost continues to slide down. It's a long way from the 13 shillings per yard quoted by Lady Hertford to 3 pennies per yard.

Even though Lady Hertford resigned herself to paying 'only' 11s. per piece, other shoppers paid much less. Lady Hertford disclaimed the notion that paper-hangings at 11s. per piece were 'rich' but it's fair to suggest that 'rich' is exactly what her choice might have represented to a different homeowner, or, a homeowner in a different mood. Yet moods are hardly scientific, and 'style' is even less so. Is there no way, then, to draw comparisons among the fragmentary data that remains?

There is. It can be done by putting all of these purchases on a material basis, i. e., by using a sq ft, roll, or sheet comparison. Of course, the things that make wallpaper most enjoyable – colour, finish, and patterns as well as that indefinable thing called 'style' – are all missing. Nevertheless, material comparisons can be done all the way back. A review shows that single sheets were current in Western Europe from earliest times and that *dominos* and *papiers de tapisseries* remained current in France until 1750 or so; single sheets were common in the Chinese trade (India pictures); they were common in the chinoiserie trade; and they were re-introduced into high-style French paperhanging around 1790 (*papiers en feuille*). In fact, single sheets did not completely vanish until the era of continuous paper began in the wallpaper trade around 1830, when the Zuber company used 'endless paper' for their 1831 season.

The statutes of the Excise Duty on Stained Paper in England fixed the size of the piece at 7 square yards. Certainly each piece (roll) of the three wallpapers mentioned by Lady Hertford contained the same number of square yards. Since stained paper was also sold in the early modern era in quires of 25 sheets (for single sheet sales) as well as in joined rolls (for regular wallpaper) they can be compared by reducing all costs to a sheet price.[267]

The highest-priced paper that Lady Hertford mentioned, assuming that around 24 sheets made up a piece, cost about 75d. per sheet. The middle-priced paper cost 25d. per sheet, and the lowest-priced paper cost close to 6d. per sheet. A wide range indeed. The results are reported in Table 1 in Appendix A. The exercise is continued below: a sheet cost is found for leather, and then compared to other costs.

## Comparison To Leather

Calculations of sheet cost for gilt leather serve as a cross-check to gauge the relative cost of another 'going rate' in the period. The going rate for gilt leather in the shops of Rowland and Hutton over a thirty-five-year span (1721 to 1756) was apparently 6 shillings per skin.

A skin was about 20" by 27" (540 sq in.) and a sheet of stained paper in the early-eighteenth century was about 19" by 22" (418 sq in.). If these are put on the same basis, a cost of 52d. is discovered for 418 sq in. of leather. This cost falls midway between the most expensive paper (75d. per sheet) and the next-most-expensive paper (25d. per sheet) mentioned by Lady Hertford. The most expensive paper could be an outlier paper (or even an imaginary paper – an empty boast by the master of the warehouse). The prices suggest that paper-hangings in this period, at least at high society levels, could occasionally be more expensive than gilded leather – a testament to the value placed on wallpaper.

## Table 1 Results

The Mellerstain bill shows seven room areas and seven wallpapers. In Table 1, the costs and sheets are totalled (less borders and shipping) and averaged. The average cost of the seven wallpapers listed on the Mellerstain bill is 5s. 6d. per piece.

Table 1 shows that Lady Hertford's choice cost 11s per piece, and that the average cost of the two wallpapers ordered by Richard Hoare was also 11s per piece. The samples are few, yet the comparisons give us some sense of what was available at retail, and how Lady Hertford's choice stacks up against other wallpaper costs.

Retail prices for paper-hangings from the 1650s to the 1750s were rarely lower than 2 shillings per piece or more than 11shillings per piece. The mid-range, 4 to 8 shillings, would seem to be the 'going rate' for a piece of figured paper in two or three colours. Wallpaper bills on both sides of the Atlantic support this price range (see Appendix A, Table 1).

# CHAPTER 14:
# The American Colonies

## 1686

*There are some very good houses in this country. Those of the peasants are all of wood. They are sheathed with chestnut plank and sealed inside with the same. As they get ahead in the world they refinish the interior with plaster, for which they use oyster shells lime, making it as white as snow; so that although these houses seem poor enough on the outside because one sees only the weathered sheathing, within they are most agreeable. Most of the houses are amply pierced with glazed windows.*[268]

This text was written by Durand of Dauphiné, a Frenchman who travelled in the American South. The shift from wood planks to plaster happened no less in America than in Europe, and, according to this witness, no less in the South than in the North. Wattle and daub had been left behind. But, conditions could be primitive. The windows in the French colonies were not always made of glass, as in this example. Even the seats of government often made do with treated paper.[269]

The same touchstones are used for the American colonies as in previous chapters: the wallpaper trade, wallpaper shopping, rooms, paperhanging, installers, and costs. In 1686, wallpaper use must have been marginal. By 1750, though there was still no domestic paperstaining trade, there were certainly wallpaper tradesmen. Two are Thomas Coleman, who plied his upholstery trade near Charleston Harbor after keeping shop near London Bridge, and the merchant Thomas Hancock of Boston.

## Shopping For Paper-Hangings

Some of the documents about early wallpaper purchases reveal an interesting quirk. Colonists often ordered paper from England in linear yards (12 yds per piece). This explains why high linear yardages (360 or 600 yd, for example) are divisible by twelve. But, when wallpaper was going in the other direction, the tax authorities invariably counted it by the square yard (seven sq yd per piece).

In America, as in Europe, paper-hangings were sold by the quire and roll. Sales of roll paper have been recorded for 1714, 1730, 1736, 1741 and 1742.[270] James Birket

Figure 22: Trade card of Thomas Coleman (1734).

observed in 1750 that in Portsmouth 'the houses that are of Modern Architecture are large & Exeeding neat this Sort is generally 3 Story high & well Sashed and Glazed with the best glass the rooms are well plasterd and many Wainscoted or hung with painted paper from England the outside Clapboarded very neatly and are very warm and Comodious houses'. In Newport, 'the houses in general make a good Apearance and also as well furnished as in Most places you will meet with, many of the rooms being hung with printed Canvas and paper &C which looks very neat Others are well wainscoted and painted as in other places'.[271] Others have commented on the affluence of Newport: 'At Newport [...] many of the settlers were wealthy men from the Bay colony'.[272]

Birket was a merchant and sea captain based in the West Indies. He made his observations after several weeks in the northern colonies during August and had arrived on the mainland with letters of introduction to elite households. His comments offer a rare glimpse into early interiors. They include a reference to 'printed canvas'. Sales of this type of decoration pepper the account books of Samuel Grant, native-born upholsterer of Boston. It's an open question if these, like most paper-hangings at that time, came exclusively from England, or whether the Low Countries may have supplied them.

Birket's remarks show that paper-hangings had penetrated upper-class culture. Yet he was describing a mercantile phenomenon more prevalent in the North. Planters in the South often enlisted family members or agents to get household goods and bespoke orders from back home. Even when commercial partners supplied these goods, custom called for a veneer of friendship, lending the transactions a familiar tone. Paper-hangings were not unknown in the South, but they were apparently less popular than in the northern cities.

Although it seems to be generally true that population growth and commercial development was more pronounced in the northern than in the southern colonies, these differences faded over time. Distribution down the coast and around to New Orleans improved, as did the shipment of goods down the Mississippi River. Though records are scarce, it seems safe to say that wallpaper was established throughout the colonies by 1750. In the South, billing records and extant samples prove that many planters, merchants, military and government officials used wallpapers. Yet this very evidence tends to reinforce an assumption that the only consumption was elite consumption.

There is still little proof of decorative elaboration for its own sake, whether paint or paper, on interior walls, whether plaster or wood, before 1700.[273] It's well established that pictures of the Old and New Testament and Lives of the Saints enhanced the teaching methods of the Jesuits: 'To the adults I explained the whole of the New Testament, of which I have copper-plate engravings representing perfectly what is related on each page'.[274] Another example reinforces that these pictures were often engraved, not painted: 'This is one of the best means that we can employ to give some idea of the mysteries of our religion to the Savages; they are in ecstasies when they see the picture of Saint Régis that I have in my room, which was engraved by Monsieur Cars; they put the hand over the mouth, which is a sign of admiration among them'.[275]

Painted papers among the European settlers may have provoked similar admiration but for more worldly reasons. Although it's likely that single-sheet paper-hangings were hung in New France and New England before 1700, recorded history has been stubborn – there is no proof. There were '7 quires of painted paper and three reams of painted paper'[276] inventoried after the death of Michael Perry, Boston bookseller and stationer in 1700. These may have been paper-hangings, albeit in the quire and ream as opposed to the roll. But what they looked like or how much they cost is unknown. The account books of Perry's successor, Daniel Henchman, offer us more. He had a long career and recorded dozens of transactions.[277] These are examined later in this chapter and in the appendices.

Some single sheets may have been paper-hangings, while others may have been *decorative paper*, *lining paper* (or, as proposed earlier, *decorative lining paper*). These were destined for trunks, drawers and small objects. Other than stationers, the conduit for wallpaper before 1750 was the upholder's shop. At least a half-dozen upholsterers mention wallpaper in colonial advertising before 1750.

## Rooms

In addition to his notes about wallpaper, Birket records lumber being transported down the Piscataway River in New Hampshire for export. Panelled and wainscotted rooms were still common in Europe around 1750, though their numbers were dwindling. Lumber was highly prized by one commentator in 1700:

> Boards are what will turn to least account of any of the Commodities I have enumerated, yet a vessel wholly laden with them would make a saving voyage from these Plantations to England [...] The boards are rarely under 25 foot in length, and from 15 to 18 inches in breadth, and more free from knots than the Norway boards are [...] With a good regulation here will be a lasting store of all these things to the end of the world.[278]

The account books of Robert Gibbs, a Boston dry-goods merchant, show that one of his main sources of income around 1700 was sales of timber. He recorded sales of '499 foot of board; 304 foot plank; 532 foot of inch @ 200 of ½ inch boards' to Theodore Atkinson, Sr.[279]

According to Birket, the principal cities of New England were 'well plasterd'. As we've seen, the proliferation of plaster walls was encouraging more paper-hangings use in Europe by 1750 – much to the chagrin of Isaac Ware and other tastemakers. No doubt the same thing was happening in the colonies. But there were many other differences between Europe and America. The improvement of dwellings with insulation, whether plaster or sheathing, evolved naturally in England. These improvements came later in the colonies, and for good reason. There was no remodelling, because there was no building stock. Everything was built from scratch. It's no exaggeration to say that many colonists in the 1630s lived in holes in the ground, or tents, for some months after arriving.[280] Yet

American styles of building evolved quickly; any perceived differences between English and American building practices are easily explained by infrastructure, resources, and conditions.

In America, oyster shell or lime plaster offered better materials and results than wattle and daub, which shrank more, and so provided less protection from drafts and cold. Colonists often raked autumn leaves around the base of their dwellings in the early years to serve as crude insulation, but this practice faded with the advent of mature lime plaster walls. Another medieval holdover was the 'black and whites', large cruck and box timber-framed structures whose beams and lime-washed daub formed patterns on the exteriors. It was not long before these were put aside in favour of clapboard. There were certain backward-looking construction practices in the late-seventeenth century, but these *recherché* overhangs and facade gables gave way to simplified forms in the new century.[281]

From earliest times, abundant forests provided wood sheathing. Generally, planks were placed horizontally on the exterior, where they shed water easily, and placed vertically on the interior. Exterior sheathing was used at first to carry shingles; later, the insulating qualities of the sheathing were recognized. Interior sheathing was largely plain, though 'creased' panelling with a small lip was also used. This was an in-between type: not as smooth as plain panelling nor as raised as other types. Creased types declined after 1700 or so. By that time it was standard practice to put plaster on three walls (on hardwood riven lathe), with vertical boards for the fourth (the fireplace wall).[282]

The earliest plaster finishes were rough, but they were an improvement over chopped straw and mud. Gradually, surfaces became smoother. The period between 1675 and 1700 witnessed the near-total finishing of residential interiors, though rooms meant only for storage lagged. There was a lifting up and improvement of the structural/finished quality, whether this resulted in lime plaster walls, plank and board partition walls, and whether those boards ran vertically or horizontally. Changes in decoration which were evident by around the first quarter of the eighteenth century in the American colonies are still somewhat mysterious. There is no easy explanation for how, from a meagre start, the situation changed so rapidly. By 1725, paint, textiles, paper or raised panelling all seem to be viable wall options for the gentry.

When builders began panelling the dado area, this was often done with horizontal boards. And when plaster came into use below chair rails, it gave birth to the baseboard. Frederick Kelly says that the dado 'shrunk' to the size of the baseboard.[283] In the South, raised panels were commonly used below the dado by 1750. They were succeeded by flat panels of wood to complement the plaster increasingly used above the chair rail. Full plaster walls came to the South, but not until the late-eighteenth century.[284]

## Paperhanging

From this survey, it seems that 'few', 'some', and 'many' can describe the trends. Few paper-hangings are likely to have been put up in the American colonies before 1700.

Some were put up 1700 to 1725. And it's likely that many were put up between 1725 and 1750.

As in Europe, fixed fabric was the precursor. Not surprisingly, the first appearances of soft furnishings are hard to trace. Early twentieth-century writers such as George Francis Dow and Norman Isham noted that wall hangings were scarce around 1650, but not unknown. Dow cites some recorded in an upper chamber in Ipswich, Massachusetts, in 1648, costing all of £2 10s.[285]

Isham describes fabric hangings in Connecticut from 1657 (the Eaton inventory) and 1707 (the Jones inventory). In 1657, 'hangings about the [green] chamber' are valued at £2. 15s. (presumably colonial pounds); 'hangings about the [blue] chamber' are valued at £1. 10s.; and hangings in Mrs Eaton's chamber, including the window curtains, are worth £1. 10s. In 1707, 'hangings of the green chamber' are worth £2, and 'hangings of the middle chamber' are valued at 30s. Some of these hangings (other than the window curtains) may have been sewn together and tacked up.[286]

In the South, William Fitzhugh of Stafford County, Virginia asked his London agent in 1683 'please to procure for me a suit of Tapestry hangings for a Room twenty foot long, sixteen foot wide, and nine high and half a dozen chairs suitable'.[287] The *en suite* treatment of the chairs is interesting – a direct infusion of continental fashion. Four years later, he mentioned that he had four rooms 'hung'. In comparison, paper-hangings were not as durable as tapestry, and many did not meet planters' requirements for display. Additionally, the South's heat, humidity, and insects were inimical to paper. The air space provided by canvas supports was one way to defeat these problems, as we've seen. But, fabric supports for wallpaper before 1750, for the North or the South, are practically unknown.

It sounds like James White, 'lately arrived from London' to Philadelphia in 1754, may have been offering canvas jobs when he advertised 'paper hangings put up, so as not to be affected by the hottest weather'.[288] The investigation of some walls in two 1760s houses in Connecticut revealed interesting substrates:

> In both cases, the paper had been applied to a smooth sheathing nailed to the plank walls of the house, which had been left unpainted and was evidently not intended to be exposed since horizontal and vertical boards were patched together and the seams were covered with strips of cloth. Practically all the sheathing boards in the Buckingham house were of whitewood, with one board of chestnut; those at Guilford were of whitewood, chestnut, and oak.[289]

Documentation for lining paper is practically unheard of in the colonial America before 1750. The reasons may include economy, expediency, and ignorance. Paperhanging proceeded by fits and starts as handymen were pressed into service. This helps to explain why so many patterns were mismatched in early America. Drop matches, to say nothing of multiple drop matches, were sometimes botched. Even when the pattern was understood, 'ye flowers' did not always join. Many paper-hangings have been found pasted directly onto wood. Hints of this widespread practice, and the problems it caused, surface in advertising. There are no ads in America in this period stating that upholsterers will do their work so that the fabric will 'stand for several years, without coming off' or that fabric will be hung 'in the most durable manner' or that fabric 'is warranted to stay up' . Yet all of these assurances are found in American ads offering wallpaper and paperhanging. That these assurances were necessary suggests that failures were common.

## Installers

'As I propose building an House and doing it upon the most easy Terms, I have taken this opportunity to [ask you] to procure me an House joiner [of] a good character both as a workman and a well behaved Man'.[290] Robert Beverley of Blandfield was writing in the 1760s from Virginia to his agent, John Backhouse, in Liverpool. The all-consuming effort of house building may have occasionally justified a search for artisans as well as finished goods from Europe. But there was little need for gentlemen to import professed upholders or painter-stainers. Up to at least 1725 or so, paper-hangings were rare, and artisans familiar with paper, fabric or leather were capable of hanging single sheets above a fireplace.

We saw that the Painter-Stainers' Company tried to monopolize paint media in England. Around 1700, impressive lists of painting materials are found in the Boston records of immigrant Painter-Stainers' Company freemen such as Thomas Child and John Gibbs. Although the Company itself did not survive the sea voyage, these Company men sought to control the art and mystery of painting, which included house-, coach-, ship-, and even portrait-painting. The transfer of the painter's knowledge to apprentices continued in America.[291]

The guild breakdown that had occurred in England was also felt in America. The colonial environment, though vastly different, was similar in this one respect, for control was no more maintained in Boston than it was in London. This is not to say that there was no control, for price controls over wages were imposed at critical times, albeit by the local government rather than a city corporation or tradesman's group. Nevertheless, the lessening of control encouraged the development of the 'mechanic branches' of the working class, especially in rural areas, where the jack-of-all-trades gained a new respectability.[292]

In America, as in England, the term *paperhanger* had a slow start. Following a familiar path, professional installers at first worked out of stationers' shops, then out of upholsterers' shops. The first installers who advertised with any consistency are self-described in innumerable ads as belonging to one of the 'branches of the upholstery trade'. Not surprisingly, the upholstery trade took root in Boston. Some must have gone to New York and Albany. A handful of upholsterers begin to advertise in the Philadelphia newspapers with some regularity around 1750. Upholsterers did the same in the Southern colonies rather later.

But at least two upholsterers were in Virginia early on, for in 1737 Samuel Bowler advertised that he 'performs all manner of Upholdsterers Work'. In 1745, Richard Caulton, from London, 'doth all Sorts of Upholsterer's Work, after the newest Fashion [...] at their Houses or at his Lodgings'.[293] Thomas Elfe announced in Charleston in 1750 that he had hired a London upholsterer. This artisan may have been Thomas Booden the younger, member of the Worshipful Company, whose dates match up. Thomas Elfe sold 'all kinds of upholsterer's work, in the best and newest manner, and at the most reasonable rates, viz. tapestry, damask, stuff, chints, or paper hangings for rooms'.[294]

An upholsterer of special interest is native-born Samuel Grant of Boston, who was charging 20 to 30 shillings colonial money in the inflationary mid-1740s for tacking up calico and 'crim. harateen' hangings. 1,000 tacks at Grant's shop cost 10s. colonial money. Samuel ran what might be called a full-service shop. He sold reams of paper, whitewash brushes and a vast assortment of fabrics, including much 'painted linen', as well as his services He 'took down and put up beds' endlessly. He 'leathered' compass chairs at 20s. each, selling a half-dozen on one occasion to his fellow tradesman Thomas Hancock.[295]

Like Thomas, Samuel sold wallpaper, though in rather small amounts and always in colonial money. It's difficult to visualize the destination of the '4 yd paper @ 30/' (1739) or the '1 role paper @ 13/' (1741) that he sold – perhaps these were hung over a mantle? The transaction of 6 September 1739 is more understandable. He charged Rowland Cotton 28s. per piece for 4 pieces of paper and 3s. per yd for 4 ½ yd of border. This number of yards would have generated about 135 linear feet of narrow border, and about 250 sq ft of sidewalls. These could have decorated a small anteroom or hall.

European training was mentioned in the following upholsterers' ads: Job Adams (1732); Walter Rowland (1741); Richard Caulton (1745); Stephen Callow (1749); James Huthwaite (1750); James White (1750); Thomas Booden (1756) and Thomas Coleman (1766).[296] We've seen that some professed decorators came to America; the painter Thomas Child arrived in 1685.[297] Child's widow, Katherine, continued his business, then leased it to Edward Standbridge, who arrived in Boston before 1714. Standbridge ran the painting business from 1725 until his death in 1734.[298]

The painter-stainers found themselves in vastly different circumstances after crossing the ocean, but they didn't really change their stripes. Like joiners, brick-makers and timber-framers, they soon took up their familiar duties in a new land.[299] Child, Gibbs and Standbridge assumed the important roles of shopkeepers and custodians of raw materials such as oil and pigments. What of the upholders? Karin Walton lists Job Adams coming into the Worshipful Company by servitude in 1729. Thomas Booden was admitted in 1720 by servitude, and his son, also named Thomas Booden, was admitted in 1750 by patrimony. Thomas Coleman was admitted by servitude to the Worshipful Company in 1733. These three upholders advertised their services in the New World:

Job Adams (Philadelphia)

1732: Whereas Job Adams, upholder, lately arriv'd from London, living in Front-street near the Croocked-Billet; makes and sells all sorts of upholders goods, viz. beds and beding, easy chairs, settees, squabs and couches, window-seat cushions Russia leather chairs, with all sorts of upholders goods, at reasonable rates.[300]

Thomas Booden (Charleston):

1756: Lately imported from London, several sets of fine figured paper hangings for rooms, ceilings, and screens, some India pictures and mash work fit for ornamenting walls, etc. Likewise all sorts of upholsterers work done, chairs stuffed, and rooms hung in as neat and good a manner as can be done in England and at the lowest prices. Any person directing to me, at the sign of the Royal-Tent in Elliot Street, may depend on being punctually waited on by Thomas Booden, Upholsterer from London.[301]

Thomas Coleman (Charleston):

1766: Thomas Coleman, Working Upholsterer from London, takes this Method of returning thanks to those ladies and gentlemen that have favoured him with their commands; and at the same time acquaints them, that he still continues to carry on all the various branches of the upholstery business, on the most reasonable terms, at Mr Benjamin Hawes, painter, behind St. Philips Church. Paper hung in the most durable manner as cheap as in London.[302]

# Costs

The bill titled 'Invoice of Sundries' shows Philip Schuyler's wallpaper purchases. He made his only shopping trip to England in 1761 while his brick house was being built in Albany, New York. The house endures but no wallpaper remains. The wallpaper was bought at the shop of 'William Squire, at the Three Tents and Lamb in the Poultry'.[303] The 'three tents' (arms of the Worshipful Company) was a popular trade icon. Squire later described himself in court documents as a paperstainer[304] and may have been a freeman of the Painter-Stainers' Company.

By his own reckoning Schuyler spent £1,425 16s. on furnishings throughout the house. Mayhew and Myers describe this as 'showering expense'.[305] It's not clear if these are pounds sterling or New York notes, which in 1760 were worth 167 colonial pounds for every £100 pounds sterling.

The papier-mâché ceiling was expensive at £6. 6s. The costs sound comparable to those quoted by London upholder Mackay in 1755 to his client Patrick Duff for a papier-mâché ceiling in Scotland (see Texts: The Duff/Mackay Correspondence). No doubt Schuyler's ceilings included centre rose, medallions, and ornaments. Schuyler's

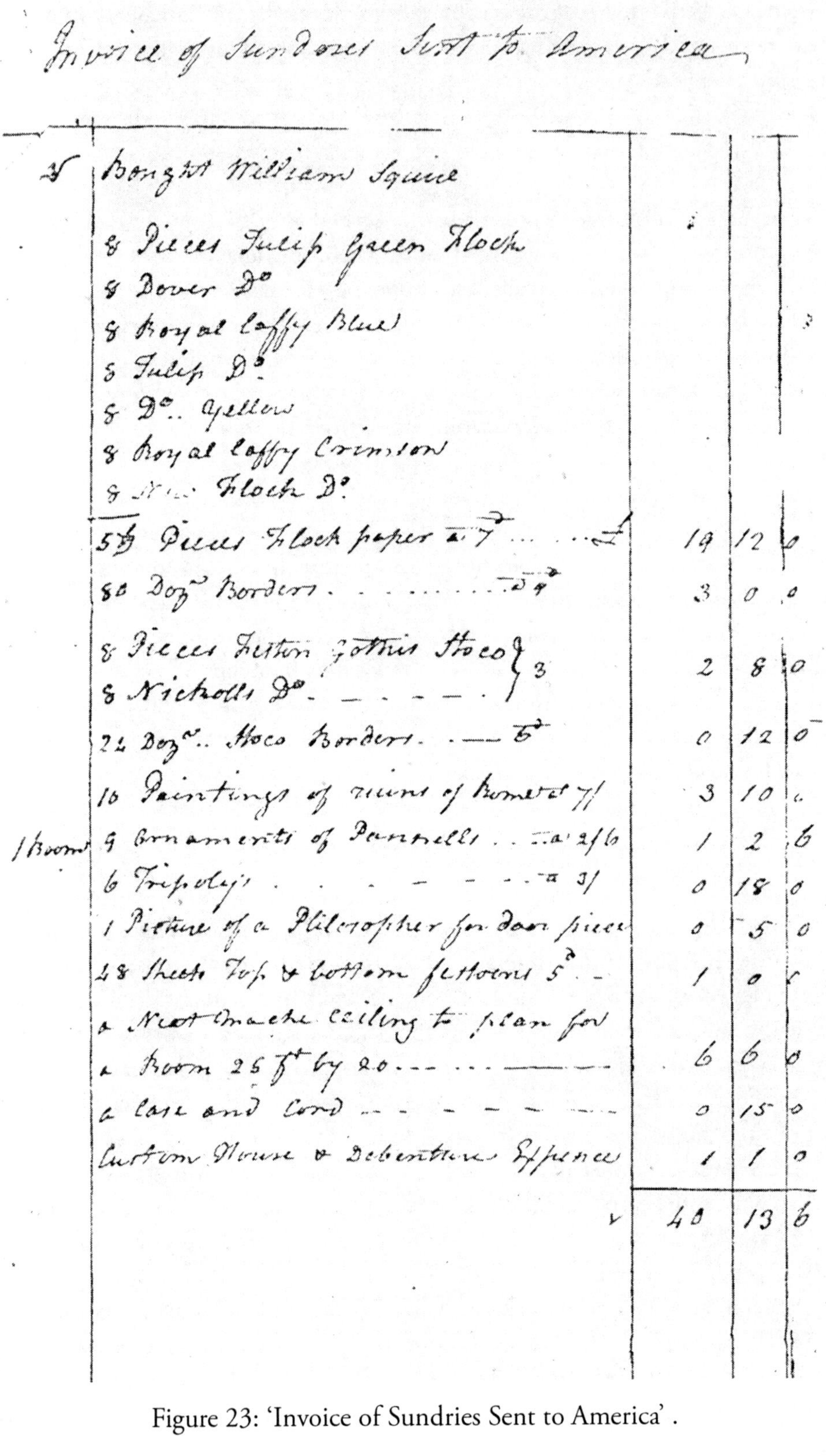

Invoice of Sundries Sent to America

| | | £ | s | d |
|---|---|---|---|---|
| ✓ | Bought William Squire | | | |
| | 8 Pieces Tulip Green Flock | | | |
| | 8 Dover Do | | | |
| | 8 Royal Caffy Blue | | | |
| | 5 Tulip Do | | | |
| | 8 Do.. yellow | | | |
| | 8 Royal Caffy Crimson | | | |
| | 8 New Flock Do | | | |
| | 56 Pieces Flock paper at 7/ .......... | 19 | 12 | 0 |
| | 80 Dozn Borders ..........at 9d | 3 | 0 | 0 |
| | 8 Pieces Fetton Gothic Stoco } 3 | | | |
| | 8 Nicholls Do. _ _ _ _ . } | 2 | 8 | 0 |
| | 24 Dozn.. Stoco Borders. ___ 6d | 0 | 12 | 0 |
| | 10 Paintings of ruins of Rome at 7/ | 3 | 10 | 0 |
| 1 Room | 9 Ornaments of Pannells . . . at 2/6 | 1 | 2 | 6 |
| | 6 Tripolys . . . _ _ _ _ . at 3/ | 0 | 18 | 0 |
| | 1 Picture of a Philosopher for door piece | 0 | 5 | 0 |
| | 48 Sheets Top & bottom festoons 5d. - | 1 | 0 | 0 |
| | a Neat Mache ceiling to plan for | | | |
| | a Room 25 ft by 20 --- ... ______ | 6 | 6 | 0 |
| | a Case and Cord -- - - - - --- | 0 | 15 | 0 |
| | Custom House & Debenture Expence | 1 | 1 | 0 |
| | ✓ | 40 | 13 | 6 |

Figure 23: 'Invoice of Sundries Sent to America' .

flock papers at 7s. per piece seem only moderately expensive. 7s. could probably have bought a small or mid-sized repeating pattern in one or two colours. The 80 yards border cost 9d. per yard (so, 9s. per piece). These inexpensive small borders, almost invariably put up in 10 or 12 courses per width, would have provided plenty of yardage to have run around the ceiling and woodwork to enclose the flocks. Typical borders of this period used a palette of greys, browns, blacks and whites.

The landscape scenes (Ruins of Rome) are only 7s. each, but the accompanying festoons, overdoor (Picture of a Philosopher) and ornaments raise the price for the wallpaper for that room close to £15. The set of similar-sounding landscape paper-hangings bought by his kinsman, Stephen van Rensselaer II, for a larger room at the end of the 1760s cost close to £21.[306] These are substantial costs, for substantial papers. The price structure is naturally much foggier for earlier wallpaper purchases, especially the single-sheet types.

Conflicted evidence about the earliest wallpaper in American comes from Michael Perry's shop in Boston. After Perry's death, the business was continued by his relative, Daniel Henchman. Although Michael's and Daniel's stock is referred to as 'painted paper', this seems to have been an unselfconscious reference to coloured paper which could have been either decorative paper or wallpaper. The term appears to have no connection to the mid-eighteenth century designation of *papier peint* (lit. 'painted paper') which came to stand for French wallpaper. If there were paper-hangings in the quire in early America, as seems likely, their costs were probably close to those of roll paper, since they served similar functions. Therefore, where 'painted paper' was recorded at costs approaching roll paper, those sheets were probably paper-hangings. Where 'painted paper' cost much less, those sheets were probably decorative papers. Yet, there seem to be no records showing that 'painted paper' in the quire was costly.

There is no easy explanation for this contradiction. Could the roll have commanded a higher price because it saved labour? Was it viewed as an engineering marvel? Or, once again, is there simply too little information? It's odd that even in Western Europe so little documentation has been collected about single sheets. In summary, roll paper in America seems to have come at a premium.

There are many records of the sale of 'painted paper' starting in 1712. Quite by coincidence, this is the year that the Excise Duty on Stained Paper began in England. Just as the new regulations helped in understanding Lady Hertford's transactions, they help in determining a universal sheet cost for single-sheet and joined paper.

The Watkins article ('The Early Use') about early paper-hangings includes ten transactions (1714 to 1742) in which Daniel Henchman sells 'painted paper'. In the absence of better records, these transactions are used as a basis for the cost of colonial paper-hangings. The data is summarized in Appendix A, Table 2. No discussion about costs in Massachusetts in the early-eighteenth century can omit the rampant monetary inflation from 1714 to 1749. Yet, tables are available to correct for it.[307] More information about the methods for figuring sheet and roll costs is found in Appendix B: Notes On Costs.

## The Passing Of The Torch

Thomas Coleman is a unique figure because he appears to have advertised his upholstery business on both sides of the Atlantic. His last known ad appeared on 28 February 1769. A week later, in a 'most melancholy accident', Coleman and three others drowned in Charleston Harbor. The snow Portland was returning from the Hobcaw rice plantation on 4 March, a Saturday night, between 7 and 8 p.m. when a sudden squall filled the boat with water. A few months later, in a poignant passing of the torch, American paper-hangings were advertised for the first time. Philadelphian Plunkett Fleeson confidently touted 'American Paper Hangings [...] not inferior to those generally imported' along with a long list of imported goods.[308] Thus American upholsterers began providing American paper-hangings alongside European models as they carried the trade forward.

Plunkett Fleeson's relationship to Europe is unusual. While advertising his upholstery services and wares on 1 August 1739 in the Philadelphia Gazette he claimed to be 'lately from London and Dublin, at sign of Easy Chair'. However, Plunkett (1713–1791) was the son of an Irish immigrant merchant who provided him with an excellent education.[309] Perhaps part of his seasoning was an extended trip to the commercial capitals of Europe. He would have been twenty-five years old in 1739 and just setting up shop. The Irish researcher David Skinner has found that a Plunkett Fleeson was baptized in Dublin at St. Peter's church on 7 March 1713, the son of Thomas Fleeson of Butter Lane and Dorcas Bowles, daughter of a family of prosperous Dublin property owners and aldermen. Perhaps the Fleesons lived in both the Old World and the New at various times. His European experience may have given him an advantage over his competitors. Plunkett made good on his ambition. He became the upholsterer to the elite, and a respected, if minor, politician and judge. The career of Thomas Bromwich springs to mind.

Prior to Plunkett's 1769 announcement there were two instances of American paperstaining, by John Hickey and John Rugar. Hickey described himself in a 1756 New York ad as a 'silk-dyer and scourer, lately from Dublin' who 'stamps or prints paper in the English manner and hangs it so as to harbour no worms'.[310] However, this ad appears to record his solitary attempt at the paper-hangings trade. Hickey had been advertising his services as dyer and scourer in Philadelphia from 1754. Soon after 1765 he moved up the Eastern seaboard and continued to follow a somewhat checkered career in Boston and Portsmouth until around 1777.[311]

In 1765, wallpaper was reportedly produced by Rugar for the newly formed Society for Arts, Manufactures, and Commerce, a political response to the punitive Townsend Acts. An early-nineteenth century commentator gave an overview:

> The acts of 1764, by abolishing in some cases, and diminishing in others, the drawbacks on goods exported from England to the colonies, had a tendency to raise the prices [...] The Americans made considerable efforts to introduce new manufactures, and to extend those already established. A society of arts, manufactures, and commerce, on the plan of that established in London,

was instituted at New York, and markets opened for the sale of home made goods; by which it soon appeared, says Mr Coombe, '[that] linens, woollens, some of the coarser kinds of iron ware, malt spirits, paper hangings, &c, were produced to the society, and, when offered for sale, were greedily purchased'.[312]

Who was the first paperhanger in America? This honour may have been won before 1700, but there is no record. The earliest on the books is a job done for the 'Province of Massachusetts Bay' in 1741.[313] In October, bookseller Samuel Robinson was paid £4 10s. colonial money for work at the Province House in Boston, a grand home built by Peter Sergeant in 1680 and later converted to official use. One of Robinson's jobs was 'New papring one roome below stairs'; the other was 'New Tacking the paper hanging above in the chamber'.[314]

The second job proves that tacks were just as important in America as in Europe. The 'New Tacking' may have been done to arrest sagging. The hangings must have been tacked to battens or the perimeter of a panelled room. Borders were likely used to cover the tacking. The hangings must have been strong in order to withstand re-tacking and may well have been monolithic for each wall. Everything suggests that they were lined with canvas.

By our terminal date of 1750, English upholders and painter-stainers were active in most colonies, and must have started training native apprentices. The colonies had caught the taste for wallpaper, but the sole sources were still England and France, respectively, for New England and New France. It would be many more years before American wallpaper would appear, but the foundation had been laid.

Just imported,

By THOMAS COLEMAN, Upholsterer and Paper-hanger,

In the Schooner Three Brothers, Capt. Fitch,

A SMALL but GENTEEL ASSORTMENT of the NEWEST PATTERN PAPERS, which he will dispose of on the most reasonable terms. Any orders for the above will be immediately complied with, by sending word to Mr. Robert Bolton's.

N. B. He has also to dispose of, A FEW SETS of VENETIAN WINDOW BLINDS, with a WINDSOR CHAIR, an ITALIAN CHAIR, and SEVERAL CHAIR BODIES.

Newspaper ad of Thomas Coleman (Georgia Gazette, 15 April 1767).

# CHAPTER 15:

# Canada And The North American Wholesale Trade

This chapter is largely based on newly discovered wholesale costs for the Canadian and American colonies. The Canadian documents from the 1760s through the 1780s include a bonus: the number of rolls in the shipments. This comes as a welcome counterpoint to the sparse information about the colonies to the south for this same period. But first, there is one final set of data for the American colonies for the first half of the eighteenth century, and it concerns Thomas Hancock.[315]

In 1737, Thomas wrote to a business associate in London, John Rowe, concerning a fine chinoiserie scenic paper. In November 1746 he was again writing to 'John Rowe & Co.', asking for:

| | |
|---|---|
| 1 role parchment | |
| 2 rolls forest (?) | |
| 50 p painted paper No. 7B | @ 2/6 |
| 30 do. 22 | do. 4/ |
| 30 do. 23 | do. 4/ |
| 30 do. 25 | do. 6/ |
| 50 do. 5 | 4/9 |
| 30 do. 6 | 3/3 |
| 30 do. 7 | 3 |

The following year, in August, he requests:

| | |
|---|---|
| 1 Role writing parchment | |
| 30 Roles painted paper N 7B | @ 2/6 |
| 30 p do. 5P | 4/9 |
| 30 p do. 6 | 3/3 |
| 30 p do. 7 | 3/ |

| | |
|---|---|
| 30 p do. 22 | 4/ |
| 30 p do. 23 | 4/ |

Per Scarborough
I am Gentl. Your Most Ob. Hum. Servt. TH
To Messrs. John Rowe & Co.

These items, which Thomas does not bother to total up, establish that he was ordering paper-hangings by pattern number: this shows that he was a wholesale dealer in paper-hangings. After receiving these rolls (250 pieces in 1746 and 180 pieces in 1747) he could have sold them to a local storefront or disposed of them in Halifax, Quebec or Newfoundland (but perhaps not in heavily trafficked New York or Philadelphia). From the fact that each pattern matches up with a consistent price, these might be called his stock-in-trade.

The range of price (2s. 6d. to 6s.) is interesting as well. Since Massachusetts was in the throes of rampaging inflation, these low values are most likely given in pounds sterling. Based on the tables in the appendices, they suggest respectable but not inordinately expensive paper. The highest priced paper at 6s. (# 25, in the 1746 order) was the only pattern not renewed in the 1747 order. Was it a little rich for the territory?

We saw earlier that Thomas fit Defoe's definition of a *merchant*. Though these paper purchases are tiny, they're part of a pattern. Thomas was a generalist, as one writer put it: 'Thomas tried specializing in potash, whale oil and other commodities, but his success as a business man was mainly because of a willingness to shift quickly from one project to another as opportunities opened'.[316] Thomas Hancock no less than Thomas Bromwich was catching the spirit of the time and exploiting a growing taste for paper-hangings.

The last time paper-hangings appear in Thomas's account book is 12 September 1748. His postscript to another letter to John Rowe & Co. states: 'If not too much trouble & no expense to you a few misc patterns of Role paper of any new fashion pretty cheap wont be amiss'. Thus the account book of Thomas Hancock and the American colonies are left behind as he places an order for 'new fashions' – sight unseen.

His request is not blind faith but a fair hunch based on decades of familiarity. He knew how much wallpaper cost, what it would bring, and how attractive it would be to his fellow colonists. How fitting a conclusion to the getting-acquainted period for the American colonies and what a harbinger for the coming years, during which paper-hangings would rise in popularity to levels that no one, not even Thomas Hancock, could have imagined.

At first, early wallpaper consumption in Canada seems like a blank white space. Part of the reason for the blankness is quite literal – printing presses were forbidden in New France despite repeated requests. French colonists were not encouraged to be independent thinkers or avid consumers of competitive products, but rather faithful suppliers of natural resources to the mother country.

The records in Canada are slight, but it's probably significant that the first issue of Quebec's first newspaper (*The Quebec Gazette*, 21 June 1764) mentioned wallpaper.

The issue carried an ad by the Englishman John Baird touting 'an assortment of goods suitable to the country, recently arrived from London'. In 1752 paperhangings were advertised in the *Halifax Gazette* the first year the newspaper was printed: 'To be sold by Frances Martin, at Mr Fairbanks store near the south gate, wholsale or retail, at the very lowest rates (as he intends shortly to leave this colony) [...] All sorts of paper hangings for rooms'.[317]

As mentioned earlier, there were many French upholsterers in colonial Quebec – at least a half-dozen before 1700. Even if they left few marks, it seems likely that they were engaged from time to time with fabric and wallpaper. By 1750, the population of the city had grown to almost 8,000. Professional upholsterers were also living in Louisbourg during 1749–67.[318] A 1736 document mentions a 'velvet' fabric being planned to decorate either a closet or a closet door at the Golden Dog Hotel, also called the Philibert House, in Quebec.[319] Wallpaper was used in Canada, Felicity Leung asserts, 'even against bare sod walls'.[320]

Wallpaper imports to New England were almost exclusively English products up to the Revolutionary War, and, logically enough, the imports to New France seem to have been mainly French. This held true, at least officially, until 1763, when the changeover from French to British rule took place. 'Re-exporting' (redistribution of export goods in North America by coastal traders) ensured that paper goods from Western Europe and China could have easily reached areas comprising Canada from 1650 to 1750.

These areas included major ports in New France: Montreal, Quebec City, Three Rivers, and Louisbourg, as well as Acadia, Newfoundland, and Nova Scotia. Regular wallpaper use may have begun around 1689. By then, the European population of New France had reached 12,000. According to Felicity Leung, 'a period of peace began, and trade with France grew as fish, furs, hemp, tar, potash, iron, and coal were exported and France manufactures were imported'.[321] These facts argue strongly for the use of easily transportable single-sheet painted paper and paper tapestry, which after all were specialities of the French nation.

One interesting finding of Leung is that the amount of wallpaper shipped to Canada in 1777 was seven times more than the amount shipped during the fateful year of 1776.[322] No doubt the seven-fold increase was quickly re-distributed. But whether wallpaper came from France or England is probably not as important as the events at the end of the French and Indian War.

The Treaty of 1763 gave England all of North America east of the Mississippi. A British proclamation converted Canada, which had been part of New France, to the Province of Quebec. Political stability and population growth followed. While the French were just getting started with roll paper, English paperstainers were poised to deliver the goods. A flurry of statistics establish that many thousands of rolls were shipped from England to Canada in the mid-1760s through the 1780s.[323]

Those arriving in the mid-1760s came through the port of Quebec. The documentation links these paper-hangings to a list of trading companies known by their initials, two of whom were revealed to be John Baird and Moore & Finlay some time later when those merchants started advertising their wares in the pages of *The Quebec Gazette*. Records indicate that seventeen cases and four casks of 'stained paper', 'stamped paper', and 'paper hangings' came from London in 1763 and 1764. A minimum estimate of the rolls in the twenty-one containers is 2,310 pieces, based on the smallest amount for one case, which was 770 sq yd (110 pieces). Another contained 508 pieces, indicating that the total could have climbed to 10,000.[324]

Others who traded in wallpaper at this time were Robert and John Stenhouse. These merchants of Montreal probably came from England.[325] From what's known about their business, even rough and ready pioneers liked to pick out wallpaper. Robert Stenhouse procured nine pieces of wallpaper costing 3s. each for fur traders Benjamin and Joseph Frobisher in 1774. The wholesale price paid by the Stenhouses in the mid-1760s for a total of 549 pieces ranged from 11d. per piece to 2s. 4d. per piece. These goods were bought from Thomas Harris in London.[326] The higher cost papers included:

| | |
|---|---|
| fine stone chintz | @ 2/4 |
| odd flock paper | @ 2/- |
| green and red | @ 2/- |
| red on stone | @ 1/8 |
| red and yellow | @ 1/8 |
| blue on stone | @ 1/6 |
| pink on stone | @ 1/6 |
| green on stone | @ 1/6 |

The largest quantity (432 pieces) is not described by pattern. These were evidently the cheapest at 11d. per piece and classified as 'odd paper hangings'. Leung suspected that many of them were ungrounded or grounded in off-whites with few foreground colours. The accountant who figured the duty for the entire order in 1767 noted in the margin that about seventeen sheets of 'elephant paper' comprised a piece of paperhanging.[327] This number of sheets would dictate a sheet height of about 25 ½" for a piece measuring 12 yards long. These elephant sheets had not yet reached the 28" or 30" heights of later years.

Summing up, the documented rollage for Canada during the 1760s was at least 91,533 sq yd, or 13,076 pieces. This compares to a total of 233,810 sq yd (33,401 pieces) in the 1770s. In the 1780s, volume almost doubled from the previous decade: 416,314 sq yd were shipped (59,473 pieces).[328]

The 1780s are the end of the line for statistics. Leung found that those for the 1790s through the 1820s are 'sparse and incomplete'. It's worth noting that military men in Canada became prolific users of the product. British military rulebooks of a somewhat later date confirm a tradition of furnishing first-class through fourth-class quarters with wallpaper.[329]

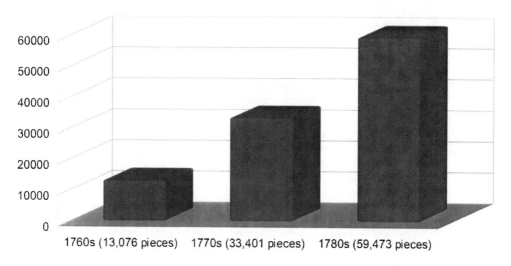

Figure 25: Wallpaper shipments to Canada for three decades.

Taken all together it's quite likely that wallpaper as defined in this book was used in some quantity in Canada prior to 1750. Wallpaper shipments increased significantly in the 1760s, 1770s, and 1780s. The diversion of shipments during the American Revolution may have encouraged more use. Since the Canadian population continued to increase (from 70,000 in 1760 to over 190,000 by 1790), it's possible and even probable that the use of wallpaper continued to grow right through the turn of the century.[330]

# CHAPTER 16:
# Bringing The Backstory Forward

The papering job in the eighteenth-century Irish parlour is done. The paperhangers have thrown out the trimmings and wheat paste, cleaned and put aside the brushes and shears, and carted the ladders away. Everyone in the family, each in their own way, has come to grips with the huge red flowers blossoming on Hannah Shaw's parlour walls. Some thought of the cost. Some pronounced themselves satisfied. Some just smiled.

As we turn back to the present – and to the wallpaper on our computer screens – we might ask: are our rooms so different from Hannah's parlour? Even though our homes have fewer doors and our rooms are unlikely to be wrapped up like pretty packages with borders running round, we still have walls. And where there is wall, there is a need to decorate that wall. Like Hannah, we need to feather our nests and make them our own.

Wallpaper was a new idea in 1650, and it evolved from handicraft – not design studios. Paperstainers came from the painting trade, their methods, tools, and stock came from papermakers and calico-makers, their goods were sold by stationers, and the installers were upholders. Wall surfaces changed drastically over a hundred years, yet this was no hindrance. Wallpaper easily kept pace. Nor was the lack of trained paperhangers a problem. If a John Schaw was not available, then a William Reid or a Mr Thorburn would do. Even Catharine, or perhaps the 'negro boy named Devonshire' could tackle the job.[331] If there was wallpaper to hang, it got hung, even on bare sod walls in frigid climates. Wallpaper competed with cotton, silk, velvet, and leather – and won. With 'mock flock', wallpaper incorrigibly imitated itself. It crossed national boundaries with ease.

But more important than these accomplishments may be that wallpaper has always been a quintessentially domestic product. Wallpaper is now celebrated in prestigious museums as a significant cultural artefact. Yet, wallpaper in museums is always *ex situ* – out of context. To understand it, one needs to look at how it was used. Wallpaper arrived from the factory as an almost-finished product that needed to be hand-crafted into place. This background raises a question: should wallpaper be classified as a domestic art as well as a decorative art?

Three lessons can be pulled from this one-hundred-year framework:

### Wallpaper began as a folk art.

Was wallpaper, at first, 'only for the rich', as sometimes asserted? The backstory shows the opposite. Ada K. Longfield maintained that in the 1600s the peasant class in Normandy placed block printed and coloured pictures over their fireplaces with honour. Jean-Michel Papillon admitted the same about *dominos*. Jacques Savary des Brûlons wrote that wallpaper was 'used by the peasants and the poorer classes' in Paris. John Houghton reported that in Epsom, paper-hangings were being adopted in the 'houses of the more ordinary people'.

The myth that wallpaper was, at first, only for the well-to-do is therefore debunked; but it did 'trickle-down' in one important way. Elite wallpaper which was exported to countries like Sweden, Norway, and Denmark was consumed by the wealthy and educated classes. This elite wallpaper was then copied within the new country, influencing the design of the stripes and small flower types which were already being created for local use. This pattern of assimilation continued.

### Wallpaper is a demand-side product.

Wallpaper was popular because it furnished style as well as economy. Like leather panels, India pictures, and papier-mâché components, rolls of wallpaper were essentially modular. All were shipped out from workshops in boxes and wall decorations were made up on site. Wallpaper was a much-loved traveling companion for the population surging westwards from Europe and then onward to the west coast of North America. It was as easy as sticking a few rolls into a trunk or buckboard.

Yet, wallpaper designs over the first hundred years had few protections. Copying was rampant and competition was fierce. Paperstainers had to respond quickly, even instinctively, to the needs of consumers, creating new styles even as they risked capital expenditures. Thus wallpaper was not foisted on the populace by a clan of tastemakers and elite producers; it was a demand-side product. This is true despite iconic types within the market such as flock damasks and Chinese scenics.

It's interesting that throughout the first one hundred years there are no 'designer labels'. It was not until 1754 that the unfortunate John Baptist Jackson touted the connection of his goods with Albrecht Dürer and Hugo di Carpi.[332] The most important designer by far over the first hundred years was 'Anonymous'.

### All wallpaper is beautiful.

John Cornforth once called wallpaper history 'all arms and legs' because it lacked consistency – this much is a fair criticism.[333] Maybe it can never be consistent; but, there are consistent ways to study it. When wallpaper is seen through craft traditions, we learn that every wallpaper represented a choice, and was therefore beautiful to someone. Why did Queen Caroline switch from green to red flock at Hampton Court? For that matter, why did she switch from a painted surface to a papered one? The answer must lie in preference. For commoners as well as the Queen, choice matters.

Lady Hertford said that 'I have no idea of paper furniture being rich' and we must believe her, even when we know that the price for her paper *was* rich, compared to others. The same is true for the middling classes, or for the lowest of the low, respectively. Whoever the consumers are, we must put ourselves in their shoes, because the patterns of the past belong to the people of the past. The most important question about historic wallpaper design, then, may have little to do with its formal qualities. It may be: why did this pattern appeal to the one who bought it?

———————————————

In summary, what has been rediscovered about wallpaper? This account has shown that during the first hundred years – for Sarah Osborn, Henrietta Knight, John Drummond, and countless others – wallpaper was amiable, simple, portable, cheap, innocent, fragmentary, cheery, civilized, versatile, useless, redundant, and protean in its growth and dispersion.

# Glossary

'Every trade has its nostrums, and its little made words, which they often pride themselves in, and which yet are useful to them on some occasion or other' (Defoe, *The Complete English Tradesman*).

bag-cap: Cheap paper for lining and other preliminary work.

blue paper: Not art paper (Bleue Hollande or Dutch blue) nor 'blued paper' (low-quality yellowy paper dyed blue to neutralize the colour). Blue paper used for wallpaper in the late-seventeenth century was strong and thick; similar to sugar, wrapping, and ream papers.

*boiseries*: Sets of intricately carved raised wood panelling.

bordering: A name for borders; sometimes found in colonial American eighteenth century bills and correspondence.

buff: Dull whitish-yellow colour as from an ox-hide dressed with oil.

dead colour: Colours without a reflective sheen; most all distemper colours would have qualified.

decorative lining paper: Not decorative paper, not wallpaper; printing press off-cuts overprinted with mostly small patterns used for lining boxes and drawers.

*dominos*: Cheap decorative paper with simple designs sold in streets, small shops and village markets for a variety of uses.

dozens: Most often used to denote 'yards of' border. Mary Delany, writing to her brother Bernard Granville in 1751: 'I have received the 6 dozen borders all safely [...] They are for framing prints'; *Autobiography of Mrs Delany*, 1st ser., III:34.

drab: A dull light brown or yellowish-brown colour; 'Hence our drab cloth, pure and undied cloth, and they call this a drab colour in the trade'; S. Pegge, *Anecdotes of the English Language (1803)*, p. 266.

elephant: A coarse, strong paper used for paper-hangings; sheets 22" wide by 19" to 25" high were popular 1650–1750.

fillet: Narrow border running at extremities; sometimes in relief with gilt highlights.

ground, grounding, grounded: Laying a preliminary coat of colour on the paper.

grounds: Studs in the corners of rooms; fabric underlayments were sometimes tacked to them.

harn: Scottish origin; coarse linen cloth made from the refuse of flax or hemp; sackcloth. Often used as a support.

'in the white': 'It sometimes happens that they require single sheets to be stamped and charged in the white, that is, before being printed, for the purpose of hanging rooms and to be subsequently painted'; tax regulation quoted in Dagnall, *The Tax On Wallpaper*, p. 19.

lumberhand: Cheap paper for lining and other preliminary work.

M: Roman numeral for one thousand; sometimes designating a thousand tacks or nails on a bill.

marouflage: Adhering a painted mural on canvas to a substrate with adhesive.

*papier peint*: French wallpaper; lit., 'painted paper'.

*papiers de tapisseries*: French wallpaper; lit., 'paper tapestry'; the constituent sheets create a larger design once trimmed and joined on the wall.

piece: Pc, ps, piece, peice, roll, role, rool, role, rowl, furniture paper, room paper, all mean the same thing – a unit, or bolt, of paper-hangings; defined by English statute as 7 sq yd (63 sq ft).

pink'd: Scalloped; shrouds were provided by undertakers and upholders 'pink'd [...] plain and plaited'.

pumiced: Abraded; sanded smooth. Pumicing was done with volcanic stone or other rough material to remove bumps and tags from single-sheet lining paper installations; it was also done to walls and wooden mouldings before painting.

quire: A bundle of paper composed of 24 or 25 sheets.

*raboute*: French joined paper, post-1750; lit. 'end to end'.

scorched leather: Also known as damask leather, it was pressed between a mould and a heated metal plate.

selvedge: The unprinted edges of the wallpaper.

size (noun): Hide glue used for reducing porosity of plaster and paper. Purer forms were used for adhering flock, mica (spangles), and metal leaf and powders to wallpaper.

size (verb): To spread a dilute mixture of glue onto plaster or paper.

staining: Application of colour to paper; root of 'paperstainer'.

stamped paper: In Ireland, a synonym for 'block printed paper'. In England, also used to denote paper which had been stamped by the tax authorities. Hence 'stamp'd Elephant' in a bill signifies a legitimate but blank paper.

tier: (OED): the second sense of the verb 'tier' is an erroneous spelling of 'teer' – to cover or spread with earth, clay or plaster. Hence teering, plastering or daubing; especially, teering-boy, in calico-printing (whence paper-hanging), a boy who spreads a fresh surface of colour on the printer's 'pad' before each use.

# Texts

c. 1690, Edward Butling's Trade Card

4 February 1722, first letter of John Rowland

1738, *The General History of China*, by Du Halde

1747, *The London Tradesman*, by R. Campbell

1747, *A General Description of All Trades*

1755, The Duff/Mackay Correspondence


c. 1690, Edward Butling's Trade Card

[Trustees of the British Museum; Heal, 91.12, AN588972001]

At the Old Knave of Clubs, at the Bridge-foot in Southwark, liveth Edward Butling, who maketh and selleth all sorts of hangings for rooms, in lengths or in sheets, frosted or plain: also a sort of paper in imitation of IrishStich, of the newest fashion, and several other sorts, viz. flock-work, wainscot, marble, damask, turkey-work. Also shop-books, pocket books, writing-paper, brown-paper, and whited-brown paper, cards, and all other sorts of stationary wares, good and reasonable.


4 February 1721/2, first letter of John Rowland to Jan Gerrit Van Wassenaer [Koldeweij, 'Gilt Leather Hangings', p. 83.]

My Lord,

I had the Honour of Yours of the 5th instant and have here sent a pattern which is as gentile as anything that is made and in my opinion as the peices of hanging are large it will look much nobler to have a mixture of large as well as small work and the border which is att top of the pattern to go round each piece of hanging, if it is agreable to your Lordships fancy. I made Mr Netcher's hangings with figures & houses butt Sir

Matt. Decker & my lady Dentrey's hangings I made with birds & flowers agreable to the pattern I have sent and the lowest price is six shillings a skin which is near 27 inches long & 20 inches wide according to our measure when they are joyned I compute it att about 135 or 140 skins which att the last number comes to forty two pounds sterling. if Your Lordship is pleased to send the measure in the box with the pattern in peices of red tape we shall be more exact in our measure. one peice for the height and four peices each to be just the length of the breadth of each peice of hanging I having had severall measures sent from abroad that way with a writing to each peice to distinguish them as soon as I have Your Lordships answer I will Immediately put them in hand and they shall be compleated neatly according to Your Lordships time if, I have a speedy answer.

I am My Lord Your Lordships most obedient Humble Servant

John Rowland


## 1738, *The General History of China*, by Du Halde

[Du Halde, *General History of China*, II:419-20. First published in 1735 and based on dairies of Jesuit missionaries; Samuel Johnson said it was 'the most copious and accurate account, yet published, of that remote and celebrated people'.]

It is certain that the Chinese paper is preferable to that of Europe, because the sheets are made of a very great length [elsewhere he estimates sheets as long as 30 to 50 feet], and being full as white is much softer and smoother [...] The consumption of paper in China is so great that it is not surprising they make it of all sorts of materials, for besides the prodigious quantity that is used by the learned and students, who are almost innumerable, and to stock tradesmens shops, one cannot conceive how much is consumed in private houses; one side of their rooms is nothing but windows of sashes covered with paper; on the rest of the walls, which are of plaister, they paste white paper, by which means they preserve them white and smooth; the cieling is made of frames cover'd with paper, on which they draw divers ornaments: if it has been justly said that the Chinese apartments are adorn'd with that beautiful varnish which we admire in Europe, it is also true that in the greatest part of the houses there is nothing to be seen but paper; the Chinese workmen have the art of pasting it very neatly, and it is renewed every year.

## 1747, *The London Tradesman*, by R. Campbell, p. 169

Chapter 32: Of the Upholder and the Trades employed by him

I have just finished my house, and must now think of furnishing it with fashionable furniture. The upholder is chief agent in this case. He is the man upon whose judgment I rely in the choice of goods; and I suppose he has not only judgment in the materials, but taste in the fashions, and skill in the workmanship. This tradesman's genius must be universal in every branch of furniture; though his proper craft is to fit up beds, window-curtains, hangings, and to cover chairs that have stuffed bottoms.

He was originally a species of the taylor; but, by degrees, has crept over his head, and set up as a connoissieur in every article that belongs to a house. He employs journeymen in his own proper calling, cabinet-makers, glass-grinders, looking-glass frame-carvers, carvers for chairs, testers, and posts of bed; the woolen-draper, the mercer, the linen-draper, several species of smiths, and a vast many tradesmen of the other mechanic branches.

The upholder, according to this description of his business, must be no fool; and have a considerable stock to set up with: however, a young man who has a mind only to be a mere upholder and has no prospect of setting up in the undertaking [supervising] way, does not require such a universal genius as I have been speaking of: he must handle the needle so alertly as to sew a plain seam, and sew on the lace without puckers; and he must use his sheers so dextrously as to cut a valence or counterpain with a genteel sweep according to a pattern he has before him.

All this part of the work is performed by women, who never served an apprenticeship to the mystery, as well as men. The stuffing and covering of a chair or settee-bed is indeed the nicest part of this branch; but it may be acquired without any remarkable genius. All the wooden-work they use is done by the joiner, cabinet-maker, and carver. A tradesman who is a good hand in the upholder's own branch is paid twelve or fifteen shillings a week; and the women, if good for any thing, get a shilling a day.

1747, *A General Description of All Trades*, pp. 159, 214.

Paper-Makers

[the Paper-Makers] goods go chiefly into the hands of the wholesale stationers, who vend them to the retailers, booksellers, printers, & c. [...] There are likewise hangings for rooms made by colouring and embossing of thick paper, the making and dealing in which is now become a considerable branch of trade; the masters in this part seldom take an apprentice with less than 10 l. at the working part of which a journeyman can get 15 or 18 s. a week, and a shopman has generally 10, 15, or 20 l. a year and his board. To set up in this branch compleatly will take up 500 l.

Upholders, the 49th [company]

Most frequently called upholsterers, who are the absolute necessary tradesmen for decently or sumptously furnishing an house and a large branch of business it is, the working part of which is not hard, but clean and genteel; (and if they were not so, what would the nice ladies do with them?) therefore fit for smart youths, who have no strength to spare; for they even employ woman to do some of the needle-work.

Besides performing this part many of them are great shop-keepers, who have abundance of ready-made goods for sale always by them. Most of them are also appraisers (which see before) and several of them are undertakers too.

The upholsterers take with an apprentice generally from 20 to 30 l. who work from six to eight; pay a journeyman in common 2 s. 6 d. or 3 s. a day; or, if by the year, 15, 20, or 30 l. and his board. If a master only does business in a private way 100 l. may serve his occasions; but if he keeps a stock of upholstery ware and materials for funerals he had need have 500 l.

Arms. On a chevron between 3 tents as many roses.

1755, The Duff/Mackay Correspondence

[Aberdeen (Scotland), Aberdeen University Library, Montcoffer Papers, MSS, courtesy of Captain Alexander Ramsay. Patrick Duff of Premnay commissioned the furnishings for his new Drawing Room in the Castlegate, Aberdeen, from James Mackay, a London upholder. The parts extracted here were transcribed by Dr Ian Gow who comments 'Of Mackay little is known but [...] in comparison with Duff of Premnay's crabbed questioning, Mackay, with his polished hand filling up the page neatly, comes across as suave, confident and breezy and with a relish for the fantastic ornamental vocabulary of the chinoiserie rococo as well as a penchant for the novelties made possible by papier-mâché'.]

Duff to Mackay:

It is proposed that the Spaces betwixt A: and B on the South end of the room betwixt the Chimney and west syde wall, as also all the west syde wall to [the Nitch or place for a Buffette], and likewise all the North wall above the pedestal...be lining with India paper. I send you a pattern of three kinds, one scarlet, one straw colour with some guilt ornaments, and one blue and gold [all which I have]. Its the blue and gold I truly care to make use of. Its to be pasted on canvas and the wall Lynd with [plain] wood to keep off damp, and then fitted to the wall and fixd wit a narrow frame of guilt leather and guilt nails [and a small plain moulding of wood guilt round each piece]. Write me if ye approve of this method, or if ye can advise me of any better method for putting up the China paper, and what is the prettiest kind of paper for hangings in such a room in use with you, and what it would cost and if you think it much prettier as what I have, send me a small pattern of it. Are myne true India paper [...]

Mackay to Duff:

A description of the Inside of a Room 24 x 20 as in the Scheme [...] The whole Room hung with paper all round above the Surbase to the foot of the Cornish close to the architrave of the Doors and windows &c., and the Carving of the several pieces of furniture put upon the paper or damask &c., the architraves, Surbase and bass are Sketched out with the manner of ornaments put upon them [...] The following Sketches are made of paper Brought to a paste and formed by a mould to put up in any Room.

A and B, in the Sketch for a cove of a Room, are Joyned in about 3 feet Long: being first painted to what colour desired, all round the Room, above the Cornish and has a good Effect at that Distance, being much in fashion here and comes at about 30 pence per foot, being much cheaper and better than Stuko and will Laste 2 or 300 years. This may be thought a Romance, But in repairing Westminster Abbey this was Discovered, and has Brought it into the Esteem of every body of Judgment, first, because it is Easy removed from one place to another; and then may be Cut in any place and fashioned as you please without the Least trouble or Expence.

In the Sketch for a Ceiling of a Room above the Cove you have Six Different patterns Viz.:

| | |
|---|---|
| The Corner A; 12 feet by 10 feet | 2.12.06 |
| The Same without the moulding | 2.12.00 |
| The Corner B; without the moulding | 1.15.00 |
| The Corner C2. | 15.00 |
| The Corner D2. | 15.00 |

If the Compartment for the middle of the Ceiling if the Fig: E is liked best or the Fig: F it makes no Difference, Either will come to: 4.04.00

These ornaments painted white, upon a deep yellow ground of the Ceiling has a good Effect, or all white both are in fashion here [...] Article of palm branches are not understood by you I did propose to put them round the India paper instead of your gilt leather and brass nails – see the pattern – you Imagined them Branches or Girandoles for Candles 2 pairs of such are sent with the Chairs – See the bill [...] Your method of covering the walls with plain wood is certainly the best; and put up strong mearns Linen under the paper in Stead of canvas and paist a coat of writing paper upon it before the India paper is put up, otherwise you'll see all the threads of the linen thro' the India papr. The India paper that is most in use here, has a white ground and full of flowers, birds and trees etc.. The Sheets Some are 9 feet long by 3 feet wide; at 10 shilling each, others 4 feet 6 Inches Long by 22 or 23 Inches wide at 3 Shillings each. But those prices Depends on the Sale in the India houses.

Palm branches at 15 d Per foot in lead as the Pattern.

If made in Papier Machier 14 pence pr foot and both Gilded

If made in Paper and painted white without Gilding at 6d per foot and will look very neat and set off the paper

Duff to Mackay:

As for the Papier Machier I do not know Sufficiently about it, not having seen any that was good, And therefore will only at present desire you to send some of it to the Value of ten shillings Sterling in either two or four ornaments of Separate pieces That can be put up in either of the Corners or sides of a Room above the Ceiling with directions how its to be put up and fixed, that I may be the better able to judge of I shall use any more of it or not.

Mackay to Duff:

I do not much approve of your India paper, The gold dust, thats done on it, is of no Substance, and by being Exposed to the air will tarnish, and become black in a Short time […] I have only sent you 2 patterns of flock paper which is much esteemed here for its durableness, and may be made of any colour.

Duff to Mackay:

I believe the paper of which ye sent me patterns may be very good and durable, but I love my India paper much better I think it looks handsomer, and I have some of it of twenty years standing as fresh and free of tarnish as it was at first so that I am determined to use it.

Mackay to Duff:

The method of puting up the palm branches is to joyn them all neatly and fix them on with Small Sprigs round the outside of the paper then paint or gild them in oyl gold.

# Appendix A: Table 1

**Appendix A, Table 1 - Comparison Shopping: 4 colonial 'roll paper' transactions compared to Lady Hertford's shopping trip and Robert Dunbar's charges for the Mellerstain estate (Scotland) and Richard Hoare, London.**

| year | buyer | cost | sheets* | sheet cost Col. d. | piece cost Col. d. | piece cost Col. £ | exch. rate | exch. rate % | sheet cost d. | piece cost d. | piece cost £ | av. piece cost |
|---|---|---|---|---|---|---|---|---|---|---|---|---|
| 1714 | Thomas | 600 | 188.96 | 3.17 | 73.52 | 0.6.2. | 153 | 0.653 | 2.07 | 47.94 | 0.4.0. | |
| 1736 | Hatch | 3900 | 231.60 | 16.83 | 390 | 1.12.6. | 430 | 0.232 | 3.90 | 90.42 | 0.7.6. | |
| 1741 | Province House | 1296 | 92.64 | 13.98 | 324 | 1.7.0. | 548 | 0.182 | 2.53 | 58.71 | 0.4.11. | |
| 1742 | Robinson | 480 | 46.32 | 10.36 | 240 | 1.0.0. | 550 | 0.181 | 1.87 | 43.42 | 0.3.7. | £0.5.3.** |
| | | | | | | | | | | | | |
| 1741 | Hertford high | 1728 | 23.16 | | | | | | 74.61 | 1728 | 7.4.0. | |
| 1741 | Hertford med. | 576 | 23.16 | | | | | | 24.87 | 576 | 2.8.0. | |
| 1741 | Hertford low | 132 | 23.16 | | | | | | 5.69 | 132 | 0.11.0. | |
| 1741 | Hertford choice | 132 | 23.16 | | | | | | 5.69 | 132 | 0.11.0 | |
| 1741 | Mellerstain hi | 120 | 23.16 | | | | | | 5.18 | 120 | 0.10.0. | |
| 1741 | Mellerstain lo | 36 | 23.16 | | | | | | 1.55 | 36 | 0.3.0. | |
| 1741 | Mellerstain all | 3686 | 1281.21 | | | | | | 2.87 | 66 | 0.5.6. | £0.5.6. |
| | | | | | | | | | | | | |
| 1740 | Hoare paper 1 | 566 | 99.39 | | | | | | 5.70 | 132 | 0.11.0. | |
| 1740 | Hoare paper 2 | 22 | 3.86 | | | | | | 5.70 | 132 | 0.11.0. | £0.11.0 |

Hoare paper 1: '51 ½ yd. 2 Green on Mantua'. Hoare paper 2: '2 yd. 2 Blew on Yellow Mantua'. Entwisle, *Book of Wallpaper*, plate 27.

* Sheets per piece are calculated at 23.16 sheets per piece, see Appendix B: Notes On Cost.

** Piece costs for four sales total nearly 241d. sterling. When divided, the average piece cost is 60.25d, which is rounded to £. 5s. 3d.

Narrative: When the 'Hertford high' cost of 1728d. (12s. per piece x 12d.) is divided by 23.16 sheets, the sheet cost is 74.61d. each. The cost of the piece in pounds sterling is £7 4s. Preferring to economize, Lady Hertford chose the lowest priced paper mentioned, which cost 132d. (11s. per piece x 12d.), or 11s. per piece. This cost is the same as the average paid by Richard Hoare, and far more than the average paid by the Mellerstain Estate. It is also far more than the average price paid for four transactions for roll paper in the American colonies.

# Appendix A, Table 2

**Appendix A: Table 2 - Ten Transactions from Daniel Henchman's Shop, 1712 - 1742 (after Watkins\*)**

| year | buyer | cost d. | sheets** | sheet cost Col. d. | piece cost Col. d. | piece cost Col. £ | notes | exch. rate | rate % | sheet cost d. | piece cost d. | piece cost £ |
|---|---|---|---|---|---|---|---|---|---|---|---|---|
| 1712 | Dupee | 48 | 50 | 0.96 | 22.23 | 0. 1.10. | 2 quires | 150 | 0.666 | 0.640 | 14.82 | 0.1.3. |
| 1712 | Boone | 132 | 150 | 0.88 | 20.38 | 0. 1.6. | 6 quires; bookseller | 150 | 0.666 | 0.586 | 13.57 | 0.1.2 |
| 1713 | Belknap | 48 | 50 | 0.96 | 22.23 | 0. 1.10. | 2 quires | 150 | 0.666 | 0.640 | 14.82 | 0.1.3. |
| 1714 | Thomas | 600 | 188.96 | 3.17 | 73.52 | 0. 6.2. | pieces, quires | 153 | 0.653 | 2.070 | 47.94 | 0.4.0. |
| 1734 | Maverick | 285 | 105 | 2.71 | 62.86 | 0. 5.3. | quires, sheets, shop | 355 | 0.281 | 0.761 | 17.63 | 0.1.6. |
| 1734 | Robinson | 48 | 50 | 0.96 | 22.23 | 0. 1.10. | quires; bookseller | 355 | 0.281 | 0.269 | 6.25 | 0.0.6 |
| 1736 | Robinson | 120 | 50 | 2.40 | 55.58 | 0. 4.8. | quires; bookseller | 430 | 0.232 | 0.556 | 12.89 | 0.1.1 |
| 1736 | Hatch | 3900 | 231.60 | 16.83 | 390 | 1.12.6. | pieces; homeowner | 430 | 0.232 | 3.904 | 90.42 | 0.7.6. |
| 1741 | Province H. | 1296 | 92.64 | 13.98 | 324 | 1. 7.0. | pieces; government | 548 | 0.182 | 2.535 | 58.71 | 0.4.11. |
| 1742 | Robinson | 480 | 46.32 | 10.36 | 240 | 1. 0.0. | pieces; bookseller | 550 | 0.181 | 1.875 | 43.42 | 0.3.7. |

\* See Appendix B: Notes On Cost for each transaction as quoted in Watkins, 'The Early Use'.

\*\* Number of sheets are calculated at 25 per quire, and sheets per piece are calculated at 23.16 sheets, see Appendix B: Notes On Cost.

Narrative: Dupee bought 2 quires (50 sheets) from Henchman for 4s., or 48d. in colonial currency. The cost per sheet is .96 of a colonial penny.

When this is multiplied by 23.16 sheets. the price of a piece is 22.23d. When this is expressed in colonial pound notation, the result is 1s. 10d.

When the colonial currency is adjusted for pounds sterling, the exchange rate of 150 is used (McCusker. Money and Exchange. p. 140).

This percentage (.666 for the year 1712) yields an adjusted sheet price of .640d. in pounds sterling.

When this is multiplied by 23.16 sheets. the price of a piece is 14.82d. When this is rounded to pound sterling notation, the result is 1s. 3d.

The table shows that roll paper is significantly higher in cost than 'painted paper' in the quire.

## Appendix B: Notes on Costs

Ten Transactions From Daniel Henchman's Shop as quoted in Watkins, 'The Early Use':

13 September 1712, John Dupee, two quires painted paper, 4s.

November 1712, Nicholas Boone, bookseller, six quires painted paper, 11s.

August 1713, Joseph Belnap, two quires painted paper, 4s.

7 October 1714, Isaac Thomas, six rolls painted paper and two quire, £2, 10s.

1734, John Maverick, shopkeeper: four quires and five sheets, £1 3s. 9d.

1734, Samuel Robinson, bookseller, two quires painted paper, 4s.

1736, Samuel Robinson, bookseller, two quires painted paper, 10s.

1734, Colonel Estes Hatch, ten rolls painted paper, £16 5s.

October 1741, Province House, four rolls painted paper, £5 8s.

1742, Samuel Robinson, bookseller, two rolls of paper, £2.

## Methods

This section describes a method for determining costs of early wallpaper in England and America. Both painted paper in quires and painted paper in rolls are of interest. Those in rolls are assumed to be wallpaper. It's difficult to know whether a documentary record of painted paper in quires refers to wallpaper or to decorative paper intended for other uses. Another question is whether prices for wallpaper varied between England and the colonies. Cost comparisons may help answer these questions.

Catalog entries No. 33, 34, 36, and 50 of Wells-Cole, *Historic Paper Hangings* include data about the size of the sheet for each sample of wallpaper. These four were created between the years of 1714 and 1750, and have tax stamps. Each sample is presumed to have originally belonged to a 'piece' (or roll) of paper which was 12 yards long – thus making up the required 7 sq yd which constituted a 'piece' under the Excise Duty on Stained Paper. All of the samples are about 22" wide. Three of these samples have sheet heights of 19" high, but those of # 36 are about 27.5" high; since sheets of this size have rarely been found before 1750, # 36 was removed from consideration.

Allowing a little leeway for overlaps, selvedges, and varying shop practice, it seems likely that No. 33 consisted of 23 sheets, No. 34 consisted of 23 sheets, and No. 50 consisted of 23.5 sheets. The average number of estimated sheets is therefore 23.16.

It seems from Dagnall, *The Tax On Wallpaper* and other sources that the length of 12 yards was observed as a standard, notwithstanding the fact that an unprinted width of 21, 22 or 23 inches would have changed the square yardage of a piece overall. Seemingly, the tax was laid only on the printed portion of the piece, perhaps because the sheets making up the piece had already been taxed.

## Lady Hertford's Shopping Trip

In Chapter 13, Lady Hertford's shopping trip to a warehouse is described, during which she learned of three prices for wallpaper. The most expensive wallpaper cost 12s. per yd. (the 13s. per yd. paper is ignored). Assuming 12 yards per piece, the piece cost 144s., or 1728 pennies. Assuming the piece contained 23.16 sheets, each sheet cost 74.6 pennies, rounded to 75d.

Since each piece contained 9072 sq in., the 23.16 sheets contain 391.709 sq in. per sheet. If each sheet of paper is put on an inch-for-inch basis, the result is that the most expensive paper cost .191d per sq in. This figure is arrived at by dividing the sheet area of 391.709 sq in. by the cost of 75d. The result is a per sq in. cost of .191d.

## Leather Costs

In Chapter 10, the leather cost mentioned by Rowland and Hutton is 72d. per skin (6s. x 12d. = 72d.). The area of the skin is 540 sq in. When the cost of 72d. is divided by the sq in., the result is .133d per sq in. The leather cost is .133d. per sq in.

If the sq in. price for leather of .133d. is multiplied by the 391.709 sq in. area of the paper sheets, the result is 52.09. The price of a skin of leather, if it were as large as a typical sheet of paper, would be 52d. This cost is about midway between the costs of 75d. (for the highest priced wallpaper mentioned by Lady Hertford) and 25d. (for the next highest priced wallpaper). The type of wallpaper that she chose is much lower in cost – only 5.69d. per sheet. When this is multiplied by the 23.16 sheets in a piece, the result is 132d., or, 11s.

## Exchange Rates

The question of equalizing the currencies of the pound sterling and the colonial pound is a large one; Massachusetts was racked by inflation in this period. I've followed John McCusker's *Money and Exchange*, which includes tables for basic calculations. His tables give yearly exchange rates. Table 1 and Table 2 give examples in a narrative form. One of McCusker's other books, *How Much Is That In Real Money?* was also used for guidance.

Taking the example of Hatch's purchase of ten rolls of painted paper for colonial money of £16. 5s.: Using the figure of 23.16 sheets per roll, the number of sheets are 231.60; the colonial money is converted into pennies (3900); when this is divided by the number of sheets, the sheet cost is 16.83 pennies; when this is multiplied by 23.16 sheets, the piece cost is 390 pennies or £1. 12s. 6d. in colonial money.

Switching to the conversion of this amount to pounds sterling, the exchange rate for the year 1736 is 430 (McCusker). A percentage is found by dividing this into 100. The answer, .232, is the percentage to be applied to the sheet price of 16.83 pennies. When this is done, the sheet cost in pounds sterling is 3.904. When this is multiplied by 23.16, the result gives us the piece price in pounds sterling: 90.42 pennies, or £0 7s. 6d.

The Mellerstain bill references seven rooms, each with its own wallpaper. There are also charges for borders and for shipping, but those were dropped from the totals. I totalled up the number of pieces (55.32) and the pounds sterling (£15.7s. 2d.) and averaged them out.

Included in Table 1 are three examples from the Mellerstain bill: the paper with the highest cost (10s. per piece), the paper with the lowest cost (3s. per piece), and the average cost. The bill is transcribed in Chapter 13 as: 'The Mellerstain Bill'. The two Richard Hoare samples seem weighted toward the high end, like the Lady Hertford references. Yet, being from the same year, they provide some context. These are tiny samples, yet the tables as a whole tend to suggest that the 'going rate' of a sidewall paper with figures and perhaps 2 or 3 colours might have been anywhere from 4s. to 8s. per piece.

In Table 1, the choice of Lady Hertford (11s. per piece) and the average from the Mellerstain bill (5s. 6d. per piece) support the possibility that the 7s. 6d. paid by Colonel Hatch indicates a wallpaper of considerable quality. At the other end of the scale, in Table 2, the cost of the quires of painted paper stand out. These costs are much less than the cost of roll paper.

It's hard to see how Dupee's, Boone's, and Belknap's purchases could have been wallpaper. Their low prices instead suggest decorative paper meant for small objects like trunks, boxes and the like. The great gap in price between the sheets of quires and the sheets of roll paper may also indicate that single-sheet installations were not common in the American colonies.

# Bibliography

Adams, Blaine, *Artisans at Louisbourg* (Ottawa: Parks Canada, 1972)

Anderson, Judy, *Glorious Splendor* (Donning, 2011)

Archer, Chloe, 'Festoons of Flowers for fitting up print rooms', *Apollo* (December 1989), pp. 386–391

Arnold, A. P. and A. G. Ingram, *History of the Painter-Stainers Company of London, Volume II* (London: Painter's Hall, 1988)

Arnot, Hugh, *The History of Edinburgh...to the year 1780* (Edinburgh: Thomas Turnbull, 1816)

*The Autobiography and Correspondence of Mary Granville, Mrs. Delany...*, ed. by Augusta Llanover, 1st ser., 3 vols (London: Richard Bentley, 1861), 2nd ser., 3 vols (London: Richard Bentley, 1862)

Ayers, James, *Domestic Interiors: The British Tradition, 1500–1850* (New Haven: Yale University Press, 2003)

Bailey, Anthony, *Vermeer: A View of Delft* (New York: Henry Holt, 2001)

Baty, Patrick, 'A Documented Review of the House-Painting Trade in London ca. 1660–1850' (unpublished thesis, University of East London, 1993)

Baxter, William, *The House of Hancock, Business in Boston, 1724–1775* (Boston: Harvard University Press, 1945)

Beard, Geoffrey, *Craftsmen and Interior Decoration in England, 1660–1820* (London: Bloomsbury Books, 1986)

——, and Annabel Westman, 'A French Upholsterer in England: Francis Lapiere, 1653–1714', *The Burlington Magazine*, 135, no. 1085 (August 1993), pp. 515–24; <http://jstor.org/stable/885586>

——, *Georgian Craftsmen* (New York: A.S. Barnes, 1967)

——, 'Three Eighteenth-Century Cabinet-Makers: Moore, Goodison and Vile', *The Burlington Magazine* 119, no. 892 (July 1977), pp. 478–86; <http://jstor.org/stable/878898>

——, *Upholsterers and Interior Furnishings in England 1530–1840* (New Haven: Yale University Press, 1997)

Beckmann, Johann, *A History of Inventions and Discoveries*, trans. from German by William Johnston, 4th edn, 2 vols (London: Bohn, 1846); <http://books.google.com>

Berg, Maxine, 'From Imitation to Invention: Creating Commodities in Eighteenth-Century Britain', *Economic History Review*, New Series 55, no. 1 (February, 2002), pp. 1–30; <http://jstor.org/stable/3091813>

Birket, James, *Some Cursory Remarks Made By James Birket In His Voyage To North America, 1750–1751* (New Haven: Yale University Press, 1916); <http://books.google.com>

Bondaroy, Fougeroux de Auguste Denis, *Art de travailler les cuirs dorés ou argentés* (Paris: Desaint, Saillant & Nyon, 1762)

Bristow, Ian, *Interior House-Painting Colours and Technology, 1615–1840* (New Haven and London: Yale University Press, 1996)

Broström, Ingela, and Elisabet Stavenow-Hidemark, *Tapetboken: Papperstapeten I Sverige* (Stockholm: Byggförlaget, 2004)

Brückle, Irene, 'Historical Manufacture and Use of Blue Paper', *AIC Book and Paper Group Annual* 12 (1993), unpaginated

Brûlons, Jacques Savary des, and Philemon-Louis Savary, *Dictionnaire universel de commerce*, 3 vols (Paris: Estienne, 1723); <http://books.google.com>

Butterfield, Lindsay, in *The Artist* magazine (New York, 1898–1902), September 1898

Calhoun, Jeanne A., and others, 'The Geographic Spread of Charleston's Mercantile Community, 1732–1767', *South Carolina Historical Magazine* 86 no. 3 (July 1985), pp. 182–220

Calnan, Christopher and Mariabianca Paris, 'Scorched or Damask Leather', in *The Conservation of Gilt Leather Post-Prints*, ed. by Theo Sturge, pp. 6–10; published by ICOM-CC Working Group, 'Leather and Related Materials', 2007; <http://lulu.com/content/810780>

Campbell, R., *The London Tradesman* (London: 1747)

Chatto, William Andrew, *A Treatise on Wood Engraving, Historical and Practical* (London: Charles Knight and Co., 1839); <http://books.google.com>

*The Chronicles of London Bridge, by An Antiquary* (Richard Thompson), 2nd edn (London: Thomas Tegg, 1839)

Churchill, W. A., *Watermarks in Paper* (Amsterdam: 1935)

Clouzot, Henri, and Charles Follot, *The History of Wallpaper in France* (Paris: Charles Moreau, 1935)

Colville, Olivia Spencer-Churchill, *Duchess Sarah, Being the Social History of the Times of Sarah Jennings, Duchess of Marlborough* (London: Longmans, Green and Company, 1904); <http://archive.org>

Conybeare, Anthony J., 'Boxing Clever: a brief look at lining papers', *Wallpaper History Society Review (WHSR)*, (1996/7), pp. 10–12

Cornforth, John, 'Arms and Legs of Wallpaper', *Country Life* 183 (20 April 1989), pp. 168–71

——, *Early Georgian Interiors* (New Haven: Yale University Press, 2004)

——, 'Putting Up With Georgian D-I-Y', *Country Life* 186 (9 April 1992), pp. 54–56

Coulter, Calvin B., Jr, 'The Import Trade of Colonial Virginia', *William and Mary Quarterly*, 3rd ser., 2, no. 3 (July 1945), pp. 296–314; <http://jstor.org/stable/1921454>

*Covent-Garden Journal*, by Sir Alexander Drawcansir, Knight Censor of Great Britain (Henry Fielding), ed. by Gerard Edward Jensen, 2 vols (New Haven: Yale University Press, 1915)

Craske, Matthew, 'Plan and Control: Design and the Competitive Spirit in Early and Mid-Eighteenth-Century England', *Journal of Design History* 12, no. 3 (1999), pp. 187–216 <http://jstor.org/stable/1316282>

Crossman, Carl, 'Decorative Painted Wallpapers to 1850', Chapter 15 in *Decorative Arts of the China Trade* (Suffolk, England: Antique Collectors Club, 1991), pp. 390–449

Cummings, Abbott L., 'Colonial and Federal America: Accounts of Early Painting Practices', in *Paint In America*, ed. by Roger Moss (Washington: Preservation Press, 1994), pp. 12–41

——, *The Framed Houses Of Massachusetts Bay, 1625–1725* (Cambridge: Harvard University Press, 1979)

——, 'The Use and Manufacture of Wallpaper in New England 1700–1820', in *Wallpaper in New England*, by Richard Nylander and others (Boston: Society for the Preservation of New England Antiquities, 1986), pp. 3–27

Dagnall, H., *The Tax on Wallpaper: An Account of the Excise Duty on Stained Paper, 1712–1836* (Middlesex, England: self-published, 1990)

Defebaugh, James Elliott, *History of the Lumber Industry*, 2 vols (Chicago: The American Lumberman, 1906)

Defoe, Daniel, *The Complete English Tradesman*, (Edinburgh: 1839); <www.gutenberg.org/ebooks/14444>

Donnell, Edna, 'The Van Rensselaer Wall Paper and J. B. Jackson: A Study in Disassociation', *Metropolitan Museum Studies* 4, no. 1 (February 1932), pp. 76–108

Donnis, Erica, 'Puzzling Together the Wallpaper Pieces', *Old House Journal* (January-February 2006), pp. 60–65

Dossie, Robert, *The Handmaid To The Arts*, 2 vols, 2nd edn (London: Nourse, 1764); originally published 1758; the section 'On The Manufacture of Paper-Hangings' first appears as part of the appendix to Volume II of the 1764 edition, pp. 445–62

Douglas, Audrey W., 'Cotton Textiles in England: The East India Company's Attempt to Exploit Developments in Fashion, 1660–1721', *Journal of British Studies* 8, no. 2 (May 1969), pp. 28–43; <http://jstor.org/stable/175215>

Dow, George F., *Every Day Life In The Massachusetts Bay Colony* (Boston: Society for the Preservation of New England Antiquities, 1935)

——, ed., *The Arts and Crafts in New England, 1704–1775* (Topsfield, MA: Wayside Press, 1927)

Du Halde, Jean-Baptiste, trans. by Richard Brookes, *The general history of China, containing a geographical, historical, chronological, political and physical description...*, 3rd edn corr., 4 vols (London: J. Watts, 1739–41)

*Edinburgh Encyclopedia*, ed. by Sir David Brewster, 18 vols, 1st American edn, 1832

Englefield, William, *History of the Painter-Stainers Company of London, Volume I* (London: Chapman and Dodd, 1923)

Entwisle, E. A., 'The Blew Paper Warehouse In Aldermanbury, London', *Connoisseur*, May 1950, pp. 94–98

——, *The Book of Wallpaper: A History and An Appreciation* (London: Arthur Baker, 1954)

——, 'Eighteenth Century London Paperstainers: Thomas Bromwich at the Golden Lyon on Ludgate Hill', *Connoisseur*, October 1952, pp. 106–110

——, 'XVIIIth-Century Paper-Stainers' and Decorators' Bills', *Connoisseur*, September 1943, pp. 38–41

——, *A Literary History of Wallpaper* (London: Batsford, 1960)

Fabry, Philippe de, 'La Fabrication Des Papiers De Tapisserie Au XVIIIe Siecle Un Example Particulier: Papillon', in *Technique et Papier Peint*, ed. by Bernard Jacqué, pp. 68–78

Faulkner, Harold, review of *House of Hancock* by William Baxter, *The American Economic Review*, 35, no. 5 (December 1945), p. 951

Fowler, John, and John Cornforth, *English Decoration in the 18th Century* (London: Barrie & Jenkins, 1974)

*A Frenchman In Virginia; being the memoirs of a Huguenot refugee in 1678*, Durand of Dauphiné trans. by Fairfax Harrison (Richmond, VA: self-published, 1923)

*A general description of all trades...*(London: T. Waller, 1747)

Gilbert, Christopher, 'Chippendale's Harewood Commission', *Furniture History* 9 (1973)

——, *The Life and Work of Thomas Chippendale*, 2 vols (New York: Macmillan, 1978)

Glassie, Henry, 'Folk Art', in *Material Culture Studies in America*, ed. by Thomas Schlereth, (Nashville: American Association for State and Local History Press, 1982), pp. 124–140

Glendinning, Miles, R. MacInnes, and A. MacKechnie, *A History Of Scottish Architecture, From The Renaissance To The Present Day* (Edinburgh: Edinburgh University Press, 1996); <http://books.google.com>

Gottesman, Rita Susswein, *The Arts and Crafts in New York*, 3 vols (New York: The New-York Historical Society, 1938, 1954, 1965)

Greysmith, Brenda, *Wallpaper* (New York: Macmillan, 1976)

Hamel, Nathalie, 'Un papier peint inspiré de l'Orient dans une ville coloniale d'amérique: Présence de la chinoiserie dans la maison estèbe à Québec au milieu du XVIIIe siècle', *Material Culture Review* 68, North America, (June 2008)

Hamilton, Jean, *An Introduction to Wallpaper* (London: H. M. Stationery Office, 1983)

——, 'Early English Wallpapers', *Connoisseur*, July 1977, pp. 201–06

Heal, Ambrose, 'Paper-Stainer's of the 17th and 18th Century', *Country Life*, 22 July 1949, pp. 258–60

Heijbroek, Jan Frederik, and T.C. Greven, eds, *Sierpapier: Marmer-, Brocaat- En Sitspapier in Nederland* (Amsterdam: Uitgeverij De Buitenkant, 1994)

Hills, Richard, *Papermaking in Britain 1488–1988* (London: Athlone Press, 1988)

Hoskins, Lesley, ed., *The Papered Wall: The History, Patterns and Techniques of Wallpaper*, 2nd edn (New York: Abrams, 2005)

Houston, J. E., *Featherbedds And Flock Bedds: A History Of The Worshipful Company Of Upholders Of The City Of London*, 2nd edn (Bedfordshire: Three Tents Press, 1999)

Hunter, George L., *Decorative Textiles* (Philadelphia and London: J. B. Lippincott, 1918)

Huth, Hans, 'English Chinoiserie Gilt Leather', *The Burlington Magazine* 71, no. 412 (July 1937), pp. 25–35; <http://jstor.org/stable/867067>

Innocent, C. F., *The Development of English Building Construction* (Cambridge: Cambridge University Press, 1916)

Isham, Norman M. and Albert F. Brown, *Early Connecticut Houses* (Providence: Preston and Rounds Company, 1900; repr. New York: Dover, 1965)

Jackson, John Baptist, *An essay on the invention of engraving and printing in chiaro oscuro, as practised by Albert Dürer, Hugo di Carpi, &c. and the application of it to the making paper hangings of taste, duration, and elegance* (London, 1754); <http://archive.org>

Jacqué, Bernard, 'De la manufacture au mur: Pour une histoire matérielle du papier peint (1770–1914)', (unpublished doctoral thesis, Université Lumière, Lyon, 2002);

<http://theses.univ-lyon2.fr/documents/lyon2/2003/jacque_b/info>

——, ed., *Le Papier Peint En Arabesques* (Mulhouse, France: Musee du Papier Peint, 1995)

——, 'From 'papiers en feuille' to 'decor': The Industrialisation of Decoration', in *New Discoveries, New Research,* ed. by Elisabet Stavenow-Hidemark (Stockholm, Nordiska Museet, 2007), pp. 8–19

——, ed., *Technique Et Papier Peint,* Bulletin de la Société industrielle de Mulhouse (BSIM) 823 (Mulhouse, France: 1991)

Jobe, Brock, 'The Boston Upholstery Trade', in *Upholstery in America and Europe from the Seventeenth Century to World War I,* ed. by Edward S. Cooke Jr, (New York: Norton, 1981), pp. 65–90

Johnson, Thomas, *One Hundred and Fifty New Designs* (London: Robert Sayer, 1761)

Jourdain, Margaret and R. S. Jenyns, *Chinese Export Art in the Eighteenth Century* (London: Country Life Limited, 1951)

——, 'English Wall-papers', *Architectural Review* 49 (January-June 1921), pp. 14–17

*Journal of the Commissioners for Trade and Plantations...preserved in the Public Record Office; 1749, 1750–1753* (London: H. M. Stationery Office, 1920–38), vol. 60, p. 329

*Journals of the House of Commons*, vol. 18 (London: Great Britain House of Commons, 1803); reprinting deliberations during Geo. I's reign 1714–18

Kafker, Frank and Serena, 'The Encyclopedists as individuals: a biographical dictionary of the authors of the Encyclopédie', *Studies on Voltaire and the Eighteenth Century* 257, 1988, p. xxv

Kainen, Jacob, *John Baptist Jackson: 18th Century Master of the Color Woodcut* (Washington: United States National Museum, 1962)

Keatinge, Charles T., 'The Guild of Cutlers, Painter-Stainers and Stationers, Better Known As the Guild of St. Luke the Evangelist, Dublin', *Journal of the Royal Society of Antiquaries of Ireland* 30 (1901), pp. 136–47; <http://books.google.com/books>

Keith, Elmer, 'An American Wallpaper Discovery', *The Magazine Antiques*, September 1952, pp. 216–17

Kellett, J. R., 'The Breakdown of Gild and Corporation Control over the Handicraft and Retail Trade in London', *The Economic History Review,* New Series, 10, no. 3 (1958), pp. 381–94; <http://jstor.org/stable/2591259>

Kelly, J. Frederick, *Early Domestic Architecture of Connecticut* (New Haven: Yale University Press, 1924, repr. New York: Dover, 1963)

Kimball, Fiske, *American Domestic Architecture* (New York: Charles Scribner's Sons, 1922); <http://books.google.com>

Kirkham, Pat, 'The London Furniture Trade 1700–1870', *Furniture History* 24 (1988), pp. 1–219

Koldeweij, Eloy, M. Knuijt, and E. Adriaansz, *Achter Het Behang* (Amsterdam: Simons and Partners bv, 1991)

——,'Gilt Leather Hangings In Chinoiserie and Other Styles: An English Speciality', *Furniture History* 36 (2000), pp. 61–101

——, 'High Fashion Through the Ages', lecture, Cooper-Hewitt National Design Museum, 17 June 1992

——, 'The Marketing of Gilt Leather in Seventeenth-century Holland', *Print Quarterly* 13 no. 2 (1996), pp. 136–48

Krakovitch, Odile, *Arrêts, déclarations, édits et ordonnances concernant les colonies, 1666–1779 : inventaire analytique de la série Colonies A* (Paris: Archives nationales, 1993)

Law, Ernest, *The New Historical Guide to the Royal Palace and Gardens of Hampton Court* (London: George Bell and Sons, 1902); <http://books.google.com>

Le Comte, Louis, *Nouveaux memoires sur l'état present de la Chine*, 2 vols (Paris: J. Anisson, 1696)

Leahy, George W., *L'ornementation dans la maison québécoise aux XVIIe et XVIIIe siècles* (Sillery: Éditions du Septentrion, 1994)

Leath, Robert, 'After the Chinese Taste: Chinese Export Porcelain and Chinoiserie Design', *Historical Archeology* 33, no. 3 (1999), pp. 48–61

*Letters of Horace Walpole, Earl of Orford, to Sir Horace Mann*, ed. by Lord Dover, 3 vols (London: Richard Bentley, 1833)

Leung, Felicity L., 'Wallpaper in Canada' (Ottawa: Parks Canada, microfiche, research report series 208, 1983)

Longfield, A. K. (later Mrs Leask), 'Old Wall-Papers In Ireland', *Journal of the Royal Society of Antiquaries of Ireland* 78, no. 2 (December 1948), pp. 157–169

——, 'History of the Dublin Wall-Paper Industry in the 18th Century', *Journal of the Royal Society of Antiquaries of Ireland* 77, no. 2, (December 1947), pp. 99–120

Luxborough, Henrietta Knight, *Letters Written by the Late Right Honourable Lady Luxborough to William Shenstone, Esq.*, ed. by John Hodgetts (London: J. Dodsley, 1775)

Lynn, Catherine, *Wallpaper in America: From the Seventeenth Century to World War I* (New York: Norton, 1980)

Lyson, Daniel, *The Environs of London: Counties of Herts, Essex & Kent,* 4 vols (London: T. Cadell, 1796)

Macky, John, *Memoirs of the Secret Services of John Macky, Esq....* (London: 1733)

MacMichael, J. Holden, 'The London Signs and their Associations', *Antiquary* 40 (1904), p. 368

Mayhew, Edgar, and Minor Myers Jr, *A Documentary History of American Interiors* (New York: Scribner's, 1980)

McClelland, Nancy V., *Historic Wall-Papers: From Their Inception to the Introduction of Machinery* (Philadelphia: Lippincott, 1924)

McCusker, John, *How Much is That in Real Money?*, 2nd edn (Worcester: American Antiquarian Society, 2001)

——, *Money & Exchange in Europe and America* (Williamsburg: Institute of Early American History and Culture, 1978)

McCutcheon, Roger, 'John Houghton, a Seventeenth-Century Editor and Book-Reviewer', *Modern Philology* 20, no. 3 (February 1923), pp. 255–60

Michie, Audrey, 'Upholstery in All Its Branches', *Journal of Early Southern Decorative Arts* 11, no. 2 (1985), pp. 21–84

Millar, Oliver, 'Artists and Craftsmen in the Service of Sir Stephen Fox and His Family', *The Burlington Magazine* 137, no. 1109 (August 1995), pp. 518–28; <http://jstor.org/stable/886538>

Miller, Marla, 'Gender, Artisanry, and Craft Tradition in Early New England: The View through the Eye of a Needle', *William and Mary Quarterly*, 3rd ser., 60, no. 4 (October 2003), pp. 743–76

Mitchell, Anthony, 'Leather Hung Rooms Surviving In Situ', in *The Conservation of Gilt Leather Post-Prints*, ed. by Theo Sturge, published by ICOM-CC Working Group, 'Leather and Related Materials', 2007, pp. 36–37; <http://lulu.com/content/810780>

Montgomery, Florence M., *Textiles in America, 1650–1870: A Dictionary Based on Original Documents...* (New York: Norton, 1984)

Mora, P., L. Mora, and P. Philippot, *Conservation of Wall Paintings* (London: Butterworths, for the International Centre for the Study of the Preservation and Restoration of Cultural Property (ICCROM), 1984)

Morris, Rosie, 'The "Innocent and Touching Custom" of Maidens' Garlands: A Field Report', *Folklore* 114, no. 3 (December 2003), pp. 355–87; <http://jstor.org/stable/30035124>

Moss, Roger, ed., *Paint In America* (Washington: Preservation Press, 1994)

Moxon, Joseph, *Mechanick Exercises, or the Doctrine of Handy-Works,* 3rd edn 1703; <htpp://books.google.com>

Mungello, David, *The Great Encounter of China and the West, 1500–1800,* 4th edn (Lanham, Maryland: Rowman and Littlefield, 2013)

*Notes and Queries* (Scottish), ed. by John Bulloch, 2nd ser., 3 (July 1901–June, 1902), p. 13

*Notes and Queries, A Medium of Inter-Communication,* 2nd ser., 2 (July–December 1856), pp. 7–8

Nylander, Richard C., Elizabeth Redmond, and Penny J. Sander, *Wallpaper in New England* (Boston: Society for the Preservation of New England Antiquities, 1986)

Oman, Charles, and Jean Hamilton, *Wallpapers: an international history and illustrated survey* (London: Abrams, 1982)

Pannabecker, John R., 'Representing Mechanical Arts in Diderot's Encyclopedie', *Technology and Culture* 39, no. 1 (January 1998), pp. 33–73; <http://jstor.org/stable/3107003>

Papillon, Jean-Michel, *Traité historique et pratique de la gravure en bois,* 3 vols (Paris: 1766); <http://books.google.com/books>

Plomer, Henry, *A Dictionary Of The Printers And Booksellers Who Were At Work In England, Scotland And Ireland From 1668 To 1725* (Oxford: Oxford University Press, 1922)

*Political and Social Letters of a Lady of the Eighteenth Century*, ed. by Emily Osborn (New York: Dodd, Mead and Company, 1891); <http://books.google.com>

Pollard, Mary, *A Dictionary of Members of the Dublin Book Trade, 1550–1800* (Great Britain: The Bibliographical Society, 2000)

Postlethwayt, Malachy, ed., *Universal Dictionary of Trade and Commerce* (London: 1751)

Prime, Alfred Coxe, ed., *The Arts & Crafts in Philadelphia, Maryland and South Carolina, 1721–1785* (The Walpole Society, 1929)

Pritchard, Earl, review of *Chinese Export Art* by Margaret Jourdain and R. S. Jenyns, *The Far Eastern Quarterly* 14 no. 2 (February 1955), pp. 267–70

Pritchard, Margaret and Willie Graham, 'Rethinking Two Houses At Colonial Williamsburg', *The Magazine Antiques,* January 1996, pp. 166–75

Pyne, William H., *The History of the Royal Residences*, 3 vols (London: A. Dry, 1819)

Ratzki-Kraatz, Anne, 'A French Lit de Parade "A la Duchesse" 1690–1715', *J. Paul Getty Museum Journal* 14 (1986), pp. 81–104

Rickman, Catherine, 'Conservation of Chinese Export Works of Art on Paper: Watercolours and Wallpapers', in *The Conservation of Far Eastern Art: preprints of the Kyoto Congress,* 19–23 September 1988, pp. 44–51; published by the International Institute for Conservation of Historic and Artistic Works, 1988

Rock, Joe, 'Scottish Wallpaper', *WHSR*, 2004/05, pp. 3–6

Rosenband, Leonard, 'Jean-Baptiste Réveillon: A Man on the Make in Old Regime France', *French Historical Studies* 20, no. 3 (1997), pp. 481–510

Rosoman, Treve, *London Wallpapers: Their Manufacture and Use, 1690–1840* (London: English Heritage, 1992)

Russell, Archibald, 'A Seventeenth Century Wall-Paper at Wotton-under-Edge', *The Burlington Magazine* 7, no. 28 (July 1905), pp. 309–11

Sanborn, Kate, *Old Time Wall Papers* (New York: Dutton, 1908)

Saunders, Gill, *Wallpaper in Interior Decoration* (London: Victoria and Albert Publications, 2002)

Savary, Jacques, *Le parfait négociant ou Instruction générale pour ce qui regarde le commerce des marchandises de France et des pays étrangers* (The Perfect Merchant or General Instruction regarding the mercantile trade of France and foreign countries), 2 vols (Paris: 1675)

Schopfer, Hermann and Philippe de Fabry, 'Un Paysage de Dominos du Milieu du XVIIIe Siecle' *Cahiers* no. 1, Musee du Papier Peint, Rixheim, France, 1993

Scott, William R., 'The Society of the White-Writing and Printing Paper Manufactory of Scotland, Established in 1694' *Scottish Historical Review* 3, no. 9 (October 1905), pp. 71–76; <http://jstor.org/stable/25517691>

——, *The Constitution and Finance of English, Scottish and Irish Joint-Stock Companies to 1720*, 3 vols (Cambridge: University Press, 1911)

Simpson, Henry, *The Lives Of Eminent Philadelphians, Now Deceased* (Philadelphia: C. Sherman and Son, 1859); <http://archive.org>

Skinner, David, 'Irish Period Wallpapers', *Irish Arts Review* 13 (1997), pp. 53–61

Smith, Charles Saumarez, *Eighteenth-Century Decoration* (London: Weidenfeld and Nicolson, 1993)

Smith, John, *The Art of Painting in Oyl* (London: Samuel Crouch, 1687)

Somerset, Frances Thynne Seymour, and Henrietta Louisa Jeffreys Fermor Pomfret, *Correspondence between Frances, Countess of Hartford and Henrietta Louisa, Countess of Pomfret, 1738–1741*, 3 vols (London: R. Phillips, 1805); <http://books.google.com>

Statistics Canada; <http://www.statcan.gc.ca/pub/98-187-x/4151287-eng.htm>

Stavenow-Hidemark, Elisabet, ed., *New Discoveries, New Research, Papers From The International Wallpaper Conference* (Stockholm, Nordiska Museet, 2007)

Stuart, Catherine M., and Margaret Fox, *A Family Life Revealed* (Traquair House, Scotland, 2012)

Styles, John, 'Product Innovation in Early Modern London', *Past & Present* 168, no. 1 (August 2000), pp. 124–69

Sugden, A. V., and J. L. Edmundson, *A History of English Wallpaper, 1509–1914* (London: B.T. Batsford, 1925)

Sullivan, Michael, *The Meeting Of Eastern And Western Art,* 2nd edn (Berkeley: University of California, 1989)

Symonds, R. W., 'Domestic Furnishings in the Time of Charles II', *The Burlington Magazine* 81, no. 474 (September 1942), pp. 218–22; <http://jstor.org/stable/868584>

Taylor, Clare, 'Chinese Papers and English Imitations in 18th Century Britain', in *New Discoveries, New Research,* ed. by Elisabet Stavenow-Hidemark (Stockholm, Nordiska Museet, 2007), pp. 36–53

Teynac, Françoise, Pierre Nolot, and Jean-Denis Vivien, *Wallpaper: A History* (New York: Rizzoli, 1982)

*Peter Kalm's travels in North America; the America of 1750; the English version of 1770, rev. from the original Swedish and edited by Adolph B. Benson* (New York: Wilson-Erickson Inc. 1937; repr. New York: Dover, 1966)

*The Scots Magazine*, vol. 50 (1788), Deaths and Preferments, p. 103

*The Statutes at Large From the Magna Charta, to the End of the Eleventh Parliament of Great Britain, Anno 1761* [Continued to 1807], vol. 45, Part 1 (London: Danby Pickering, 1807)

*The Statutes of the United Kingdom of Great Britain and Ireland: from Magna Carta to the union of the kingdoms of Great Britain and Ireland,* vol. 20 (G. Eyre and A. Strahan, 1811)

*The Trial At Bar Between Campbell Craig . . . and the Right Honourable Richard Earl of Anglesey...,* Issue 92 Historical Trials (London: R. Walker, 1744); <http://books.google.com>

Thornton, Jonathan, 'The History, Technology and Conservation of Architectural Papier Mache', *Journal of the American Institute for Conservation* 32, no. 2 (Summer, 1993), pp. 165–76

Thümmler, Sabine, *Die Geschichte der Tapete: Raumkunst aus Papier: aus den Beständen des Deutschen Tapetenmuseums Kassel* (Eurasburg: Edition Minerva, 1998)

Thwaites, Reuben C., ed., *The Jesuit Relations and Allied Documents,* 73 vols (Cleveland: Burrows Bros., 1896–1901)

*A Transcript Of The Registers Of the Company Of Stationers of London,* by Charles Robert Rivington and others, 5 vols (London: self-published, 1894), V (index)

Van Gulik, R. H., *Chinese Pictorial Art* (New York: Hacker Art Books, 1981)

Velut, Christine, 'Between Invention and Production', *Journal of Design History* 17 no. 1 (2004), pp. 55–69

——, *Décors de papier: Production, commerce et usages des papiers peints à Paris, 1750–1820* (Paris, Éditions du Patrimoine, 2005); see also Bernard Jacqué's review in *Studies in the Decorative Arts,* vol. 14, no. 2 (Spring-Summer, 2007),182–85

'Voel and South Grove House', in *Survey of London*, vol. 17, the parish of St Pancras, part 1, the village of Highgate (1936), pp. 63–66; <www.british-history.ac.uk/report.aspx?compid=65013>

*Wallpaper History Society Review*, ten compilations of the Wallpaper History Society (Manchester, England, 1989–2012); <http://wallpaperhistorysociety.org.uk>

Walsh, Claire, 'Shop Design and the Display of Goods in Eighteenth-Century London', *Journal of Design History* 8, no. 3 (1995), pp. 157–76

Walton, Karin, 'An Inventory of 1710 from Dyrham Park', *Furniture History* 22 (1986), pp. 25–80

——, 'The Worshipful Company of Upholders of the City of London', *Furniture History* 9 (1973), pp. 41–79

Waterer, John, 'Dunster Castle, Somerset, and its Painted Leather Hangings', *Connoisseur* 164 (March 1967), pp. 142–47

Watkins, Walter K., 'The Early Use and Manufacture of Paper-Hangings in Boston', *Bulletin of The Society for the Preservation of New England Antiquities* 12 (July 1921-April 1922), pp. 109–19

Webb, Cliff, *London Apprentices, Vol. 19: Upholders' Company 1704–1772* (Great Britain: Society of Genealogists, 1998)

Webber, Mabel L., comp., 'Death Notices', *South Carolina Historical and Genealogical Magazine* 34, no. 2 (April, 1933), pp. 88–95

Webber, Pauline, and Meryl Huxtable 'The Conservation of Eighteenth Century Chinese Wallpapers in the United Kingdom', in *The Conservation of Far Eastern Art: preprints of the Kyoto Congress,* 19–23 September 1988, published in 1988 by the International Institute for Conservation of Historic and Artistic Works, pp. 52–58

Wells-Cole, Anthony, *Historic Paper Hangings from Temple Newsam and other English Houses* (Leeds: Leeds City Art Galleries, 1983)

Wharton, Edith, *The Decoration of Houses* (London: Batsford, 1898)

*Wilson's Tales of the Borders and of Scotland...*, revised by Alexander Leighton, 6 vols (London: William MacKenzie, 1900); <http://archive.org>

Wolfe, Richard J., *Marbled Paper: Its History, Techniques, and Patterns: With Special Reference to the Relationship of Marbling to Bookbinding in Europe and the Western World* (Philadelphia: University of Pennsylvania Press, 1990)

Woods, Christine, '"An Object Lesson to a Philistine Age": The Wall Paper Manufacturer's Museum', *Journal of Design History* 12, no. 2 (1999), pp. 159–71; <http://jstor.org/stable/1316311>

## archival and manuscript references:

Aberdeen, Scotland, Aberdeen University Library, Montcoffer Papers, MSS, courtesy of Captain Alexander Ramsay

Boston, Massachusetts, The Massachusetts Historical Society, Thomas Hancock letterbook and receipt book, Hancock family papers

Edinburgh, Scotland (Reference GD 220/6/1806/1): The Royal Commission On The Ancient And Historical Monuments of Scotland

London, British Museum, Lansdowne MSS., vol. 487, No. 222

London, 1 Jas. I, c.20: The Plaisterers' Act

London, Victoria and Albert Museum, The Duppa Account Books, MSS, (Letter Book 86.AA.14)

Worcester, Massachusetts, American Antiquarian Society, Robert Gibbs Business Records: 1669–1708, MSS

Worcester, Massachusetts, American Antiquarian Society, Samuel Grant Account Book: 1737–1760, MSS

# Endnotes

1    *The Trial At Bar*, p. 242. Full references are given in the bibliography.

2    *Notes and Queries, A Medium*, pp. 7–8; Bailey, *Vermeer: A View of Delft*, p. 19.

3    In *Marbled Paper*, pp. 32–33, Richard Wolfe makes useful distinctions among many paper types, but few others have made the attempt.

4    Heijbroek and Greven, *Sierpapier*, pp. 152–54.

5    Brûlons, *Dictionnaire universel de commerce*, I:717: 'Les feuilles imprimées & séchées, on les peint & on les rehausse de diverses couleurs, en détrempe, puis on les assemble pour en former des pièces; ce que font ordinairement ceux qui les achètent; se vendant plus communément à la main, que montées'.

6    Longfield, 'Dublin Wall-Paper', pp. 101–02.

7    *Sanborn, Old Time Wall Papers*, p. 106; Lindsay Butterfield's article about the fragments is found in the *Artist* magazine (September 1898); fragments and reconstructions are illustrated in Sugden and Edmundson, *A History of English Wallpaper*, plates 13–15; the installation is dated 1600 by Greysmith, *Wallpaper*, p. 29.

8    Jourdain, 'English Wall-papers', vol. 49, p. 14.

9    Small decorative sheets are explored by Geert Wisse in the chapter 'Manifold Beginnings' in Hoskins, *The Papered Wall*. See also Wolfe, *Marbled Paper*; and the voluminous literature on buntpapier, sierpapier, and carte decorate.

10   Teynac, *Wallpaper: A History*, p. 50.

11   Heijbroek and Greven, *Sierpapier*, p. 153.

12   It's been asserted that this reference appears in vol. 4, p. 76 of *Dictionnaire de l'ameublement et de la décoration*, but this could not be confirmed.

13   Chatto, *Treatise on Wood Engraving*, p. 593 for Papillon, p. 443 for Le Sueur. Chatto's book is a cross-check against the extravagant claims of Jean-Michael Papillon's 1766 work, *Traité historique et pratique de la gravure en bois*, (hereafter, *Traité*). Chatto's account is only slightly less heated but it was the standard work for the Victorian era.

14   Savary, *Le Parfait Negociant*, I:556–57.

15   As quoted in Leung, 'Wallpaper in Canada', p. 21.

16   Leung, 'Wallpaper in Canada', p. 22, n. 55, citing the *Jesuit Relations*.

17   Postlethwayt, *Universal Dictionary*; entry for 'dominotier'; Jacques Savary des Brûlon's study from 1723 was translated and published with additional material by Postlethwayt in 1751.

18   Leung, 'Wallpaper in Canada', p. 22, n. 58, citing the *Jesuit Relations*.

19     Leung, 'Wallpaper in Canada', p. 34, citing *Peter Kalms Travels,* pp. 444, 455, 470.

20     The Wienhausen/Rosenvinge paper is illustrated in *The Papered Wall,* ill. 4; the Läckö paper is illustrated in the *Wallpaper History Society Review* (hereafter *WHSR*), 2004/05, p. 36.

21     Entwisle, *The Book of Wallpaper,* plate 25 illustrates Minnikin's ad.

22     Hamilton, *An Introduction to Wallpaper,* p. 7.

23     As part of his review of *Achter Het Behang,* an exhibition and book about the Dutch industry; *WHSR,* 1992, p. 58. See also *The Papered Wall,* passim, especially the chapter 'Manifold Beginnings'. For Germany see Thummler, *Die Geschichte der Tapete,* reviewed in *WHSR,* 2001, p. 56.

24     Clouzot and Follot, *Wallpaper in France,* p. 1.

25     See Anthony Conybeare, 'Boxing Clever', pp. 10–12.

26     A Transcript Of The Registers, p. lv (55).

27     Dagnall, *The Tax On Wallpaper,* p.1.

28     As quoted in Sugden and Edmundson, *A History,* p. 40; *London Gazette* 21 August 1693.

29     Rickman, 'Chinese Export Works', p. 45.

30     As quoted in Hills, *Papermaking in Britain,* p. 49; Patent 284, 6 Nov. 1691.

31     Brückle, 'Blue Paper', not paginated.

32     Ibid. Brückle states that brazilwood and cochineal (reds) when combined with blue dyes produced purple paper.

33     Scott, *Constitution and Finance,* III:72.

34     The ad appeared in the back pages of *The Elements of Arithmetic;* this reference courtesy of Dr Joe Rock.

35     Sugden and Edmundson, *A History,* p. 39; Entwisle, *Book of Wallpaper,* Blue Paper Warehouse Ad, plate 18.

36     Dagnall, *The Tax On Wallpaper,* p. 1.

37     Oman and Hamilton, *An International History,* p. 17.

38     See Rosoman, *London Wallpapers,* plate 28, the papers at the Jeremiah Lee Mansion in Marblehead, Massachusetts, Anderson, *Glorious Splendor,* p. 23, and the Van Rensselaer wallpaper now at the Metropolitan Museum of Art.

39     Wells-Cole, *Historic Paper Hangings,* passim, but especially No. 33, 34 and 50, which have English tax stamps and are presumed to date before 1750.

40     Churchill, *Watermarks in Paper,* # 187. This mark is similar to the earliest elephant mark (# 5946) recorded by Briquet, which was found in Italy.

41     Bristow, *Interior House-Painting,* table 1, p. 4.

42     Ibid., p. 3.

43     As quoted in Baty, *House-Painting Trade,* p. 10.

44     As quoted in Watkins, 'The Early Use', p. 110.

45     Fabry, 'La Fabrication Des Papiers', in *Technique et Papier Peint,* p. 70.

46     *Traité,* I:535.

47     Ibid.

48 Beckmann, *History of Inventions*, I:384.

49 For alum and Von Gulick, see Webber, 'Conservation of Chinese Wallpapers', p. 53.

50 Sugden and Edmundson, *A History*, pp. 114, 135.

51 Dagnall, *The Tax On Wallpaper*, p. 5.

52 'They have received advice from Russia that one Butler, an Englishman, who had some time ago settled there had introduced the manufacture of paper hangings to the great prejudice of our trade, and had lately made application to the Russia Senate totally to prohibit the importation of foreign paper hangings there, and therefore praying such redress and directions therein as the Board shall think proper. Messrs. Goadby, Herring and Kite [...] acquainted the Board that the manufacture and exportation of paper hangings had within these few years greatly increased chiefly to Russia, and that it was become the more important, as the greater part of it was now manufactured with English paper made in Kent and Hampshire'; Journal of the Commissioners for Trade and Plantations, 1749, vol. 60, p. 329.

53 Broström, *Tapetboken*, p. 16.

54 Hills, *Papermaking*, p. 52.

55 *Col. State Papers (Domestic)*, 28 January 1692, p. 115, as quoted in Longfield, 'Dublin Wall-Paper', p. 107; see also *Notes and Queries (Scottish)*, ed by John Bulloch, 2nd series, 3 (July 1901-June, 1902) p. 13.

56 Scott, 'Society of the White-Writing and Printing Paper Manufactory', p. 72.

57 Arnot, *History of Edinburgh*, p. 465.

58 Jacqué, 'From "papiers en feuille" to "decor"...' p. 8.

59 Pannabecker, 'Representing Mechanical Arts', p. 41. Diderot's account is found in his 'Encyclopédie' article (p. 641), which is not to be confused with the *Encyclopédie* itself. Pannabecker dates the article to 1755 which is confirmed by Frank and Serena Kafker who date it to November (see bibliography).

60 *Traité*; extracts are from I:ix, III:7, and I:83.

61  But see *WHSR*, 1993–4, p. 35 (8-panel proto-scenic dating from 1742 found in Switzerland); and Chapter 1, 'Manifold Beginnings' in *The Papered Wall*, ill. 16, 17.

62 *Traité*, I:310: 'On lui doit l'invention à Paris des papiers de tapisseries qu'il commença à mettre en vogue environ l'an 1688; il les sçavoit poser en place avec goût, beaucoup d'art & de propreté. Il a porté cette invention au plus haut point où elle ait jamais été, de sorte que de son tems, & depuis lui tous ceux qui se sont mêlés de ce commerce ont contresait ses desseins, parce qu'ils étoient goûtés & en grande réputation'.

63 See Fabry, 'Papiers De Tapisserie' for a complete account.

64 Ratzki-Kraatz, 'A French Lit de Parade', p. 85, fig. 4.

65 See Teynac, *Wallpaper: A History*, pp. 28–34 for a complete set of the plates with annotations.

66 For the equivalency of the first two terms, see Wisse, 'papiers peints en arabesques sur le mur', in Jacqué, *Arabesques*, p. 82; for the distinctions among them, see Jacqué, 'papiers en feuille', p. 14.

67 As quoted in Entwisle, *Literary History*, p. 24.

68 Plomer, *A Dictionary Of The Printers And Booksellers*, p. 51.

69 Entwisle, *Literary History*, plate 22.

70 See Sugden and Edmundson, pp. 72–79.

71    See Koldeweij, 'Gilt Leather Hangings', Appendix 3, for a list of Bromwich's apprentices.

72    *London Gazette, Boston Evening Post, Boston Post Boy,* and *The Boston News-Letter and New-England Chronicle.*

73    His obituary ran in the *Gentleman's Magazine,* July 1787. Bromwich's house is profiled in 'Voel and South Grove House', *Survey of London,* pp. 63–66.

74    Defoe, *The Complete Tradesman,* preface. All emphasis in this section is added. All quotes are from an unpaginated 1839 edition at: <www.gutenberg.org/ebooks/14444>

75    Baxter, *The House of Hancock,* passim.

76    Entwisle, 'The Blew Paper Warehouse', p. 95.

77    Ibid.; Kainen, *John Baptist Jackson,* pp. 43, 48.

78    Campbell, *The London Tradesman,* pp. 116–18.

79    Ibid.

80    *Journals of the House of Commons,* vol. 18 (Great Britain House of Commons), p. 416, for 9 April 1716.

81    Dagnall, *The Tax on Wallpaper,* pp. 1–4.

82    Russell, 'A Seventeenth Century Wall-Paper'; see *The Papered Wall,* ill. 70.

83    Dagnall, *The Tax On Wallpaper,* p. 9.

84    *The Statutes of the United Kingdom of Great Britain and Ireland,* Volume 20, pg. 66, 287 (1806?). See also for Ireland: *The Statutes at Large From the Magna Charta, to the End of the Eleventh Parliament of Great Britain, Anno 1761* [Continued to 1807], Volume 45, Part 1, pp. 34, 66, 122, 126–27, 486.

85    See Wells-Cole, *Historic Paper Hangings,* especially commentary on the 1680–1700 Epsom papers, p. 22.

86    Craske, 'Plan and Control', p. 208, n. 74.

87    This discussion is based on the work of Christine Velut: 'Between Invention and Production'. Her article explores design as a 'negotiation' between public and paperstainers in Paris around 1800.

88    As quoted in Longfield, 'Dublin Wall-Paper', p. 107; Messink's ad is from *Pue's Occurrences,* 17 June 1746. For Ashworth: 'Dublin Wall-Paper', p. 108, n. 16.

89    See Craske, 'Plan and Control', pp. 195 and 190–96 generally.

90    Houghton, 'A Collection', No. 356, 19 May 1699.

91    Houghton, 'A Collection', No. 362, 30 June 1699.

92    McCutcheon, 'John Houghton', p. 256.

93    1697? 'James Brooke, Stationer, at Ye Anchor and Crown, near the Square on London Bridge, sells all sorts of Books for Accounts, Stampt Paper, and Parchments, variety of Paper Hangings for Rooms, and all sorts of Stationery Wares, Wholesale and Retail, at Reasonable prices'; As quoted in MacMichael, 'The London Signs and their Associations' which cites *The Chronicles of London Bridge,* by An Antiquary, 1839, pg. 278. See also Heal, 'Paper-Stainer's of the 17th and 18th Century', *Country Life,* 22 July 1949, p. 258.

94    Wells-Cole, *Historic Paper Hangings,* p. 22.

95    Smith, *Eighteenth-Century Decoration,* p. 43.

96    Watkins, 'The Early Use', p. 110.

97    Jobe, 'The Boston Upholstery Trade', pp. 65–66. If the £600 refers to colonial money, it was worth about £200 sterling in 1728.

98    Walsh, 'London Shop Design', p. 161.

99    Craske, 'Plan and Control', p. 208.

100    Walsh, 'London Shop Design', p. 167.

101    As cited in Walsh, p. 167; Corporation of London Record Office, OCI 3178.

102    Ibid., 160.

103    Berg, 'From Imitation to Invention', p. 2.

104    *Hamlet*, Act 5, scene 1, lines 255–57.

105    Morris, 'Maiden's Garlands', table 1 and p. 373.

106    Ibid., p. 362. See also *WHSR*, 2001, pp. 4–6, with 6 photographs.

107    Longfield, 'Dublin Wall-Paper', p. 108.

108    As quoted in Longfield, 'Dublin Wall-Paper', p. 107; *Pue's Occurrences,* 17 June 1746.

109    As quoted in Longfield, 'Old Wall-Papers', p. 157; *Universal Advertiser,* 10 January 1754.

110    For 'stiff duties': Krakovitch, *Arrêts, déclarations, édits*, p. 385; for 'sweeping search': Hamel, 'Un papier peint inspiré', section 28.

111    *Covent-Garden Journal*, 27 June 1752, vol. 2, no. 51, p. 42.

112    Clouzot, *Wallpaper in France*, p. 18.

113    *Political and Social Letters*, p. 50. Other quotes in this section are from pp. 52, 71, and 95.

114    Innocent, *English Building Construction*, fig. 44, p. 115.

115    Cummings, *The Framed Houses*, pp. 174–78, fig. 237.

116    Moxon, *Mechanick Exercises*, pp. 108–09.

117    As quoted in Ayres, *Domestic Interiors*, p. 55. The text is cited as the 1677 edition of *Mechanick Exercises or the Doctrine of Handy-Works.*

118    Beard, *Craftsmen and Interior Decoration*, p. 29.

119    Ayers in *Domestic Interiors*, p. 54, suggests the opposite: that the fashion for large central wood panels may have evolved from the use of wood supports under fabric and paper-hangings.

120    Walton, 'An Inventory of 1710 from Dyrham Park', *Furniture History*, p. 40. The comparison is made by taking the figure of 2s. 6d. per piece found in Entwisle, *Book of Wallpaper*, Blue Paper Warehouse Ad, plate 20, and converting it into square yards, the standard method of estimating painted work and lumber in this period. Paper-hangings were ordinarily billed by the running yard or 'piece' of 12 linear yards.

121    This section is indebted to Ayers' observations about panelling in *Domestic Interiors*, pp. 54–60.

122    See Cornforth, *Early Georgian Interiors*, fig. 431.

123    This quotation courtesy of Dr Joe Rock from Buchanan MSS.

124    Cummings, *Framed Houses*, p. 3, 44.

125    Kimball, *American Domestic Architecture*, pp. 115–16.

126    Law, *The New Historical Guide*, pp. 79–80.

127    Ibid.

128    As quoted in Rock, 'Scottish Wallpaper', *WHSR* 2004/05, p. 4.

129    Ibid.

130    Edinburgh, National Archives of Scotland, GD112/21/78 bundle 277. More of this story is told in Rock's article in *WHSR* 2004/05, p. 5. Harn is 'coarse linen cloth made from the tow-hards' (refuse of flax) according to *Wilson's Tales of the Borders and of Scotland* VI:7.

131    Illustrated in Entwisle, *Book Of Wallpaper*, plate 36.

132    Watkins, 'The Early Use', p. 110.

133    Entwisle, *Book of Wallpaper*, plate 27.

134    Beard, *Upholsterers and Interior Furnishings*, pp. 303, 158.

135    Ibid., p. 145.

136    Mora, *Conservation of Wall Paintings*, p. 156.

137    Houghton, 'A Collection', No. 362, 30 June 1699.

138    Broström, *Tapetboken*, p. 50. A PDF showing the process is on the website of the Skansen Living History Museum: <http://www.skansen.se/artikel/vandspikning-av-tapeter>

139    Waterer, 'Dunster Castle', p. 147. For sewing and installing canvas underlayments (late 1760s) see Gilbert, 'Chippendale's Harwood Commission'.

140    Montgomery, *Textiles in America*, p. 224.

141    Mellerstain Account Books (Scotland), this reference provided by Dr Joe Rock. See Chapter 13 for transcription.

142    The example assumes that the borders are put up in 10 to 12 courses. A common border width for the early-eighteenth century was 1 3/8". It's hard to ignore that this measurement yields exactly a 'dozen' borders per 22" width.

143    London, Victoria and Albert Museum, MSS, The Duppa Account Books (Letter Book 86.AA.14). Correspondence to Thomas Couldhart, Wales (8 May 1819).

144    Michie, 'Upholstery In All Its Branches', p. 48.

145    *The Trial At Bar*, pp. 15, 17, 242, 378.

146    See Walton, 'The Worshipful Company', pp. 49–50.

147    Ibid., p. 47.

148    Innocent, *English Building Construction*, pp. 143-44.

149    Baty, 'House-Painting Trade', p. 2.

150    Arnold, *History of the Painter Stainers Company*, p. 91.

151    1 Jas. I, c.20: <u>The Plaisterers' Act.</u>

152    Lansdowne MSS, as quoted in Baty, p. 7.

153    Arnold, *History of the Painter Stainers Company*, p. 91.

154    Baty, 'House-Painting Trade', p. 6.

155    Kellett, 'Gild and Corporation Control', p. 384.

156    Ibid.

157    Baty, 'House-Painting Trade', p. 8.

158    Symonds, 'Domestic Furnishings', p. 221.

159  Ibid, p. 218.

160  Ibid., p. 218.

161  Walton, 'The Worshipful Company', p. 41.

162  Ibid., p. 45.

163  As quoted in Taylor, 'Chinese Papers', p. 45.

164  Macky, *Memoirs of the Secret Services*, p. 18.

165  See Gilbert, *Life and Work of Chippendale*, I:225. Letter from 23 Jan 1771.

166  Entwisle, 'XVIIIth Paper-Stainers", p. 40.

167  Ibid.

168  Rock, 'Scottish Wallpaper', p. 4.

169  Beard and Westman, 'A French Upholsterer in England', p. 523.

170  Beard, *Upholsterers and Interior Furnishings*, pp. 145, 301.

171  Prime, *Arts & Crafts*, p. 199. It is unlikely that this is a different person from the Job Adams admitted to the Worshipful Company in 1729; see Walton, 'The Worshipful Company', pp. 9, 51.

172  Hamel, 'Un papier peint inspiré de l'Orient', table 1.

173  Kellett, 'Gild and Corporation Control', p. 390.

174  Ibid., p. 389.

175  Ibid.

176  Walton, 'The Worshipful Company', pp. 48–50.

177  Campbell, *The London Tradesman*, The Cabinet-Maker, especially p. 171.

178  Gilbert, 'Chippendale's Harewood Commission'. Indeed, Reid worked almost continuously at Harewood for two years, eight months (p. 9). In contrast, there is a solitary reference to Chippendale's presence at Harewood.

179  Worcester, American Antiquarian Society, MSS, Samuel Grant daybook entry dated 17 December 1746.

180  See Texts: Campbell; see also Kirkham, 'London Furniture Trade', p. 35.

181  Miller, 'Gender, Artisanry, and Craft', pp. 746; emphasis in original. Other contributors to literature about early North American women artisans include Adrianna Hood and Laurel Ulrich.

182  This information is found in Hamel, 'Un papier peint inspiré de l'Orient', sections 21–4.

183  Keatinge, 'The Guild of Cutlers, Painter-Stainers and Stationers', p. 136.

184  Pollard, *Dublin Book Trade*.

185  Prime, *Arts & Crafts*, p. 280.

186  As quoted in Koldeweij, 'Gilt Leather Hangings', p. 83; Letter of John Rowland to Admiral van Wassenaer.

187  Waterer, 'Dunster Castle', p. 143.

188  As quoted in Calnan and Paris, 'Scorched or Damask Leather', p. 6. Peder Mansson translated the recipe book into Swedish around 1520.

189  Huth, 'Chinoiserie Gilt Leather', p. 26. For the information about modular types he cites

Fougeroux de Bondaroy, *L'Art de travailler des cuirs dorés ou argentés*.

190   Waterer, 'Dunster Castle', p. 146.

191   This paragraph is based on information found in Koldeweij, 'Marketing of Gilt Leather', pp. 137–48.

192   Mitchell, 'Leather Hung Rooms', p. 37.

193   As quoted in Walton, 'Dyrham Park', p. 34.

194   Ibid., p. 41.

195   Koldeweij, 'High Fashion' lecture.

196   Ibid.

197   Koldeweij, 'Gilt Leather Hangings', Appendix 3. A 'Mr Asgill' was paid £12 for hangings in 1670 by Sir Stephen Fox (see Millar, 'Artists and Craftsmen'). This job may have been done by Henry or his father John. The type of hangings are not specified.

198   See Appendix 3 (table of masters and apprentices) in Koldeweij, 'Gilt Leather Hangings'.

199   As quoted in Koldeweij, 'Gilt Leather Hangings', p. 86.

200   As quoted in Koldeweij, 'Gilt Leather Hangings', p. 83.

201   Ibid., p. 65–66.

202   Ibid., p. 84.

203   Ibid. Prices are given on pp. 62, 63, 70 and 83. The size of the pattern (not the panels) extant at Ham House is 6.3" by 5.3".

204   Wells-Cole, *Historic Paper Hangings*, p. 6.

205   As quoted in Leung, 'Wallpaper in Canada', p. 9, n. 13. See Du Halde, *General History of China*, pp. 415–30 for an engrossing account of paper production and Texts: *History of China* in this volume.

206   LeComte, '*Nouveaux memoires*', I:314.

207   Mungello, *The Great Encounter*, p. 37.

208   Glassie, 'Folk Art', p. 139.

209   Rickman, 'Chinese Export Works', p. 45.

210   Some information has come to light about how this company influenced the design of textiles coming from the East. See Styles, 'Product Innovation', pp. 132–36 for a case study about decorated cotton textiles, 1660–1700. Work like this raises some hope for research about the origin and evolution of export paper-hangings.

211   The account in this paragraph appears in Rickman, 'Chinese Export Works', p. 46, and is partly based on Van Gulik, *Chinese Pictorial Art*.

212   Earl Pritchard, review of *Chinese Export Art*, p. 268.

213   Saunders, *Wallpaper In Interior Decoration*, plate 21.

214   Ibid., plate 60.

215   Hamel, 'Un papier peint inspiré', section 1.

216   Catalogue No. E.1852-1919 at the Victoria and Albert Museum. See also figure 72, Hoskins, *The Papered Wall*, and figure 60, Sugden and Edmundson, *A History*.

217   Cited in Leung, 'Wallpaper In Canada', p. 56.

218   Illustrated in Rosoman, *London Wallpapers*, plate 8.

219   Kainen, *John Baptist Jackson*, p. 40.

220   Pyne, *Royal Residences*, II:75.

221   Houston, *Featherbedds*, Part 3. Phill is profiled in Beard, *Upholsterers*, p. 145.

222   Longfield, 'Dublin Wall-Paper', p. 102.

223   Colville, *Duchess Sarah*, p. 165. 4,755 yards were ordered at a cost of £2,139. This computes to exactly 9s. per yard.

224   Douglas, 'Cotton Textiles in England', p. 33.

225   Ibid.

226   See colour plates in Rosoman, *London Wallpapers*.

227   Wharton, *The Decoration of Houses*, p. 44. Nevertheless, Wharton used ingrains (guest suite) and varnished tile (bathroom) wallpapers in her own home. See Donnis, 'Puzzling the Pieces', *Old House Journal*. Wharton would likely have approved of the more centralized way of installing wallpaper 1650–1750.

228   Cornforth, *Early Georgian Interiors*, plate 63.

229   Extant in an upstairs bedroom at the Wentworth-Coolidge house in Portsmouth, New Hampshire.

230   R. Campbell, *The London Tradesman*; see Texts.

231   As quoted in Glendinning, *History Of Scottish Architecture*, p. 114.

232   As quoted in Cornforth, *Early Georgian Interiors*, p. 192.

233   Wells-Cole, *Historic Paper Hangings*, p. 28.

234   Cornforth, *Early Georgian Interiors*, pp. 95, 192. For America, see Nylander, *Wallpaper in New England*, pp. 41–43.

235   Campbell, *The London Tradesman*, p. 119.

236   Eric Entwisle believed that 'Moore' was Benjamin Moore of Newgate Street in London, a paperstainer and producer of gilt embossed and stencilled endpapers, see p. 73 and plate 30, *Book of Wallpaper*; Moore's endpaper dated 1765 is at the National Library of Scotland, ref. 00002736. However, in *Lady Luxborough's Letters*, p. 213, Moore is a 'stucco-man', hired by her to decorate some rooms in relief.

237   Luxborough, *Lady Luxborough's Letters*, p. 236.

238   Cornforth, 'Putting Up With Georgian DIY', fig. 6.

239   Luxborough, *Lady Luxborough's Letters*, p. 223.

240   See Texts: The Duff/Mackay Correspondence.

241   Postlethwayt's *Universal Dictionary*, 1751, as quoted in Entwisle, *Book of Wallpaper*, p. 71.

242   As quoted in Entwisle, *Literary History*, p. 29.

243   As quoted in Beard, *Craftsmen And Interior Decoration*, p. 38.

244   Longfield, 'Dublin Wall-Paper', p. 109.

245   Thornton, 'Architectural Papier Mache', p. 166.

246   Ibid., p. 175.

247 Dover, *Letters of Horace Walpole*, III:46.

248 Perhaps they came from Robert Dunbar's 'Paper Warehouse', which supplied 247 yards of paper-hangings to the Cardigan household in 1740, see Entwisle, *Literary History*, p. 24. Goodison is characterized as pious in Beard, 'Three Eighteenth Century Cabinet-Makers', p. 485.

249 Jourdain, *Chinese Export Art*, p. 31; cited in Cornforth, *Early Georgian Interiors*, p. 207, n. 55.

250 Smith, *Eighteenth-Century Decoration*, p. 43.

251 Sullivan, *The Meeting Of Eastern And Western Art*, p. 99. He cites Jourdain, *Chinese Export Art*. A discussion about the primary documents of the Company (*General Commerce Journals; General Ledger; China Factory Records;* and *Letter Books*) is found in Earl Pritchard's review of *Chinese Export Art* in *The Far Eastern Quarterly*.

252 As quoted in Leath, 'After the Chinese Taste', p. 54.

253 As quoted in Saunders, *Wallpaper in Interior Decoration*, p. 83.

254 See Archer, 'Festoons of Flowers'.

255 Llanover, *Autobiography and Correspondence*, 2nd ser., III:166.

256 Entwisle, 'XVIIIth Century', p. 38, Letter of Mrs Philip Lybbe Powys describing a visit to Mrs Freeman's Fawley Court, Buckinghamshire.

257 *Hoey's Dublin Mercury* 6 November 1770, ad of Ryves, Darkin and Co.

258 See illustrations in Archer, 'Festoons of Flowers'.

259 I am indebted throughout this section to Dr Joe Rock's work in the Traquair archives.

260 For records of Buchanan House, Edinburgh, Scotland (Reference GD 220/6/1806/1), The Royal Commission On The Ancient And Historical Monuments of Scotland. His son, also named Charles Esplin, was recorded as 'paper-stainer', at his death in 1788. In 1784 the business was styled 'Charles Esplin & Co'. After the death of Charles the younger it changed to 'Esplin & Forbes' and included James and John Forbes. For obituary, The Scots Magazine, vol. 50 (1788), Deaths and Preferments, p. 103.

261 Stuart, *A Family Life Revealed*.

262 Somerset, *Correspondence, Countess of Hartford*, III:5–6.

263 Sugden and Edmundson, *A History*, pp. 39–40.

264 Luxborough, *Letters of Lady Luxborough*, p. 22.

265 Wilk's chinoiserie wallpaper was envied by Thomas Hancock, see Chapter 6. For Cardigan, see Entwisle, *Literary History*, p. 24. See British Museum catalog #AN588653001 (1744) for bill made out to 'Mr Alderman Hoare'. This may be the Richard Hoare who was Lord Mayor of London in 1745, and noted as Sir Richard Hoare, banker, in Entwisle, 'XVIIIth-Century Paper-Stainers' and Decorators' Bills'.

266 The '51 ½ yds 2 Green on Mantua' are ascribed to Mr Richard Hoare by Entwisle; the bill is shown in Entwisle, *Book of Wallpaper*, Plate 27.

267 If the cost of the piece and the average number of sheets making it up is known, we can calculate the cost of each sheet. This universal cost of a sheet can be used to assess the cost of painted papers in the North American colonies, provided that the exchange rates are taken into consideration. The actual number of sheets in a piece of wallpaper in the early-eighteenth century is 23.16, based on three examples of tax-stamped paper in Wells-Cole, *Historic Paper Hangings*. For more discussion, see Appendix B: Notes on Cost.

268  Harrison, *A Frenchman In Virginia*, p. 112.

269  Two government buildings whose windows and walls were frequently papered were Chateau St. Louis in Quebec (1773–79) and the Government House (formerly la Masion des Indes) in Montreal (1777).

270  For the years of 1714, 1741, 1743, Watkins, 'The Early Use', pp. 109–10. For 1730 and 1736, Dow, *Arts and Crafts*, p. 150. See also Cummings, 'The Use and Manufacture', p. 3.

271  Birket, *Some Cursory Remarks*, p. 8 (Portsmouth); p. 28 (Newport).

272  Isham, *Early Connecticut Houses*, p. 5.

273  For paint, see Cummings, *The Framed Houses*, p. 168. For wallpaper, see Cummings, 'The Use and Manufacture', pp. 3–4 and Lynn, *Wallpaper In America*, pp. 22–24.

274  *Jesuit Relations*, Letter from Father Jacques Gravier, 15 February 1694, LXIV:225.

275  *Jesuit Relations*, Letter from Father du Poisson, 3 October 1727, LXVII:321.

276  Watkins, 'The Early Use,' p. 109.

277  Ibid.

278  Report by Richard Coote, colonial Governor of New England, in Defebaugh, *History of the Lumber Industry*, II:13.

279  Worcester, Massachusetts, American Antiquarian Society, Robert Gibbs Business Records, 1669–1708.

280  Cummings, *The Framed Houses*, pp. 18–19.

281  Ibid., pp. 114–16.

282  Cummings, *The Framed Houses*, pp. 169, 178. See also diagram on p. 175, which shows 3 varieties of interior wall sheathing.

283  Kelly, J. Frederick, *Early Domestic Architecture*, p. 147.

284  I am indebted for many details in this section to discussions with Maximilian Ferro.

285  Dow, *Every Day Life*, p. 56.

286  See Isham, *Early Connecticut Houses,* pp. 107, 290–91. The colonial pound was near parity in 1657. In 1707, 150 colonial pounds were equal to £100.

287  As quoted in Lynn, *Wallpaper In America*, p. 19.

288  White's ad is from 4 July 1754, *The Pennsylvania Gazette*. He also offered 'funerals furnished, and shrouds ready made, pink'd [scalloped] as in London, or plain and plaited, and sheets [...] and some patterns of papers to be seen as abovesaid.'

289  Keith, 'American Wallpaper', *The Magazine Antiques*, p. 217.

290  Robert Beverley, as quoted in Coulter, 'Import Trade', p. 312; the quote is found in Robert Beverley's undated letter, p. 59, Robert Beverley's letter book, Library of Congress.

291  See Cummings, 'Colonial and Federal America', pp. 18–20.

292  Cummings, *The Framed Houses*, p. 42.

293  Quoted in Michie, 'Upholstery In All Its Branches', p. 34; *Virginia Gazette*, 6 April 1739 and 28 November 1745.

294  Ibid., p. 33; *South Carolina Gazette*, 7 January 1751.

295  Worcester, Samuel Grant Account Book, p. 289 and entries for 21 April 1744 and 28 June 1745.

296   For Adams, *American Weekly Mercury*, 18 May 1732, as cited in Prime, *Arts and Crafts*, p. 199. For Rowland, p. 211 of Prime, *Arts and Crafts*. It's not known if Rowland is any relation to John Rowland, gilt leather maker. In Gottesman, *Arts and Crafts*, Stephen Callow's ad appears in I:134, and James Huthwaite's in I:138.

297   Cummings, 'Colonial and Federal America', p. 18.

298   Ibid., pp. 19–20; Katherine was also related to Edward Standbridge.

299   Cummings, *The Framed Houses*, pp. 40–44.

300   Quoted in Prime, *Arts and Crafts*, p. 199; *American Weekly Mercury*, 18 May 1732.

301   It's probably the younger who placed this ad in the *South Carolina Gazette*, Charleston, 28 October 1756. Thomas Booden is listed as an upholsterer in Charleston, 1756–61, in Calhoun, 'The Geographic Spread', p. 217.

302   Prime, *Arts and Crafts*, p. 201, *South Carolina Gazette*, 16 June 1766. See Webber, 'Death Notices', p. 88. Although it is unlikely that two different men with the same name and profession advertised on both sides of the Atlantic, it is not impossible.

303   His bill-head is illustrated in Lynn, *Wallpaper in America*, figure 3-8.

304   See 'Proceedings of the Old Bailey', 17 January 1770; Squire presses charges for the theft of 30 pieces of his paper; the convicted man was transported; <www.oldbaileyonline.org>

305   Mayhew and Myers, *A Documentary History*, p. 54.

306   This set is currently installed at the Metropolitan Museum of Art. See Donnell 'A Study In Disassociation' for an illustration of the bill. The bill is rendered in pounds sterling and the conversion to colonial pounds (£38. 12s. 8½d.) is done at the rate of 80%; see McCusker, *Money and Exchange*, p. 317.

307   McCusker, *Money and Exchange*, pp. 133, 316. The value of £100 was 160 colonial pounds in 1715, then rose steadily to 334 colonial pounds in 1731. It then tripled to 1,033 colonial pounds by 1749 before resetting to 133 colonial pounds after the adoption of the silver standard.

308   The phrase 'most melancholy accident' is from the *South Carolina Gazette* 9 March 1769. Fleeson's ad was in the *Pennsylvania Gazette*, 19 October 1769.

309   Simpson, *Lives Of Eminent Philadelphians*, p. 373.

310   *New York Mercury*, 13 December 1756.

311   Hickey was incarcerated while up North.

312   *The Edinburgh Encyclopedia*, vol. 18, pp. 383–85.

313   Information about installers as opposed to upholsterers is frustratingly scarce. The earliest record of a stand-alone installer appears in the obituary of Daniel Starr, 'who has been for many Years employed in Papering Rooms' according to the Boston News-Letter of 23 September 1762.

314   Watkins, 'The Early Use', p. 110. £4 10s. colonial was around £2. 18s. 9d. pounds sterling taking inflation into account.

315       All transcriptions which follow are from the business accounts of Thomas Hancock, see Boston, The Massachusetts Historical Society.

316   Faulkner, book review, *House of Hancock*, p. 951.

317   *Halifax Gazette*, 1752, as cited in Leung, p. 37. Leung noted that 'Thomas Hancock [...] was engaged in supplying manufacture goods and produce to Louisbourg and Halifax in the 1740s. Perhaps some of his trade was in paperhangings', p. 41. There is every reason to believe that her

hunch was correct.

318 Francois Larcher (1749) and Louis Greffin, (1751–57), in Adams '*Artisans at Louisbourg*', p. 109, cited in Leung, 'Wallpaper in Canada', p. 35.

319 Leahy, George W., *L'ornementation*.

320 Leung, 'Wallpaper in Canada', p. 2.

321 Leung, 'Wallpaper in Canada', p. 20.

322 I'm deeply indebted throughout this chapter to Felicity L. Leung, who compiled a research report about early wallpaper for Parks Canada in 1983.

323 The statistics are largely from the Public Archives of Canada (PAC). Figures for the 1760s as cited by Leung, n. 4, for cargo lists (British export records): PAC, MG18, F40A-703, 'List of all the ships and vessels which have entered inwards in the port of Quebec in Canada...', undated; and n. 6, PAC, RG4, A3, vol. 1, Ships and cargoes at Quebec, pp. 5, 12, 16, 32, 49, 56, 103, 132, 151–52, 161, 171.

 Figures for the 1770s as cited by Leung, n. 15, PAC, Customs 17, MG40D, 'Accounts of the Goods, Wares, and Merchandise being British Produce and Manufacture exported from England to [...] Newfoundland, Canada and Nova Scotia', 5 Jan. 1772 to 5 Jan. 1779, Reels B3911–19.

 Figures for the 1780s as cited by Leung, n. 38: PAC, Customs 17, MG40D, 'Accounts of the Goods, Wares, and Merchandise being British Produce and Manufacture exported from England to [...] Newfoundland, Canada and Nova Scotia', Reels 3913 to 3914.

324 Leung, 'Wallpaper in Canada', p. 51.

325 A tomb in the churchyard at Leyton, England, is marked 'John Stenhouse, merchant of Montreal, 1780', see *The Environs of London*, IV:172.

326 As cited in Leung, n. 8, PAC, MG19 A2 Series 3 vol. 83 pg. 66 'Bought of Mr Thomas Harris, London, 18 March 1767' and n. 9, PAC, MG19 a2 series 3, vol. 83 Invoice Book B, Robert and John Stenhouse, 1764, p. 97.

327 Leung, 'Wallpaper in Canada', p. 52.

328 Leung, 'Wallpaper In Canada', p. 51. The per capita consumption can be worked out for at least one year (1775) when square footage of 245,322 based on 3,894 pieces were imported from England (Hills, *Papermaking*, p. 85). Since the European population of Canada was about 90,000 (Statistics Canada) the rate was 2.725 square feet of English wallpaper per person.

329 Great Britain, Public Record Office, WO49 vol. 248, p. 404; these regulations date from 1807.

330 Population figures are from Statistics Canada; <http://www.statcan.gc.ca/pub/98-187-x/4151287-eng.htm

331 The entry in the daybook of Samuel Grant is dated 17 December 1746, Worcester, American Antiquarian Society.

332 *Whitehall Evening Post* [London] 1–3 January 1754.

333 Cornforth, 'Arms and Legs of Wallpaper', p. 168.

# Index

CPSIA information can be obtained at www.ICGtesting.com
Printed in the USA
LVOW11*1710270114

371148LV00013B/235/P